TECHNOLOGY TOOLS MATH INSTRUCTION

Teaching outside the box

Grades K–12

Second Edition

PATRICIA DICKENSON • LORELEI CODDINGTON

Kendall Hunt
publishing company

Cover image © Patricia Dickenson

www.kendallhunt.com
Send all inquiries to:
4050 Westmark Drive
Dubuque, IA 52004-1840

Contents

2. The Foundations and Principles of CCSS   23

3. Understanding Design   45

6. Project-Based Learning   163

7. Problem-Based Learning 197

8. Math Centers   237

9. Putting It All Together   261

Introduction

Technology for Teaching and Learning

The concept of using technology in the classroom is certainly not anything new or even a current fad; technology is, after all, the "methods, systems and devices which are the result of scientific knowledge being used for practical purposes" (Collins Dictionary, n.d.). In 1564, the invention of the pencil revolutionized how information was recorded and shared, and so the function of teaching and learning also changed. Technology shapes how teachers do their jobs, and the tools teachers bring into the classroom influence not only how learners learn, but how they demonstrate what they have learned to others.

The role of the teacher and student continues to evolve as new technology permeates the classroom and provides access to different ways to express, represent, and engage today's learners. Although the classroom looks much different today than in 1564, the pencil still has a place and the role of the teacher as classroom leader, role model, and education expert remains constant. In the math classroom, access to tools can determine how students solve problems, express their understanding, and learn new concepts. New technology tools, such as learning management systems, virtual reality, personal tablets, handheld devices, computers and smart notebooks, have the ability to simulate, engage, and motivate young learners, even before they begin to read.

As the classroom teacher, you have the power to make instructional decisions in your classroom. The decisions you make influence student outcomes and can have a profound impact on their future and readiness to enter college and careers that may not even exist yet.

The role of the teacher is paramount in the implementation and integration of technology across content areas. Successful technology use requires teachers who have the technical skills and content expertise to design instruction that is developmentally appropriate and engaging. We believe technology application for student use requires teacher modeling and explicit instruction in technology skills. Although there is a belief that today's students are "digital natives," applying digital tools in the context of subject matter is not intuitive, but it is necessary for us to prepare students to be college and career ready.

Integrating Technology into Your Math Practice

Mathematics pedagogical practices have been established for some time, but these practices must be rooted in 21st century skills and technologies to motivate young learners and prepare them for an ever-changing workforce. Technology is another tool in our toolbelt that can be used to provide students with the support, resources, and representations they need to learn and grow in their math knowledge and confidence. Blended learning provides us with the means to meet individual learners where they are, not just what their grade level standards dictate. Whether we provide additional challenge or remediation, this process is facilitated with greater ease with technology. With digital resources at their fingertips, students' thinking can become visible. Whether students construct what they know using digital models, share their thinking with collaboration tools, or present their understanding in a variety of ways, we can examine students' thinking with a different lens. Students' screencasts give us data and inform us as to what our students know and express, whereas web-based construction tools allow us to examine how they perceive a math concept. Traditional worksheets do not always reveal our students' misconceptions and why they struggle, nor do they tell us if they understand the concept when they have the correct answer.

© MNStudio/Shutterstock.com

As teachers we might not have the digital experiences as our young learners in the classroom, but we have the ability to develop the technical skill and technological pedagogical content knowledge (TPACK) to effectively use digital tools and engage young learners in the context of teaching and learning mathematics. We are teachers and life-long learners; nothing is out of our reach.

Purpose

The authors of this book are teacher educators who work with preservice teachers pursuing teaching credentials as well as inservice teachers in the area of mathematics professional development. This book fills a gap between what preservice teachers lack when they enter the field and what inservice teachers search for when they are in the classroom. The focus of this book is developing pedagogical practices that integrate technology as a tool for teaching and as a way for students to express what they know. The focus is on five mathematics research-based pedagogical practices: daily routines, open-ended tasks, project-based learning, problem-based learning, and math centers. These practices are anchored in the standards for mathematical practice, developmentally appropriate for K-12 classrooms, and support both conceptual understanding and procedural fluency.

As teacher educators, we know teachers enter the classroom with state-adopted curriculum, pacing plans, benchmark tests, and state standards, but we often hear via social media, professional development, and coaching, that teachers need support determining what mathematics pedagogical practices will best meet the needs of the diverse learners in their classroom. We believe teachers should be empowered to make instructional decisions that will best support the learners in their class regardless of the curriculum they receive. Teachers need to make pedagogical decisions that will support, challenge, and accommodate the students they teach year after year. This process requires teachers to have knowledge of how to design mathematics instruction, determine specific areas for growth, and understand where current curriculum is lacking in meeting the needs of learners. Moreover, teachers need to be aware of strategies and technology resources that can motivate, engage, and scaffold learning.

Grade-level content is no guarantee that students have acquired the fundamental skills and concepts in previous years that are required to master a standard. That is why teachers need to be aware of what pedagogical practices and technology resources best support learners. Furthermore, teachers need to know how to make instructional decisions that integrate technology to not only support student learning, but provide a means for students to create, explain, and apply mathematics.

© wavebreakmedia/Shutterstock.com

How We Organized this Book

This book guides the reader through each chapter by first introducing the math pedagogical practice in the context of teaching and learning and then explaining the practice and how it is valuable for student learning. We share research related to each math practice and ways technology can enhance and support each practice. We also explore each practice through the lens of writing, assessing, speaking, questioning, and classroom discussions. We introduce foundational information first and then build understanding upon the foundational concepts one strategy at a time. Throughout the book, the reader is asked to consider the various strategies in light of their learning and to commit to technology integration and elements of active, student-centered learning. Each chapter includes a place for teachers to reflect, write responses, and hear what the research says about the topic. We also unpack each strategy and provide practical examples and advice about organizing and implementing each practice in the classroom. Every chapter provides practical tools for technology integration and examples to support teachers' integration of tools within the math content across grade levels.

Self-Reflection: Each chapter begins with a question to prompt your thinking before reading the chapter. We encourage you to keep a journal to record your thinking and promote active reflection throughout this book.

 Think About It! Throughout the book, you will see these prompts which will require you to apply what you are learning about in the context of teaching and planning instruction.

 Stop and Reflect These prompts allow you to make connections with big ideas and concepts within each chapter.

 Watch It When you see this prompt, you can see the content in action. We have included classroom videos and screencasts where we explain big ideas in further detail.

 View It These hyperlinks will take you to presentations and documents that allow you to explore an idea or apply a concept in greater detail.

 Snag It We have included lessons and additional digital resources for you to include in your teacher toolbox.

 Try It! This will take you to web-based activities where you can try digital lessons and technology resources for exploration, practice, and student use.

 Make the Tech Connection We share best practices for integrating technology in the context of writing, assessing, representing and support students in making the digital connection. We also share resources for organizing your digital footprint.

 Across the Curriculum Teach for transfer by supporting interdisciplinary connections in other content areas that will not only build math skills but provide real-world connections.

Chapter Contents

Chapter 1: The Case for Technology in the Mathematics Classroom
The focus of this chapter is on making the case for technology in the classroom. It delves into how technology can be used to support teachers in their mathematical practice and what commitment teachers must make to use technology in their classroom. The authors share research in teacher preparation with technology as well as using the TPACK model as a framework for shaping teachers' practice.

Chapter 2: The Foundations and Principles of CCSS
This chapter explores the role of the Common Core State Standards (CCSS) in shaping teachers' practice and how teachers can approach designing instruction with the Common Core Mathematics and Standards for Mathematics Practice. This chapter supports teachers in unpacking a standard and identifying the knowledge and skills within each standard. Teachers explore resources for planning and designing instruction with the Common Core mathematics.

Chapter 3: Understanding Design
The focus of this chapter is to build understanding for instructional design of mathematics lessons with purposeful technology integration. Concepts, such as Bloom's Taxonomy, cognitive demand of tasks, Universal Design for Learning, are discussed within instructional design of mathematics lessons along with technology integration. Included in this chapter is an overview of the Big 5 research-based pedagogical strategies.

Chapter 4: Developing Daily Routines in Your Mathematics Practice
The focus of this chapter is on understanding and unpacking practical daily routines that can be established to build student confidence, develop computational fluency and engage in mental math strategies. Teachers will learn how to select a daily routine and establish goals for continuous improvement and assessment of student progress.

Chapter 5: Open-Ended Tasks
The focus of this chapter is on open-ended tasks and how teachers can leverage this practice to promote mathematical language and student confidence in problem solving. Teachers will learn how to select an open-ended task aligned to a standard for mathematics practice and Common Core Standard and establish goals for continuous improvement and assessment of student progress.

Chapter 6: Project-Based Learning
Within this chapter we build understanding of Project-Based Learning through classroom examples. Theoretical underpinnings and research are explored for why this is a critical design for learning. We discuss the value of productive struggle and rigor within mathematics instruction as encountered by PjBL. Specific types of PjBL tasks are highlighted and examples are given to structure and maintain student engagement as well as effectively integrate technology to support student achievement.

Chapter 7: Problem-Based Learning

This chapter explores the purpose, structure, and organization of problem-based learning. It examines various forms of problem-based learning and provides assistance in structuring and implementing this approach across the grade span with resources and tools for technology integration. We ground the discussion of planning problem-based learning in understanding students' developmental needs as represented by the learning progressions.

Chapter 8: Math Centers

This chapter highlights various ways to organize and structure math centers to support students' mathematical learning. We examine the role of math centers across grade levels and provide examples of how to use math centers as a form of instruction. Specific attention is paid to developing appropriate activities depending on the developmental needs of students and appropriate technological tools to enhance learning experience across grade levels.

Chapter 9: Putting It All Together

This chapter focuses on the needs of the teaching professional and aims to assist them in creating a math plan, determining goals, and setting targets. Ultimately, this chapter aims to support teachers as they move forward in implementing the strategies presented in the previous chapters. Teachers will be provided with additional technology resources and references to support their ongoing learning.

About the Authors

AUTHOR BACKGROUND

Dr. Patricia Dickenson is an Associate Professor of Teacher Education at National University. She is the Program Lead for the Bachelors of Arts In Interdisciplinary Studies with the Preliminary Multiple and Single Subject Credential. Her research area focuses on mathematics professional development and technology. She has worked in higher education for the past 8 years and was a mathematics coach, middle school teacher, and elementary school teacher for the Los Angeles Unified school district for over ten years. Dr. Dickenson has published two books and has over 12 book chapters and articles. She recently received the National Council of Teaching Mathematics Grant for Classroom research. Dr. Dickenson has posted on Twitter and Instagram over 100 blog posts on her blog: www.teacherpreptech.com and can be followed on twitter @teacherpreptech. She has written three Guest Blog posts in Education Week: http://blogs.edweek.org/edweek/rick_hess_straight_up/2012/01/justice_for_english_language_learners.html

Dr. Lorelei Coddington is an Associate Professor in the School of Education at Biola University in teacher preparation and has over 20 years of experience in K-12 education. She has been a post-doctorate fellow, K-12 researcher, teacher on special assignment, and elementary teacher. Dr. Coddington has worked extensively coaching and mentoring beginning teachers in effective pedagogy. Her research examines the influence of professional development on teacher knowledge growth and elementary mathematics learning and instruction. Dr. Coddington has conducted research in two multi-year research grants working directly with K-12 teachers to improve classroom learning of mathematics. Her research findings have been shared at national conferences, and she has several publications focused on mathematics instruction and learning. Dr. Coddington can be followed on twitter @2teachprof.

Chapter 1

The Case for Technology in the Mathematics Classroom

Self-Reflection

Which math teachers inspired you and what did they do to promote a love of mathematics? If you were not inspired why not? What were you most afraid of when it came to learning mathematics? What brought you the most joy?

Technology Takes Center Stage

When the COVID-19 virus struck in March 2020, educators shifted to teaching and learning with digital tools, which restructured the framework of their classrooms. No longer was technology viewed as an add-on to review skills or keep early finishers busy in the classroom, but technology became the means to keep teachers and students connected and learning. Parents also played a critical role as co-teacher, highlighting the importance of the school and home communication and informal learning in math. Although classroom research in math has consistently received more attention from teachers and researchers, there is substantial evidence to support the importance of out-of-school experiences in learning math and the value of parents and caregivers in facilitating mathematical reasoning and math engagement (Pattison et al., 2017, p. 7). Moreover, research has documented that math learning does not need to be solely formalized in the math classroom and in fact it should take place in a context that promotes situational application of math as a tool for problem-solving in everyday situations. For example, high school basketball players demonstrated their ability to problem-solve at a higher rate when given basketball math problems, and construction workers and fishermen without math training demonstrated their ability to solve proportional reasoning problems (Nunes & Bryant, 2010; Nunes et al., 1993). Math is everywhere and using technology can bridge these informal learning experiences in math into a collaborative culture of teachers, parents, and students, connecting and co-constructing in-school and out-of-school mathematics learning. "The mathematics of school and that of everyday life are seen as incommensurable, it impoverishes both contexts, separating the symbolic precision and power of math from the flexibility and creative sense-making of everyday life" (Martin & Gourley-Delaney, 2014, p. 611).

The Power of Technology

As technology continues to evolve, harnessing the informal learning experiences of our students will be the key to making math meaningful to learn. Blended learning, such as Khan Academy, provides students with an opportunity to extend their learning via computer-assisted programs at home or at school. In addition, these blended learning tools provide the teacher with just-in-time data to evaluate students' mathematical skills and create a personalized learning path for students (based on their performance in a computer-adaptive diagnostic). Math computer-adaptive diagnostics will evaluate students' skills and conceptual understanding across math domains and will determine whether students are performing below grade level or above. Never before have teachers had the ability to offer such personalized learning and differentiated instruction on demand. Clifford Maxwell states that, "The phenomenon of blended learning has its roots in online learning and represents a fundamental shift in instruction that has the potential to optimize for the individual student in ways that traditional instruction never could" (2016). The key word in that sentence is "optimize." The intentions of the blended learning model focus on providing students with intentional learning experiences that are differentiated uniquely for them!

What we know about technology is that it is constantly evolving. Exposure and experiences with technology will not only support math learning but also prepare students for careers in which technology skills determine their role and their opportunities for growth. As educators, developing a mindset of lifelong learning is paramount. Be ready to always try new things and not be intimidated by technology. Just like our students use technology as a tool to instantly find the answer to just about any math question, such as "what is the area of a circle whose radius is 4 units" retrieved via Google in 1.05 seconds, so can educators find a tutorial on just about anything. No longer must you type into a search bar; instead, you can just say "Hey, Siri" or "Hey, Google"—that is the power of technology. It is critical that we do not become attached to any one type of technology and fail to try new things. For example, blended learning may be in vogue now but, with virtual reality in the mainstream market, it will not be too long before augmented reality (AR) in math becomes part of how children learn. Check out how digital tools such as Geogebra and Desmos are using AR to create a space where real-life objects connect with mathematics.

👁 **View it:** https://bit.ly/3g9E1ns

Watch it

In this video, you will see how AR is utilized to explore the relationship between the diagonal lengths of rectangular prisms and everyday objects.

https://www.youtube.com/watch?v=mkc8Kvm5MTI

Starting With You!

Did you know your beliefs and experiences as a student influence your instructional choices and enthusiasm for teaching subject matter? The teacher who feels a rush of excitement about teaching mathematics most likely had positive experiences learning math whereas teachers who express fear or anxiety about mathematics may have had disagreeable or negative experiences as a student.

As an adult learner, we have the capacity to reflect on our experiences as students and make conscious decisions about how we approach instruction with our learners. Do we come into the classroom with fear and apathy, or do we approach the subject matter with excitement and enthusiasm for our learners?

Although your experiences as a student may shape your initial approach and beliefs when it comes to teaching math, effective teaching can be learned, developed, and mastered by developing a mind-set of continual growth and reflection. Good math instruction requires strong content knowledge, and good teaching requires understanding how learners learn, why students struggle, and what pedagogical practices can support all learners in the classroom, including English language learners and students with disabilities.

We've identified **five key mathematics pedagogical approaches** (the Big 5) that will positively shape your students' experiences and help you to create a classroom environment that promotes student mastery. In order to create a mastery-oriented classroom, students must perceive their intelligence as malleable and not fixed. What reinforces the idea of intelligence as fixed rather than malleable are the choices we make as classroom teachers, from the tasks we assign, to deciding how to evaluate and support students in demonstrating what they know. If our students only experience tasks based on worksheets and completing student textbooks/workbooks, students will view their intelligence as linear and learning as a process that begins and ends with the teacher providing information. However, if we shape our pedagogical choices based on our learners' needs, interests, and developmental readiness, we can support students in developing confidence in math with the ability to attack even the most challenging mathematical problems.

The Big 5 are research-based practices that support not just procedural fluency (being able to solve a problem with efficiency and automaticity), but conceptual understanding as well (understanding how concepts work). The Big 5 are essential to developing a solid math instructional block, and with the use of technology, these practices can be developed, explored, reflected upon, and organized in a meaningful way.

The Big 5 Pedagogies

1. Daily Routines
2. Open-Ended Tasks
3. Project-Based Learning
4. Problem-Based Learning
5. Math Centers

Why Do You Need This Book?

We have combined over 40 years of experience working as mathematics teachers, coaches, and university faculty. We believe no curriculum program is perfect because no program is written for you and your students. It is critical in your role as classroom teacher to determine what is working and where you need to tweak your curriculum to meet the needs of your students in the class. Each year your class will be different and you will need to adjust your instruction to meet your students' needs, not the other way around. This book will support you in determining what practices can best meet your learners' need so you can begin designing instruction for your students. The goal of this book is to support you in creating and understanding these best practices so you can meet the needs of your students, year after year, regardless of the grade and group of students you are working with. Designing instruction for 30+ students that fits their unique learning styles and abilities requires more flexibility from your curriculum and instruction. You might already have a district-adopted textbook for your math program but your program may not include one of the five key practices that we have identified as core instructional practices for a successful math block.

Each of the Big 5 pedagogies will infuse technology as a tool to support you in designing instruction and provide your students with the means to: practice skills, demonstrate understanding, deepen conceptual understanding, and create technology-driven products of learning. We believe every student has the capacity to create a product of learning, which can demonstrate their knowledge and abilities as well as their misconceptions and learning gaps. We view student products as evidence for teachers to analyze and use to make informed decisions about classroom instruction. Assessment can be used to help you make informed decisions about your practice and determine what your students know and can do independently. In each chapter, we will share approaches to assess your learners, which include "formative" measures that help you decide how to support your students and "summative" measures to grade and report student achievement. With technology, teachers can capture evidence authentically, virtually, and instantaneously while meeting the rigor of the state standards for math.

© Patricia Dickenson

The Power of Technology

What is exciting about technology today, that is different from the past, is the ability for students to create products of learning with web-based tools. Web tools shift the focus of the classroom from teacher-directed to student-centered. With web tools, students have the power to demonstrate their knowledge of concepts, understanding of procedures, and transfer what they know into a multimedia format. Moreover, these student-created products can be shared across classrooms for deeper learning, synthesis, and application. The idea that students are connected across classrooms, not just in their school and district but globally, is possible with technology, and this approach gives life to the multiple representations and ways of learning our students need for understanding.

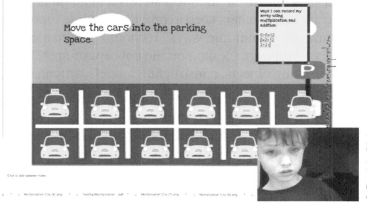

© Patricia Dickenson

Watch It

In this video Dr. Dickenson shares how students can use digital tools to learn math strategies. In addition you will see how a fourth grader explains his thinking of the area model using Google Jamboard: https://www.youtube.com/watch?v=sDwQ64GEq7M&t=33s

Think About It!

What artifacts of learning do you have from your school days? How are these artifacts preserved and cherished? What if technology could be used to capture your learning and share with your friends and family? What tools might you use to show what you know?

_____

_____

Are Kids Really Different Today?

There is an assumption that kids today learn differently than in the past. But do they really learn differently, or do we just have more ways to share information and practice skills and concepts? Anything we decide to learn, from riding a bicycle to long division, takes practice, observation, and information. With technology we can access information much more efficiently. We can watch a video, view an image, or read a web page. Long gone are the days of microfiche and card catalogs. With the touch of your smartphone and the sound of your voice, information is retrieved instantly. "Siri what is an equivalent fraction?"

What we know from brain research is that learners differ in how they perceive and comprehend information. Teachers need to provide multiple representations of concepts so learners can grasp information in multiple ways. Technology is just one tool in your toolbox. You may use technology to support a lesson on the concept of area, but your students will still need experiences manipulating objects, constructing models, articulating their thinking, and defining the formula.

From playing a game on the computer, to creating a screencast that shows how to solve a long division problem, technology allows students to play, explore, create, collaborate, and discover. The Internet is a versatile tool that does more than just display information; it allows the user to create information as well. The tasks that we design support the role and function of technology.

 Watch It

In this TED Talk "Let's Teach for Mastery Not Test Scores," Sal Khan, the founder of Khan Academy, discusses how mastery of mathematics is connected to students' mind-set about learning mathematics. Moreover, he shares how technology is changing how students access information.

Video Link: https://www.ted.com/talks/sal_khan_let_s_teach_for_mastery_not_test_scores?utm_campaign=tedspread&utm_medium=referral&utm_source=tedcomshare

Think About It!

What role does technology have in promoting student mastery in mathematics? How might access to technology influence students' lives?

_____

_____

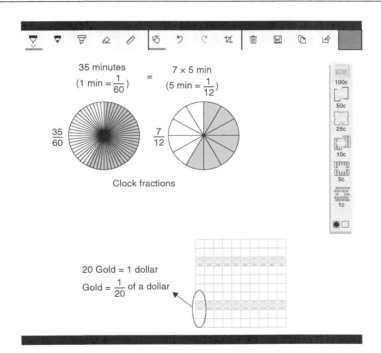

"In the above image students use a web-based tool to create a visual representation of fractions and make a connection to equivalent fractions." While children tend to struggle with fractions, web-based tools promote understanding by enabling students to create fraction representations and manipulate objects such as dragging one fraction over another to see equivalency.

Stop and Reflect

What methods and tools will you use to support your students in learning mathematics and how does this approach mirror the goals of Universal Design for Learning?

_____

_____

Technology of Tomorrow and Technology of Today

Lev Vygotsky (1978) coined the term "cultural tools" to reflect both technical tools and psychological tools that are developed and preserved in the culture. Vygotsky also believed that the purpose of education is to teach students how to use the tools that are developed and established in the culture to support children's cognitive development. Psychological tools include language, signs, and symbols which represent what things mean and how to communicate. Cultural tools include the means by which we communicate and discover information such as a pen, ruler, and protractor.

© Patricia Dickenson

In recent years, cultural tools have shifted to include more advanced technological tools such as smartphones, tablets, and web-based tools. Communication has also evolved as a result of technology to include social media, e-mail, and texting. There is no doubt that children today are growing up in a world where technology is part of everyday life, and their ability to use and manipulate such cultural tools is developing at an advanced rate. Technology holds much promise as a tool for personalized instruction, which has been found to increase motivation, engagement, and differentiating instruction. But despite such promise, technology is only as powerful as the teacher who is using it.

In 2017, Project Tomorrow conducted a survey of over 500,000 parents, educators, and students to determine how teachers are using technology and what are the barriers to technology adoption.

> The greatest barrier technology leaders face in implementing digital learning and expanding technology use is motivating teachers to change their traditional instructional practices to use technology more meaningfully with students.

Furthermore, more than two thirds of parents reported they believe technology use plays a significant role in preparing their children for colleges and careers. Teachers (68%) also shared they were better able to differentiate instruction when they used technology as a tool to support students. Whether you are a digital native (born with a smartphone in your hand) or a digital immigrant (just recently acquired one) integrating technology into your teaching practice is not an easy task. New and experienced teachers need to develop technical skills, in addition to a strong understanding of how to integrate technology, in order to purposefully include technology into their subject area.

Koehler and Mishra (2007) coined the term "TPACK," which stands for Technological Pedagogical Content Knowledge, as a framework to describe the types of knowledge teachers need to be successful with technology integration. This framework is based on Lee Shulman's (1986) idea of teacher knowledge, which includes knowledge of subject matter and knowledge of how to teach subject matter (pedagogical knowledge). Shulman argued that subject matter and teacher knowledge should not be mutually exclusive and coined the term "pedagogical content knowledge" (PCK) to address the concept of having knowledge of how to teach in a specific content area.

Mishra and Koehler (2007) built upon Shulman's (1986) notion of knowledge for teaching to include technological knowledge, technological content knowledge (TCK), and technological pedagogical knowledge (TPK). According to Koehler and Mishra (2009), TPACK is:

> the basis of effective teaching with technology requiring an understanding of the representations of concepts using technologies; pedagogical techniques that use technologies in constructive ways to teach concepts; knowledge of what makes concepts difficult or easy to learn and how technology can help redress some of the problems that students face; knowledge of students' prior knowledge and theories of epistemology; and knowledge of how technologies can be used to build on existing knowledge to develop new epistemologies or strengthen old ones. (p. 66)

Let's take a closer peek at TPACK in the context of teaching mathematics:

PCK: Pedagogical Content Knowledge refers to the knowledge of how to teach mathematics. This specialized knowledge is highly contextualized in terms of teaching math from asking a question as a way to support students in solving a problem, to launching into a math task that will engage all learners. PCK does vary across disciplines, which means what works in math might not necessarily work in your social studies class. In this book, we explore five pedagogical practices for math instruction.

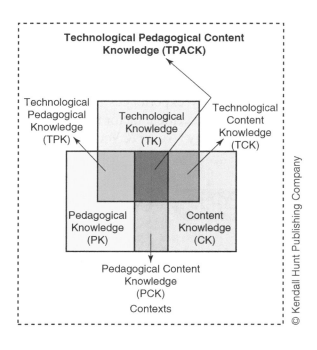

© Kendall Hunt Publishing Company

TPK: Technological Pedagogical Knowledge refers to the teachers' knowledge needed for selecting the kinds of technology to best support a teaching strategy. If students are working collaboratively on a group presentation, they might use Google Docs or Prezi as a digital tool that allows them to collaborate. If students are working independently on a skill, the teacher might choose an online math game or an online math curriculum that is personalized and adaptive based on the students' knowledge and skill.

TCK: Technological Content Knowledge refers to the knowledge about the types of technology that will best assist your students in learning content. For example, if you want students to understand equivalent fractions, you would look for virtual manipulatives that allow the students to see equivalency with different parts; provide online resources to find pictures that represent fractions; and have students create a virtual mind map, e-book, or online glossary to explain their representations.

When it comes to teaching with technology, there is no doubt that teachers need the technical skill to use digital tools, but they also need to know which tools best support the content and pedagogical practices. That is why we focus on the Big 5 practices in math and share how technology can be seamlessly integrated into each of these practices. Curating and finding resources can be a timely process that's why this book is loaded with online resources, sample lessons, and videos connected to the content you teach and is continuously curated in our online site to ensure updated links.

We've included an online resource guide that includes digital tools and apps for integration. You will also have a community of online teachers to share your ideas, ask questions, and post pictures and videos of your classroom. Please join our Facebook Group: **Teaching Outside the Box: Technology Infused Math Instruction** (URL: https://www.facebook.com/groups/techoutside/) to get connected.

© Patricia Dickenson

We know that regardless of your personal experiences using technology, knowing how technology can best support you in teaching your content areas is not intuitive. Research suggests that teachers tend to teach the way they were taught, and the quantity and quality of preservice teachers' technology experiences in teacher education programs has been found to be a critical factor that influences new teachers' adoption of technology (Agyei & Voogt, 2011; Drent & Meelissen, 2008).

Stop and Reflect

How do you think technology should be used in the classroom? What past experiences have you had that frame your beliefs about technology use in the classroom?

_____

_____

Why Technology in Mathematics?

The need to motivate and engage young learners in mathematics is more important now than ever. Some of the highest paying jobs in our country belong to workers who have one thing in common, math skills (National Association of Colleges and Employers, 2016). Furthermore, research shows students who complete a mathematics course beyond the level of Algebra II more than double their odds of pursuing and completing a postsecondary education (Adelman, 1999). Many districts require completion of an Algebra I course prior to finishing ninth grade (Loveless, 2008), but district requirements do not guarantee students are making the grade. For example, in California, many students are failing algebra; nearly one third of students scored "below basic" or "far below basic" in algebra (Terry & Rosin, 2011). Research also shows that students who fail are likely to fail again when repeating the course (Fong et al., 2014). Across the country, failure of algebra can run as high as 50%. One of the greatest predictors of success of algebra is the foundational skills that students acquire in elementary school.

Elementary teachers are laying the groundwork for students to have computational fluency, problem-solving skills, and conceptual understanding. Without a solid foundation at the elementary level, students are on a path toward failure by the time they get to middle school. In their article, "Opening a Gateway to College Access: Algebra at the Right Time," Snipes and Finkelstein (2015) state:

> Students who struggle with math in middle school and high school have a lower chance of meeting eligibility requirements in California's public universities; four years of math in high school, with a strong foundation in algebra that builds from middle school, is key to higher education access. (p. 1)

Can technology help to support your students through personalized learning, visual representations, digital tools, and online activities to support making connections and explaining their thinking?

A recent meta-analysis of the effect of technology on mathematics achievement showed statistically significant gains across the K-12 classroom (Slavin & Chung, 2013). Students who reported their teachers used computers frequently as a way to demonstrate new topics had higher levels of math achievement (House, 2011). Mathematics knowledge was also positively related to the use of multimedia strategies for elementary students (Weiss, Kramarski, & Tails, 2006). These findings suggest the role of technology does make a significant impact in students' academic achievement in mathematics. Moreover, the findings suggest the use of technology should not be limited to one instructional approach or methodology. Teachers should

© Patricia Dickenson

vary how they use technology from showing a video clip of a math-related concept to providing practice of mathematics facts and concepts through technology tools and resources.

Strong classroom practices are the key to meaningful learning experiences for students in mathematics. Throughout the years, solid mathematical practices have evolved to support students in developing computational fluency, conceptual understanding, meaningful connections, and mathematics discussions. But we know it is not enough to bridge the algebra gap. What is needed in the classroom is for teachers to bridge these practices in the context of students' lives by using culturally relevant tools that build on students' existing schemas and create a high level of interest in mathematics. We believe, and the research shows us, that technology tools at students' fingertips will elevate mathematics pedagogy in two key ways:

1. Support students in **making meaningful connections** through multiple representations, real-life application, and opportunities to express and demonstrate what they know and how they know it.
2. Provide teachers with the **efficiency to differentiate tasks, scaffold instruction, and utilize multiple measures** to assess and support student learning.

Getting Started With Technology

Throughout this book we share the best practices for using technology with math instruction. We know these tools and tips can be utilized in other subject areas. The focus of this book (as coined by Misha and Kohler) is to develop your "TPACK" that means technology is most effective when it is focused on the content knowledge and pedagogical practices in a particular subject area. To increase your efficacy in teaching mathematics with technology, we have created a master list of teaching ideas and technology resources. These ideas and resources will continue to grow and develop as new technology emerges and takes shape.

We also invite you to share your best practices and ideas for technology resources. The link below will take you to a document that is editable in Google Forms. This will allow you to include your teaching ideas and share technology resources for math. Technology tools are arranged by category so you can determine how to apply the technology in a meaningful way. In the following section, we share our classification of technology resources with an idea for integration.

Web tool Link: http://www.teacherpreptech.com/p/tech-tools.html

Category of Web Tools

1. **Digital Assessment Tools**
   Assessment tools can be used throughout instruction to understand what your learners know, need to know, and have learned. Many of the digital tools include a bank of questions categorized by content standard and the capability to create questions tailored for your students.

Digital assessment tools are highly effective at providing you with scored data that can be shared with parents and other educators.

2. **Blended Learning**

   Math instruction can be highly personalized and provide additional support or challenge using a blended learning program for every student. There are a variety of programs that are either free or charge a subscription and whereas some programs emphasize conceptual understanding, others focus on developing computation fluency. Before you sign your students up for a program we recommend you try it out.

3. **Calculation Tools**

   Digital tools support students in calculating data, displaying information, and creating pictorial and symbolic representations.

4. **Creation Tools**

   These student-centered tools allow students to express their ideas and show what they know via multimedia and video recording.

5. **Collaboration Tools**

   Tools that allow you and your students to share ideas and resources and work collaboratively on different devices at the same time.

6. **Construction Tools**

   Tools that allow students to create a mathematical model using either real-world images or virtual pieces.

7. **Connectivity Tools**

   Tools that allow students to share their ideas and/or products of learning, with other people in a virtual space.

8. **Gamify**

   Tools that create a game-based learning environment which include questions and answers to provide immediate feedback.

9. **Math Tasks**

   Rigorous math tasks that allow students to problem-solve and think deeply about a concept.

10. **Presentation**

    Web-based tools that allow you and your students to share ideas in a presentation format.

11. **Productivity**

    These kinds of tools help you and your students organize information, collaborate virtually, and communicate instantaneously.

12. **Video**

    Streaming video that can be used to demonstrate a concept or express a related math idea.

The following table is an example of the digital document you can access and contribute virtually. We are just giving you a sneak peek of what you can expect when you access this Google Sheet at https://bit.ly/3wxvXUq.

Use	TooL/URL	Description	Teaching Idea
Assessment	Woot Math https://www.wootmath.com/	Formative assessment tool and adaptive practice	Teacher selects a math concept and gives code to students as a pre-assessment to determine students' prior knowledge.
Blended Learning	ST Math https://www.stmath.com/	Adaptive learning for math	Student completes a pre-assessment to determine placement and uses program during math centers as a rotation.
Calculation Tools	PollEverywhere https://www.polleverywhere.com/	Data collection tool for graphing	Students create a survey based on a recent reading unit to determine students' beliefs about a book.
Collaborate	Padlet https://padlet.com	Students respond to a prompt or question	Create a virtual Know-Want to Know-Learned (KWL) padlet about a concept and ask students to respond.
Connect	Seesaw https://web.seesaw.me/	Online portfolio for students to share work with peers, teachers, and parents	Students share products of learning and peers' comment and provide feedback.
Construct	National Library of Virtual Manipulatives http://nlvm.usu.edu/en/nav/vlibrary.html	Students can create virtual models of math concepts	Create a virtual model of dividing fractions.
Gamify	Kahoot https://kahoot.com/	Create video or text-based questions that students respond to virtually	Students can create a Kahoot as a review to an end-of-the-unit exam.
Math Tasks	3 Acts Math Task https://whenmathhappens.com/3-act-math/	Video-based word problems that hooks students with real-life situations	Use as a warm-up to review previously learned concepts.

Use	TooL/URL	Description	Teaching Idea
Presentation	Google Slides Google Slides—create and edit presentations online, for free.	Cloud-based presentation tool for virtual sharing	Create a presentation about a concept and ask students to "make a copy," then students can add their notes and respond to questions in the presentation.

International Society for Technology in Education Standards for Students

The International Society for Technology in Education (ISTE) Standards provide a strong framework for examining how students should engage with technology. The standards call for active students' participation that is facilitated by the teacher who purposefully selects technology for student use. Technology is viewed as a tool that requires active student participation, yet participation is only possible with purposeful planning from the teacher. Each of the following ISTE Standards were considered in the design of the learning activities throughout this book.

1. **Empowered Learner**—Students leverage technology to take an active role in choosing, achieving, and demonstrating competency in their learning goals, informed by the learning sciences.
2. **Digital Citizen**—Students recognize the rights, responsibilities, and opportunities of living and working in an interconnected digital work, and they act and model in ways that are safe, legal, and ethical.
3. **Knowledge Constructor**—Students critically curate a variety of resources using digital tools to construct knowledge, produce creative artifacts, and make meaningful learning experiences for themselves and others.
4. **Innovative Designer**—Students use a variety of technologies within a design process to identify and solve problems by creating new, useful, or imaginative solutions.
5. **Computational Thinker**—Students develop and employ strategies for understanding and solving problems in ways that leverage the power of technological methods to develop and test solutions.
6. **Creative Communicator**—Students communicate clearly and express themselves creatively for a variety of purposes using the platforms, tools, styles, formats, and digital media appropriate to their goals.
7. **Global Communicator**—Students use digital tools to broaden their perspectives and enrich their learning by collaborating with others and working effectively in teams locally and globally.

👁 View It: https://www.iste.org/standards/for-students

Watch It

This is a rap video to share with your students which helps them understand the above ISTE standards for students and how they can be applied in the classroom.

https://www.youtube.com/watch?v=ooTbKEnSpIY

Designing Technology-Integrated Lessons

Another framework that is important to consider when utilizing technology is the SAMR model. Whereas the ISTE standards guide our decisions about how to use technology in our instruction, the SAMR model focuses on the rigor of technology application. Dr. Ruben Peuntedura (2006) coined the SAMR model as a way to articulate the level of technology integration across a continuum. SAMR is an acronym for substitution, augmentation, modification, and redefinition. We believe this model is important for teachers to consider as they begin to include technology in their instruction. Determining the function and role of technology will impact the instruction and support you provide students. Just like introducing a new concept to students in the classroom, their prior knowledge, skills, and abilities must be considered.

We provide an example of how the stages of the SAMR model is aligned with technology use in mathematics. The following table illustrates the use and function of Google Maps at each level of technology integration. We believe each level of technology integration is important to consider as students develop their efficacy to use a tool. Greater autonomy and choice to work independently and demonstrate more sophisticated use of the tool is achieved with practice and support (Table 1.1).

3 Stages to Connect with Tech

We have developed a simplified model for integrating technology with young learners, and surprisingly we have found a similar model also works with adults. In our experiences, the biggest predictor of technology adoption is how self-directed students are at learning a new skill. Regardless of the students' age or previous experiences, students who are self-directed will use problem-solving skills to move forward and learn the acquired skills. As math teachers, we are happy to see how much our students are willing to take risks when it comes to using technology and this has transferred into mathematics as well. Our proposed model for technology integration for student use consists of three stages.

Stage 1: *Use It or Lose It*

In the first stage, it is vital for the teacher to model the use of technology skills for student acquisition. This includes an overview of the tools and features and guided practice with students using the tool with teacher's feedback and demonstration of application.

Table 1.1   Stages of SAMR model with using Google Tours.

Level of Technology Implementation	What the Teacher Does	What the Student Does
Substitution Technology as direct tool substitute but no change to task	Shows Google Tours instead of textbook to illustrate the concept of distance	Views Google Tours and approximates distance.
Augmentation Technology as a direct tool substitute with functional improvement	Models and demonstrates how to use Google Tours and plot points to determine the distance of places using Google map tools	Students locate places on Google Tours and uses tool features to plot points and determine distance between places.
Modification Technology allows for significant task redesign	Provide students with autonomy to explore places in their neighborhood they travel to and determine distance traveled in a week	Students create a map of places traveled and shares their weekly journey with peers.
Redefinition Technology allows for creation of new tasks, previously inconceivable	Provides students with autonomy and choice to create a narrated tour of characters from a novel using Google Tours and tools.	Explore places using audio features and tools to create a narrative account of a character's journey through locating places on Google Tours.

Stage 2: *On the Surface*

In this stage, students should work independently or with a partner to utilize the tool in a context that is familiar and/or with content that students have already demonstrated expertise. For example, students create an "All About Me" with Popplet or Mindmap. In this stage, students are provided with a criteria chart to guide the use and application of tool. We view this stage as a type of formative assessment to determine if students can move forward to the next stage independently. Teachers should use this assessment to determine what re-teaching might be necessary or if grouping students during the next stage would support acquisition of technology skills while not interfering with demonstration of content knowledge.

Criteria Chart: All About Me

_____ I wrote my name in the center bubble.

_____ I shared at least two things I like to do.

_____ I have at least three pictures about me.

_____ I shared one memory and picture about a summer memory.

_____ I shared at least two things about my family.

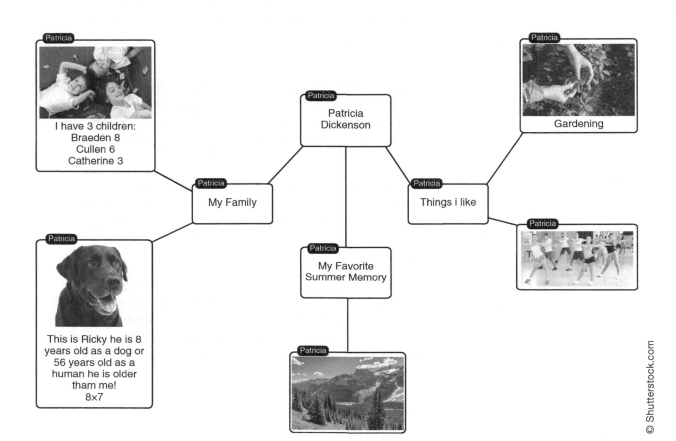

Stage 3: _Deep Dive_

In the final stage, students demonstrate their knowledge of academic content through application of the web tool. Students may use class notes, textbooks, or research to articulate their ideas, comprehension, and demonstration of learning. The teacher provides guidance and assistance to all students to ensure students have developed proficiency in technology skills. Rubrics and/or criteria charts are used to evaluate students' academic knowledge and provide feedback.

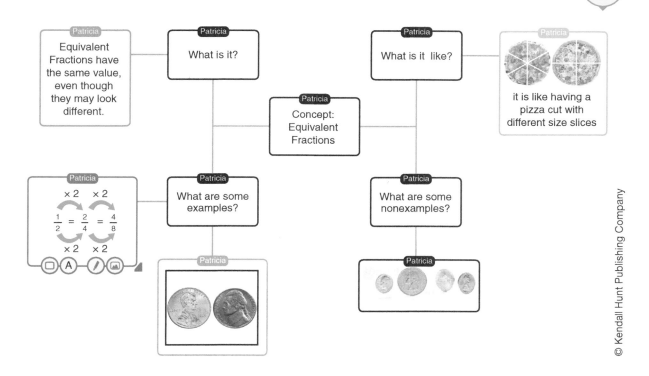

Proposed Model for Technology Integration

As highlighted, we recommend *three stages* to successful integration of technology in your classroom. Within each chapter of this book, we have included ideas for technology integration as both evidence of student learning and tools for teaching and instruction. We know that there is much to think about when integrating technology in your classroom, including what resources you have available and learning about your school policies with regard to technology. To support you in getting started with technology in your classroom, we have created a technology inventory plan for your consideration. Please reference the Appendix of this book to review our recommendations.

Five Professional Commitments to Guide Technology Integration in the Classroom

Thus far, we have explored why technology is important to make meaningful math connections. We also want you to be familiar with the principles we are using to guide our recommendations for technology. We believe teachers must make five professional commitments to make a difference in the experiences your students have during mathematics instruction. However, it is quite likely that the practices you adopt during your math period can be effective in other subject areas as well. The commitments we ask you to make are enduring issues for teachers and will greatly impact the students you serve throughout your career as an educator.

Commitment no. 1: Technology should be an active part of the student experience.

I promise to make technology a tool my students use to access and share information, create products of learning, and think critically about a concept.

Why It Matters: Students will not grow intellectually when technology is used just to display information, play a game, or assess student learning. Technology should function as a tool for students to become critical thinkers and producers of content.

Commitment no. 2: Students and teachers should use technology to collaborate meaningfully.

I promise to promote collaboration with technology tools through group work, feedback, and real-life connections grounded in the lives of the students I teach.

Why It Matters: Learning is an active task which includes listening, sharing, and hearing ideas from others. Using technology as a tool for collaboration supports students' voices and creates a classroom culture where all students feel valued and supported.

Commitment no. 3: Teachers should integrate a variety of tools to provide students with choice, creativity, and exploration.

I promise to promote choice, creativity, and exploration with access to a variety of technologies.

Why It Matters: Students are empowered by choice and can work autonomously when they have developed the efficacy to use a tool independently. Web tools that promote creativity help students make connections with content matter in a way that is meaningful and relevant to their lives.

Commitment no. 4: Teachers should include a variety of instructional approaches that apply technology as a core part of teaching and learning.

I promise to diversify the way I use technology in my classroom so students can experience how technology is used to support learning in a variety of ways.

Why It Matters: From flipped classroom to blended learning, instruction should not be a one-size-fits-all approach. Students need multiple representations and experiences with content and technology to make strong connections and transfer learning.

Commitment no. 5: Teachers should continuously learn and develop a habit of mind for technology use and application.

I promise to take an active role in my professional growth and development as a teacher and user of technology.

Why It Matters: As you continue in the teaching profession, your students will change, society will change, and technology will continue to evolve.

Developing Your Teacher Toolbox

With the birth of the Common Core and National Standards, came a new era of the modern teacher as an instructional designer, curator of content, and creator of interactive learning experiences. This shift in teaching requires teachers to become lifelong learners who are exercising 21st-century skills such as *communication* with colleagues, *collaboration* with teachers from around the world in a personal learning network (PLN), *critical thinkers* of instructional tools, and creators of personalized learning.

This book is organized around five key instructional practices (the Big 5) in mathematics that develop the habits of mind to support students in becoming mathematical thinkers and problems solvers. These practices support students in developing conceptual understanding and procedural fluency. We have selected these practices based on students' developmental readiness to engage in mathematics in ways that make sense and build upon students' existing schemas. The practices include **daily routines, open-ended tasks, project-based learning, problem-based learning, and math centers.**

In each chapter, we unpack one of the Big 5 pedagogies. We share how to plan instruction, assess and support students, and integrate technology with each pedagogical practice. We show you how to design tasks based on what you know about your learners. Do they need to deepen their conceptual understanding, develop their number sense or become more confident in explaining their ideas? Maybe they need to work on all these skills as they are just starting their journey as young mathematicians. With each instructional practices is an opportunity for teachers to integrate technology in meaningful ways and develop both conceptual and procedural fluency in mathematics.

In Chapter 2 of this book, we share the background and history of the Common Core State Standards for Mathematics and the Standards for Mathematical Practice. We believe your instruction should begin with understanding what you are teaching and why it is important. Teachers today need to do more than open a curriculum manual and read the instruction. They need to begin planning by unpacking the standards and identifying the skills they need to teach and the knowledge and skills students need to develop. They need to plan what questions they will ask to support student thinking and how they might assess learners in a variety of ways to ensure every student can explain their thinking. The Standards for Mathematical Practices inform us as to how we should teach and what habits of mind our students need to develop.

Summary

We know from research that teachers tend to teach the way they were taught, and technology is only as powerful as the teacher who is using it. We believe that technology training and integration needs to be part of teacher training and should include technical skills on how to use tools as well as subject matter integration with technology. Teacher education programs should shape the perspective of future teachers to include the knowledge and skills that are valued by society. According to Ken Kay (2010), "Today's students need critical thinking and problem-solving skills not just to solve the problems of their current jobs, but to meet the challenges of adapting to our constantly changing workforce" (NEA, p. 6). Teachers make choices about the kind of classroom they will create and the kinds of experiences their students will have. The choices you make shape the kind of teacher you become and the impact you have on your students.

Additional Activities/Discussion Questions

1. Review the TPACK model and determine what skills you need to improve in your teaching practice.
2. Which of the five professional commitments do you think will be your biggest challenge and greatest strength in the classroom?
3. Which of the Big 5 pedagogies are you most familiar with and least familiar with? How might you integrate technology into these practices?
4. Join a Twitter discussion with fellow math teachers by using the hashtag #mtbos (math teacher blogosphere)

Instructor Activities

1. Create a KWL Padlet with three sections (see instructor resources for an example): What do I know about using technology in math instruction?; What do I want to know about using technology in math instruction?; and What have I learned? At the end of each chapter have students post in the KWL chart and discuss students' posts.
2. Create a Copy of the Technology Self-Assessment in the Chapter 1 Google Folder for Instructor Resources. Have your students complete the survey and analyze the data with your class. Use the results to create heterogeneous groups based on technical skill so that peer tutoring can occur when students work collaboratively.
3. Check out the Kahoot game from the technology tools list and play in real time with your class. Share how this experience informed your practice and what you learned about your students.

Chapter 2

The Foundations and Principles of the CCSS

Self-Reflection

What are your initial thoughts about standards-based instruction? What are the benefits and drawbacks when standards mandate the skills and understandings you should teach? How might standards promote equity and access in your classroom instruction?

Starting with the Standards!

Why do I need to teach the standards?
What if my students are not ready to master the standard?
Where did the standards come from?
What are teachers supposed to do with the standards?
How do teachers use the standards to plan a lesson?

We hear the above questions from teachers as they begin to explore the Common Core State Standards (CCSS). However, as they become familiar with the underlying principles and rationale of the Common Core the fear and anxiety shifts to excitement, and creative thinking surfaces about ways to teach the math standards. Understanding the background of the CCSS and how the standards were developed is imperative and not just for teachers, but resource specialists, parents, school staff, and most importantly the students, as everyone plays a role in a child's academic success. The foundations and principles underlined in the Common Core are connected to how we plan instruction, design tasks, prepare for state assessments, and make informed decisions to parents and other constituents that impact how we support students toward mastery of grade-level expectations and beyond.

The CCSSs are the current national educational standards that define what students need to know and do in K-12 education. Your knowledge and understanding of the CCSS will help you to plan instruction for all learners and create assessment tools and activities to meet students where they are, and not just where they need to be. As the classroom teacher, you need to know more than just the grade-level standards you teach; you also need to know how the standards develop and progress in fostering mathematical understandings across the grade span.

 Think About It!

How can knowing about the development of the Common Core and the scope and sequence of the math standards across the grade span support you as a classroom teacher?

_____

_____

Plan to the Standard

When experienced teachers think about planning instruction, they consider not just what they are going to teach but who they are teaching. This requires knowing what prior knowledge, skills, and understandings students must have to become successful at mastering a new concept. Teachers must also consider how they will articulate the standard in a way that promotes meaning and value to the students.

Here are just a few ways knowing the standard will help you in the classroom.

1. **Setting Student Learning Targets**
   The math content standards are composed of concepts and skills that are built upon prior knowledge and understanding. In order to design instruction that meets the needs of your learners, you need to identify the concepts and skills you will be explicitly teaching and set student learning targets as measurable outcomes.

2. **Assessing Student Learning**
   Good teaching begins with meeting your students where they are. When unpacking a standard, identify the prior knowledge and skills your students will need and use a preassessment to determine whether students have learning gaps that need to be addressed prior to teaching the standard. Your student learning targets for the standard should lend themselves to formative and summative assessment measures. When you identify the skills and knowledge students will learn, consider how you will measure student understanding with measurable outcomes.

3. **Moving Students Toward Mastery**
   When students are given explicit, concrete feedback they are more likely to engage in an activity, seek your help, and know where they need to improve. Students' feedback matters and has been found to be directly correlated to academic achievement (Hattie, 2009).

4. **Student Self-Assessment**
   A significant amount of research shows that student self-assessment can be a powerful tool for student motivation (McMillan & Hearn, 2008). However, in order for students to self-assess in a way that is meaningful, and connected to your instruction, the assessment should be tied to the standard you are teaching.

5. **Owning It**
   Students won't own their learning if they don't understand what you are teaching and why it matters. The more you connect the standard to specific goals and targets the more students can own their learning and be responsible for what they need to know.

6. **Student Misconceptions and Common Errors**
   When you understand the expectations of a standard, you can identify common errors that students might demonstrate during instruction as well as misconceptions they might have about a concept. Knowing what to look for can help you make informed decisions about your instruction, such as what technology tools you will use, student groups, and ways of assessing.

CCSS Mathematics

The Common Core State Standards Mathematics (CCSS-M) is organized around three main principles: *Focus, Coherence*, and *Rigor*. These three principles represent the ways in which the CCSS have shifted from past standards.

Focus means time and practice are needed to give children adequate opportunities to learn the math concepts identified in the standards through deep exploration.

Coherence means standards are not only vertically aligned with previous and subsequent grades but concepts are also horizontally aligned across a single grade, linking concepts together to major topics in meaningful ways.

Rigor means an equal emphasis is placed on conceptual understanding, procedure skill, and fluency, as well as applying knowledge to real-world contexts through word problems (NGA & CCSSO, 2010).

 Stop and Reflect

How might the three main principles: Focus, Coherence, and Rigor create a shift in how teachers support and teach students in learning mathematics?

_____

_____

The CCSSM includes two types of comprehensive standards to be taught at each grade level: the CCSSs for Mathematics and the Standards for Mathematical Practice (SMP). The CCSS identify the concepts to be taught which informs us of the knowledge and skills students need to master by the end of each grade level. The SMP span the K-12 grades to indicate the habits of mind students must develop while becoming proficient with understanding the concepts. Teachers should develop these ways of thinking by embedding them in the types of activities and opportunities students have during instruction.

Unpacking the Standards

It is important to recognize how the CCSS are organized. The individual content standards are grouped by content and listed by number under a domain, or larger group of related standards. In the following given example, the domain, standards, and the standard cluster are identified. But first let's uncover what each of these terms mean in relation to a standard.

Domain: The larger concept under which the related standards are listed. This is typically the overarching topic or subject matter (e.g., Number and Operations in Base 10 3.NBT)

Cluster: A cluster or group of standards around the particular subject-matter listed together under the domain or larger concept.

Standard: Individually listed statements that include what students need to know and do related to the overarching concept (e.g., 1. Use place value understanding to round whole numbers to the nearest 10 or 100).

The individual standards are numbered. These standards are clustered because they closely relate to one another. The numbers do not mean that they must be taught in the given order, nor does the order of the domains suggest the order in which the content should be taught.

The writers of the CCSS clearly state that these standards are not curriculum or pedagogy, but rather they represent what children should know and be able to do at each grade level (NGA & CCSSO, 2010).

To record the standard in your lesson plan, you should include specific information to alert your reader to the content standards you are using. *Number and Operations in Base Ten* (domain) is referenced in the abbreviation, **NBT**. The 3 represents the grade level of the standard. In this case, it is third grade. Thus you would write **3.NBT**. If you were going to use the first standard, *Use place value understanding to round whole numbers to the nearest 10 or 100*, in your lesson plan, you would notate, **3.NBT.1**—NBT for Numbers in Base Ten, 3 to represent the grade level, and 1 to represent the first standard. Then you would write the full standard:

3.NBT.1 Use place value understanding to round whole numbers to the nearest 10 or 100.

 Try It!

When you plan a lesson, pay attention to what the standard identifies as "what students' should know" and "be able to do." The process of unpacking a standard will support you in identifying the content and skills you will need to teach. To help laser in on what students need to know, identify the nouns in the standard, which are the concepts or content that you will teach, and the verbs, which are the skills or actions that students should be able to do.

Vague Verbs Chart

Vague Verbs: "Dead Words"	Suggestions for Translating Vague Verbs
Understand	Explain, describe, demonstrate
Know	Read, explain, restate, summarize
Express	State, record, defend, explain, present, justify
Interpret	Restate, summarize, explain, paraphrase, rewrite

To begin unpacking, we will first start with the following third grade Number in Base Ten standard that we used earlier in our discussion of how to read a standard:

3.NBT.1 Use place value understanding to round whole numbers to the nearest 10 or 100.

First, identify the nouns (concepts or content that you will be teaching) by making a list.

_____

_____

Next, identify the verbs (skills) by making a list.

_____

_____

This information can be further organized by making a T-Chart:

Nouns (Concepts or content that you will be teaching)	Verb (Skills)
• Place value understanding • Whole numbers	• Use • Round (to the nearest 10 or 100)

Another way to organize the information is to highlight the nouns and underline the verbs.

Use place value understanding to round whole numbers to the nearest 10 or 100.

By pulling out this information we can clearly see that students are to use place value knowledge to round whole numbers. Consider the verb "use" and if this would be observable. As you unpack the standard you must also consider what the students will actually do to show evidence of their learning. Unpacking is not just a list of nouns and verbs. The degree of rounding is to the nearest 10 or 100. By examining what students need to know and do, we now know what to focus on when planning a lesson including specifically using place value to round whole numbers. This is a simple standard. When standards are longer, they become more complex, so practicing with a short standard like this one makes it much easier at first.

Now, it's your turn. Try unwrapping the second and third standards listed in the Number in Base Ten cluster for third grade on your own. Then view the video to compare your response.

3.NBT.2 Fluently add and subtract within 1,000 using strategies and algorithms based on place value, properties of operations, and/or the relationship between addition and subtraction.

3.NBT.3 Multiply one-digit whole numbers by multiples of 10 in the range 10–90 (e.g., 9×80, 5×60) using strategies based on place value and properties of operations.

Now watch Dr. Coddington unwrap the above standards and compare your response.

👁 **View It:** https://youtu.be/FAxGu9e0Yl4

Standards for Mathematical Practice

What we are really excited about when it comes to the Common Core math standards are the Standards for Mathematical Practice (SMP). The writers of the CCSS included eight SMPs that are consistent across grades K-12 mathematics. These standards describe the habits of mind students need to practice during the development of skills and knowledge across grades K-12 mathematics. These standards also help teachers frame how to structure activities and determine what information they should provide to support students in meeting the Mathematical Practice standard. We have taken the SMPs and provided a reference tool that includes a description of each of the standards along with a technology connection.

Standard for Mathematical Practice	Description	Technology Connection
1. Make sense of problems and persevere in solving them	Students are to explain the meaning of a problem by identifying its parts and identifying a point of entry and work toward a solution, making changes as necessary. They should persist with solving even when the problem is difficult.	Post a question using FlipGrid and students can respond by explaining their solution via video.
2. Reason abstractly and quantitatively	Students are to deconstruct a given situation by identifying quantities using symbolic representations or pictures. In addition, students should make sense of the quantities and units and make sense of them.	Provide access to digital manipulatives such as Math Learning Center and have students take a screenshot with text and annotation. Telling Time: https://itunes.apple.com/us/app/interactive-telling-time-lite/id482452233?mt=8
3. Construct viable arguments and critique the reasoning of others	Students are to justify their solutions and present their reasoned statements to others. They should also listen to other's mathematical arguments and ask questions and critique their validity.	Create a Padlet with an open ended math question which has multiple solutions. Students can respond via video or text.

Standard for Mathematical Practice	Description	Technology Connection
4. Model with mathematics	Students are to solve problems in real life by using illustrations, diagrams, or objects to show their understanding. They may also include equations to demonstrate their understanding of a given situation.	Use a learning management system such as SeeSaw or Google Classroom and have students post pictures of their illustrations or math models to share and leave comments for others.
5. Use appropriate tools strategically	Students are to select the appropriate tools and apply them to a given task. Tools may include concrete models, paper, pencil, rulers, protractors, and calculators.	Provide your students with a choice of digital tools. This supports an engaging discussion of multiple representations and ways of showing. Use this Google Deck to give choice: https://bit.ly/3clS5sH
6. Attend to precision	Students are to clearly discuss and articulate their own reasoning using mathematically accurate language. As well, students are to attend to precision in their accuracy in solving problems, specifying units, and labeling solutions.	Post a question using FlipGrid and students can respond by explaining their solution via video. Include in the directions sentence stems and/or academic language to support students in using vocabulary with precision.
7. Look for and make use of structure	Students are to find patterns and structure in numbers, equations, and in collections of objects.	Create a Jamboard for students to identify patterns on a problem type such as "Which one Doesn't Belong" students can annotate on images and post comments to share their thinking about patterns.
8. Look for and express regularity in repeated reasoning	Students are to look for numbers or calculations that are repeated to find methods and shortcuts when solving problems.	Identify an online Desmos activity for students to work through and include math chat discussions to share reasoning.

Web Tools Resource List

We have curated a list of web tools that we believe meets the Standards for Mathematics Practice and include rigorous math activities. In Chapter 1, we discuss the 12 categories we have identified and provide examples for application in your math block. We know technology continues to be developed in the education space and resources are exploding at a phenomenal rate so we encourage you to contribute to this list with any math resources you come across.

http://www.teacherpreptech.com/p/tech-tools.html

https://youtu.be/cYQiMlgKlB4

Now watch Dr. Dickenson connect the Standards for Mathematical Practice to technology tools. An explanation of how the Standards for Mathematical Practice (SMPs) influence your instruction and student actions is also shared.

👁 View It: https://bit.ly/3ioZvzf

In Chapter 3, we go deeper into planning so you can make the connection between unpacking a content standard and applying the SMPs. But for now, let's see how you might include the SMPs with the following eighth-grade content standard.

8.NS.A.1 Know that numbers that are not rational are called irrational. Understand informally that every number has a decimal expansion; for rational numbers show that the decimal expansion repeats eventually and convert decimal expansion, which repeats eventually into a rational number.

This time we will approach unpacking a standard differently. You will approach unpacking in five steps. You will copy and paste the standard into the two parts of the chart.

Step 1: Copy and paste the standard into the chart below.

Step 2: Highlight the verbs in the skills area.

Step 3: Divide the standard into statements.

Step 4: Translate Vague Verbs.

Step 5: Highlight the content knowledge. You can watch Dr. Dickenson unpack this standard with this process here: https://www.youtube.com/watch?v=26Vw80wBwaQR

Content Knowledge/Nouns	Skills/Verb

Learning Outcomes	Assessment

Think About It!

In the video you will see how Dr. Dickenson connects the unpacked standard to learning outcomes and assessment. This is the next step once you have unpacked your standard. We will discuss in greater detail how to plan your instruction in Chapter 3 of this text.

_____

_____

This standard is language-rich for students and should include activities that both scaffold descriptions and include attributes that are important to distinguish between rational and irrational numbers. We can have our students clarify understanding of rational numbers as well as use the notation for decimal expansion of irrational numbers.

When we reference the SMPs, we will want to include the following:

No. 3 Construct viable arguments and critique the reasoning of others.

No. 6 Attend to precision.

No. 8 Look for and express regularity in repeated reasoning.

We selected the above SMPs as they address students communicating precisely to others and being able to use stated assumptions and definitions to construct an argument. Furthermore, when the standard explicitly calls for students to convert then students will need to access prior knowledge about converting fractions to decimals. From this prior knowledge the teacher can connect to the skill of changing the decimal expansion of a repeating decimal into a fraction and a fraction into a repeating decimal. From a developmental perspective, having students use a graphic organizer to help students distinguish between rational and irrational numbers including in their organizer attributes of each such as descriptors and examples. The model will aid the students in using vocabulary with precision. The teacher might also include sentence frames such as:

"An irrational numbers is a decimal whose expansion does not _____ or _____."

We can integrate technology into this lesson by having students take a picture taking of their illustration and include a digital tool such as Flip Grid for them to record an explanation of their photo. The above sentence frame is an appropriate scaffold for students to use during their recording.

For teachers, these mathematical practices help us determine the kinds of evidence we should collect for student learning; however, they also help us frame the activities and tasks and the kinds of support we will need to include based on our learners' needs.

How does prior knowledge and skill impact students' learning of standards? What type of knowledge and skills do they need to be successful? There is another document called the Progression Documents for the Common Core that is useful when planning math instruction. This document gives insight into the skills needed at each level of student development.

Stop and Reflect

As a k-12 student how might the Standards for Mathematical Practice supported you in learning mathematics?

_____

_____

Balanced Approach to Instruction

What was your mathematics experience like? Did the teacher stand in front of the class and deliver instruction or were you asked to engage critically in making sense of math problems? Chances are, you experienced a more traditional teacher-centered approach in which students sat silently and passively listened. Typically, in this type of scenario, once the teacher finishes demonstrating steps of a procedure or explaining a concept on the board, it is the students' turn to try the procedure or solve the problem. Oftentimes, this problem is worked out individually in silence. What we know from research is that this type of *teacher-centered* instruction does not benefit a majority of students (Hattie, 2009). On the other hand, if you had a teacher who actively engaged you in solving problems in which you selected the approach and the method, you experienced a more *student-centered* approach that was more cognitively demanding. This type of approach engages the students actively in learning by prompting deeper understanding, allowing students to seek solutions to authentic problems and engage with peers and the teacher collaboratively. Student-centered instruction provides a more meaningful and challenging experience for students. Students move from passive recipients of information to active learners who construct understanding.

Ultimately, our goal as math teachers is to ensure *all* students understand at the conceptual level and can demonstrate the required skills and knowledge based on their development. We must make critical decisions regarding strategies and activities in which students participate so that deep learning can occur; therefore, understanding more about what students need and knowing what knowledge they should develop is critical.

The learning progressions can support our decisions on how to best plan instruction. The benefit of consulting the learning progressions is that it makes clear what students need to know prior to instruction and can be a tool for teachers to consult when moving to new concepts within the grade level. Understanding the prerequisite knowledge to meet a standard is beneficial not just when you are planning, but when students are struggling as you can identify the foundational knowledge students are missing to make new connections. Furthermore, understanding the scope of how a concept develops across the grade span will allow you to see not just what knowledge and skills students are developing, but where they are going beyond this skill. This insight will help you make informed decisions about which tasks are academically rigorous and will prepare students for where they need to go.

👁 View It: The learning progressions can be found at http://ime.math.arizona.edu/progress ions/#products.

This site provides insight into how children learn at the various grade levels, what they should know about various content at each grade, and ways of teaching math concepts across the grade levels. As we plan instruction, we must pay attention to what students know, need to know, and how to link to current knowledge with past knowledge.

👁 View It: To see how standards are connected and developed across the grade span the Coherence Map by Achieve the Core includes a mapping of standards and examples of tasks and assessments for each standard. This tool will allow you to zoom into a specific grade-level concept and see how it is developed.

https://achievethecore.org/coherence-map/

Now watch Dr. Dickenson demonstrate how to use the Coherence map to explore the progression of place value. https://youtu.be/N1NyejthxJ8

Make the Connection

Using our example of teaching students to round whole numbers to 10, we should consult the learning progressions for knowledge about what students should already know and how rounding can connect to students' prior knowledge.

3.NBT.1 Use place value understanding to round whole numbers to the nearest 10 or 100.

From the learning progressions, we understand that children have previously learned in kindergarten how to decompose 10 into pairs such as 2 + 8, 3 +7, or 5 + 5. Furthermore, kindergarteners should have learned that teen numbers can be deconstructed to be 10 ones plus some more ones. It is likely that they learned this by using the strategy of five or ten frames. Thus, when teaching rounding, we can connect to students' prior understanding of 10 from their kindergarten knowledge and use five and ten frames to help students recognize rounding numbers to the nearest 10. In the example of the number 8 in the following ten frame, students can see that the number can be rounded to 10 since it is the closest 10. There are only two circles missing.

Ten-Frame Example

8

For larger numbers, the learning progressions suggest using layered place value cards to help students see the missing 10 in numbers such as 16. Children will see 17 as the single numbers 1 and 7 rather than 10 and 7. Layered place cards make the 10 obvious by adding the missing 0.

To see the development of a math concept across the grade span watch these Graham Fletcher videos https://gfletchy.com/progression-videos/

Select a math standard that you plan to teach. Go to the learning progressions document found at http://ime.math.arizona.edu/progressions/#products and examine the knowledge students have from the previous grade on that topic. Determine how you will access this prior knowledge and connect to it purposefully through a teaching–learning activity that connects the new knowledge represented in the standard.

Stop and Reflect

How should students learn at the grade level you examined in the learning progressions? What types of approaches and materials might you use to support their learning?

_____

_____

Research

Just like children need a balanced diet, so they also need a balanced math diet. According to the National Research Council (2001), a balanced diet in mathematics means that children should be regularly exposed to conceptual understanding and procedural fluency. Conceptual understanding is practiced by reasoning about rigorous problems. Procedural fluency is practiced with an application of skills along with the ability to represent mathematical ideas in flexible ways. Moreover, children need regular opportunities for reasoning about mathematical ideas. Along the way, children should also develop positive dispositions toward mathematics in which they recognize the usefulness and benefits of math while also exhibiting self-efficacy and perseverance.

Developing conceptual and procedural knowledge according to Rittle-Johnson, Schneider, and Star (2015) is a bidirectional development, in other words, they go hand in hand and are essential in the development of skills and knowledge when learning new material. Conceptual knowledge is defined as knowledge of concepts, which are abstract and general principles and can be implicit or explicit, and thus does not have to be verbalizable. Procedural knowledge is often defined as knowledge of procedures and is a series of steps, or actions, done to accomplish a goal (Rittle-Johnson et al., 2015).

For secondary students the push for students to take Algebra 1 in middle school and Calculus in high school has resulted in inequalities as students are entering classes in which they are not prepared (NCTM, 2020) and more homogenous classes are created. Boaler (2000) has found that de-tracked students in middle school perform better as students are more likely to engage in mathematical discussions, see multiple strategies, and justify their thinking and defend their solutions.

With a solid foundation focused on number sense in middle school mathematics students are better prepared for Algebra I and beyond, thus increasing students' chances of success in four year college courses (ACT 2009; 2012). According to the US Department of Education (2012) almost 40 percent of first time postsecondary students enroll in remedial mathematics.

Building Conceptual Understanding

Research supports children's experiences with concrete materials in order to build deep and flexible conceptual understanding. For example, in the early years, when developing children's understanding of the number 8, a teacher cannot expect conceptual knowledge to be developed by just telling children about the number 8. Children will not understand the number 8 until they experience the meaning of 8 in many ways. Children will need to hold 8 of the same object, touch and move around 8 objects, and count with one-to-one correspondence the same 8 objects. If the objects are linking cubes, children can take apart (decompose) and put together (compose) 8 in various forms, such as 2 and 6, 4 and 4, 3 and 5, and 7 and 1. By touching, manipulating, and moving around objects, children begin to form conceptual understanding of the number 8. For younger children, this is not a one-time experience; rather, children need repeated and numerous experiences with a number as they build their conceptual understanding.

Similarly, older children need conceptually based concrete experiences with concepts, like multiplication. By just demonstrating or telling children what multiplication means they will not understand the concept; rather, a teacher needs to provide manipulatives (in person or virtual) for children to explore the concept of multiplication. Organizing three groups of four tiles in each group, children can count and verify that the number in total equals 12 tiles. Organizing a new set of four tiles with four in each group, children can verify that the total number equals 16 tiles. By using the concrete or virtual manipulatives, children are building their conceptual understanding. They can then move to draw and color representations of their multiplication on graph paper or on a tablet, or continue by showing just the equation that represents the quantities being multiplied. Through gathering representations of the multiplication groupings and examining patterns and structures, children will notice predictable ways that numbers are organized. They can even build their own set of multiplication tables to demonstrate this knowledge. After multiple exposures and building meaningful experiences around multiplication, children are more able to meaningfully memorize the math multiplication facts being used, building on their conceptual foundation from concrete experience.

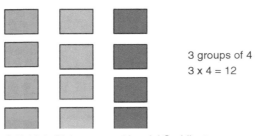

3 groups of 4
3 x 4 = 12

© Patricia Dickenson and Lorelei Coddington

The previous model was created using Google Drawing. This model can easily be illustrated by students using the shapes features to make identical rectangles for students to create and make colorful.

Similarly, secondary students can benefit from visual models that connect the big ideas of a concept into concrete representations. Manipulatives such as counters or unifex cubes which are traditionally used in primary grades can be used with older students just as effectively to teach complex skills such as subtracting integers or solving algebraic expressions.

 Watch It

In this video a 7th grader demonstrates how to use virtual counters to add integers on this Google Jamboard:

https://youtu.be/Kd7yjdoa88c

A model that is grounded in concrete materials is the CRA model. CRA stands for Concrete–Representational–Abstract; this approach calls for children to use concrete materials and objects first, followed by representations or drawings, and then finally move to mathematical symbols. Research has shown this model to benefit all students, but especially those with difficulties in mathematics (Witzel, 2005). The CRA model suggests students experience stages that move from the concrete toward the abstract. As adults, we often do not think about numbers being symbolic, or that symbols such as addition (+), subtraction (−) and all other symbols (e.g., <, >, =, x, ÷) are abstract in nature. Children are commonly rushed to use symbolic forms of math before they are ready and there is an assumption that they already know what the symbols mean. Also, there is a tendency for teachers to believe that manipulatives are just for the youngest of children; this is a myth. Manipulatives can and should be used with older children as well. Manipulatives have been found to support students' understanding of algebra concepts using algebra tiles (Witzel, 2005). Ultimately, children benefit from using concrete objects and visual representations before moving to using only numbers and other math symbols.

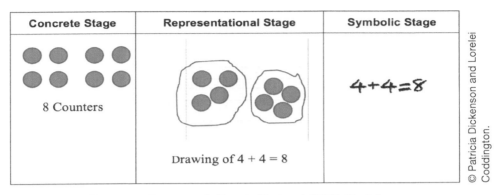

Concrete Stage	Representational Stage	Symbolic Stage
8 Counters	Drawing of 4 + 4 = 8	4+4=8

© Patricia Dickenson and Lorelei Coddington.

Figure 2.1   Concrete–Representational–Abstract (CRA) Model.

The CRA model consists of three stages (see Figure 2.1). The first stage is the *concrete stage*. This phase is characterized by children's use of manipulatives to represent the concept being taught. The second stage is the *representational stage*, in which children move from the concrete objects to drawings or illustrations of the objects. The third stage is the *abstract stage*, in which children use the numbers and operations symbolically without drawings or manipulatives as a reference. These three stages progress in order from concrete to abstract; however, children will move at their own pace through the stages; some children will move more quickly than others. Those with difficulties may need prolonged time in phase one or two for support. Even when children reach symbolic understanding, they may need to access concrete materials to review, scaffold, or support, their learning about another concept. Thus, teachers should have available to children a plethora of concrete materials that can serve as manipulatives. Such materials may include counters, beans painted in different colors, linking cubes, plastic teddy bears, blocks, Cuisenaire rods, foam tiles, tangram blocks, fraction tiles, and plastic money. Visiting a craft store or teacher supply store can provide you with many ideas of other small items that would be appropriate to use as manipulatives. Students can even make manipulatives like paper clocks with hands that turn or ten frames using egg cartons.

In this video Dr. Dickenson applies the CRA model to teaching decimals with concrete and virtual manipulatives. She also connects the learning progression of decimals to base ten blocks and why you should be consider the models and application of manipulatives to support understanding and prevent misconceptions.

https://youtu.be/RhWiOlNfBGs

Making Meaning and Virtual Manipulatives

While conceptual development is a critical component of learning, meaning-making is highlighted by Vygotsky, who promoted the importance of social interaction in the process of cognitive development (1978). According to Vygotsky, children need to learn from others (teacher, parent, or peer) who have more knowledge. Oftentimes, this theoretical perspective is applied by having children work alongside a more knowledgeable peer in a designated small group. Children can effectively learn and make meaning of experiences by working with and talking to another person.

Vygotsky also highlighted the importance of cultural tools that include both psychological tools such as language, writing, and symbols and technical tools such as computers, media, and books as paramount in shaping cognitive development. Although the technical tools you used as a student might be different than what is available today, it is important for students to experience what they observe and use in their personal life to support their learning. Furthermore, with technology at students' fingertips we believe it is possible to extend children's ability to learn from others as well as themselves. With digital recording tools, students can watch themselves explain an idea and self-correct their work. They can apply their thinking or new learning immediately with digital tools to support application. The ability to make meaningful connections can be facilitated with virtual manipulatives. Visual representations that would not be accessible in a traditional classroom are available with technology. Virtual manipulatives can support students in seeing the connection between the concrete, representational, and symbolic.

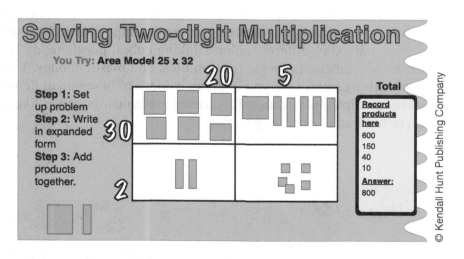

In the above screenshot, the teacher created virtual place value blocks and digits that students can move into an area model. This process will allow the teacher to determine if the student can decompose numbers with place value (ones and tens) to multiply in expanded form. Once students master this skill they can apply the standard algorithm with understanding. This process matters because students who have faulty understandings about how to multiply multi-digit numbers will likely make mistakes and be unable to explain their thinking.

🖥 **Snag It:** Two-digit Multiplication https://bit.ly/3zhJeCb

Research on Virtual Manipulatives and Student Learning

There is a significant amount of research to support the use of virtual manipulatives with students in all grades and across math concepts including geometry, algebra, fractions, and integers. In these studies not only did students demonstrate gains in academic achievement but conceptual understanding as well (Bolyard & Moyer-Packenham, 2012; Moyer, Niezgoda, & Stanley, 2005; Reimer & Moyer, 2005). This research suggests that students transfer pictorial and symbolic representations of concepts successfully. Teachers also reported an increase in student motivation and time on task when using virtual manipulatives (Jones, Uribe-Fiorez, & Wilkens, 2011).

 Watch It

In this video, Dr. Dickenson facilitates an online class of 6th graders in a lesson on rational numbers using Google Jamboard. She has crafted several tasks which include visual representations and exploration as a way to learn more about her students prior knowledge, experiences and application of rational numbers in the real-world.

https://youtu.be/_VhMqTJPCac

 Try It!

The Google presentation "Multiplication City" can be used across the grade span from first to middle school grades. From building an addition sentence to writing an equation, virtual manipulatives provide you with the flexibility to scaffold instruction and challenge others. You can create the low floor and high ceiling tasks with these tools based on your learners' needs.

📖 **Snag It:** https://tinyurl.com/yadmfhtd

When using Google Slides, please "Make a Copy" of this document to ensure it is in your Google Drive. Once you make a copy, you will "rename" it and can then share this google presentation with your students in your class. Each student will need to "Make a Copy" so they can record their ideas. In the Appendix, we included directions with screenshots on how to use Google Slides in your classroom.

Math Talk

Another area of mathematics that has a relatively new research focus is the impact of discourse or talk on student learning at the elementary level. Math talk is an essential part of mathematics instruction and has been found to influence students' conceptual understanding and achievement. It also develops students' academic language and promotes critical thinking through justification, argumentation, and collaboration. The SMPs call for students to regularly practice talking about and collaborating over mathematics, and these types of thinking and skills are important to developing healthy habits of the mind.

Webb et al. (2014) found that engaging children in mathematical discussion around comparisons and explanations was positively related to increased student engagement and achievement. These findings support Vygotsky's social learning theory and suggest that small group discussion around mathematics can produce powerful results. This study also suggested that teacher response to students' claims and questions was equally important. How teachers probed and asked questions proved to be important to student achievement. Having prompts and routines for students to engage in discussions means that math talk becomes a daily practice. For new teachers, especially, knowing how to respond to children's ideas may appear daunting; however, sentence stems or partial sentences aligned with the eight SMPs can be found in the California Common Core State Standards Frameworks Overview (CA CCSSM, 2013, pp. 18–22) at http://www.cde.ca.gov/ci/ma/cf/documents/mathfwoverview.pdf. These materials can be used by teachers to scaffold the development of students' math talk skills.

 Try It!

Select a grade level and then choose a math standard from that grade level. Use the following chart and unwrap the standard. Also consider the knowledge and skills students need before learning and the types of materials, strategies, questions, and technology you might include when planning the instruction. Be sure you consider the Learning Progressions and Common Core State Standards as referenced earlier in this chapter.

Prior Knowledge Based on Learning Progressions	Unpacking the Standard		Materials, Tools, Strategies, Questions	Technology Integration
	Content (Nouns)	Skills (Verbs)		

If you are ready for more you can begin crafting "Learning Outcomes" for the skills and concepts you identified. From Learning Outcomes we can begin to consider our assessment measures.

A New Framework...

A key aim of this framework is to address issues of inequity in mathematics learning.

- All students deserve powerful mathematics; we reject ideas of natural gifts and talents (Cimpian et al, 2015; Boaler, 2019) and the "cult of the genius" (Ellenberg, 2015).
- Students' cultural backgrounds, experiences, and language are resources for learning mathematics (González, Moll, & Amanti, 2006; Turner & Celedón-Pattichis, 2011; Moschkovich, 2013).

When students learn about brain growth and mindset, they realize something critically important—no matter where they are in their learning, they can improve and eventually excel (Blackwell, Trzesniewski & Dweck, 2007).

Summary

This chapter explored the foundational principles in teaching mathematics such as planning with standards and learning progressions; children's conceptual and procedural development; and pedagogical strategies such as the CRA model, math talk, and technology integration. We began by discussing how the CCSS originated and how the standards have shifted math instruction to include focus, coherence, and rigor. The standards also include eight SMPs that require students to engage in habits of the mind that develop skills and knowledge across the spectrum of their K-12 learning. We provided you technology tools to consider when integrating across each of the SMPs. This chapter also supported the development of your skills in unpacking the standards by examining the concepts and skills students need to know, and pointed you to consider the learning progressions and technology integration when planning of instruction. We discussed Vygotsky's theories that encourage meaningful experiences around collaborative practices to enhance a student-centered learning experience. Pedagogical approaches such as the CRA model, math talk, and technology integration were highlighted as methods to enhance and scaffold learning. These principles and practices are important to consider as we discuss the Big 5 pedagogies in chapters 4-8 as you will see how these ideas take place in the classroom.

Additional Activities/Discussion Questions

1. What are some of the larger math concepts students will need to know in the grade level you are interested in teaching? List all the knowledge and skills students need as foundational skills to learn the grade-level concepts. How might you assess students to see if they have the knowledge needed to move forward with learning the new concepts? What types of materials might you use to make students' thinking visible?

2. Explore a web tool listed for one of the SMPs. Consider these questions:
   a. What are the benefits of this tool?
   b. What are the challenges of the tool?
   c. How would you incorporate the tool into your teaching and student learning?
   d. How much instruction would you need to provide so that students can easily use the tool?
   e. How would this tool benefit English language learners?
   f. How would it benefit students with special needs?
   g. How might the tool enhance collaboration among students?

Instructor Activities

1. Ask your students to create a screencast in which they unpack a math standard and identify appropriate accommodations and modifications for a student who is an English language learner and a student with special needs.
2. Provide students with a math concept (e.g., beginning multiplication) and have them consider how they would use the Concrete–Representational–Abstract model to support students' thinking. Have students consider the learning progressions and the prior knowledge to which they must connect the new learning. Then, ask students to identify the steps in a progression of teaching from the beginning of student learning until mastery over a 10-day unit of instruction. Have your students also identify the concrete manipulatives or web tools they would use to support students' learning.
3. Present your students with several different math tasks representing various levels of Bloom's taxonomy and cognitive demand. Ask your students to classify the math tasks based on Bloom's levels. Discuss the inherent differences between the tasks based on the level of thinking required.

Chapter 3

Understanding Design

Self-Reflection

What role does teacher planning have on your learning and instruction? How does setting an agenda impact your attitude and your students' motivation?

The goal of this chapter is to highlight the habits of mind that you should consider when planning math instruction. Throughout this text we share how to plan for each of the pedagogical practices that you will be learning about. For example in Chapter 7, Problem-Based Learning, we provide you with a step-by-step process and template for planning a problem-based task. As experienced teachers, we know that planning is rooted in the students that we teach, and these characteristics can change from class to class. No matter what curriculum resources and programs your school provides, planning must be an intentional practice that is based in learning theory and connected to the students you are teaching. As a middle school or high school teacher you will see that what works in your fourth period might not be as effective for your sixth period. So, be intentional in your planning and don't be afraid to "step outside the box."

Planning is not just setting out what you intend to do, but also thinking about your learners and how you can support them so they can feel successful. Giving our students multiple ways to express what they know with multiple tools to support their expression should be part of any learning task.

Your classroom might be full of students who are around the same age, but that does not mean they learn the same way, are ready to learn, or have the prior knowledge, experience, and cognitive development to understand a concept. Our brains are wired differently. Just like the way our students range in height and development, the same is true when it comes to their brains. What works for one student might not work for another; so be flexible in your approach to designing instruction and include multiple representations of concepts, as well as student choice in how they learn, receive, process information, and express what they know.

Technology is just one tool in our toolbox that is highly adaptive for our learners and can provide us with a variety of choices in expressions of content, process of teaching, and assessment products. But remember, technology is not the only tool we have when it comes to teaching and learning mathematics. Although technology may be exciting and engaging for some children, it may not be for others. Some children will want to build, create, and express their learning in concrete ways that do not include devices. The most important thing to consider when it comes to planning is knowing your learners and what captures their attention and supports their learning process. We cannot begin planning unless we know who we are planning for.

Five Habits of Planning

Habit 1: Start With the Standards

In Chapter 2, we articulated the process of how to unpack a math standard in order to identify the content knowledge and skills that you are teaching. We also discussed the importance of examining the learning progressions to establish prerequisite skills your students should have mastered prior to teaching the standard. According to the Common Core Standards Initiative (2010), mathematics is not a list of disconnected topics, tricks, or mnemonics; it is a coherent body of knowledge made up of interconnected concepts. Therefore, the standards are designed around coherent progressions from grade to grade. Learning is carefully connected across grades so that students can build new understanding onto foundations built in previous years. The Math Standards and the Standards for Mathematical Practice are the building blocks for designing instruction, which anchor our intention and provide you with learning targets. Once you have established your learning target, then you should consider assessment. Assessment is a tool that allows teachers to determine what students know and what they do not know. How we are assessing is evident in the questions we ask, discussions our students have, and is also evident in how our students engage in activities. Assessment should not happen only at the end of your lesson, but throughout the instruction.

Habit 2: Know Your Learners

Students come to our classrooms with various skills, experiences, funds of knowledge, and opportunities for growth. Just like an architect or interior designer needs to consider who their clients are when designing their home, you too must think about your learners' interests, preferences, development, culture, and community in the design of instruction. Connecting math tasks to the backgrounds and culture of your learners is one way you can leverage students' funds of knowledge to enhance learning. Also consider additional tools, scaffolds, and resources you can use to plan and support students. Technology is a tool that we use in our design of instruction, and year after year our planning changes because technology changes and so do our learners.

Additional resources should also be gathered as you begin your initial planning. English language learners are a growing population of students throughout the United States, in fact one in four students are projected to be English language learners by 2025 (NEA, 2020). Becoming familiar with the English Language Development standards (ELD) or frameworks that are adopted by your state can help you determine the language supports you should consider while planning instruction. Likewise, the Common Core English Language Arts Standards can frame how you will infuse academic language, reading, writing, and speaking into your instruction.

Across the Curriculum

Incorporating Physical Education into math curriculum not only promotes movement, but provides students with a real world context for seeing math in their lives. Students can record their percent of accuracy for basketball shots or record their time and graph the class results in a 50 meter dash.

Social Cognitive Theory

Do you learn best by listening to a teacher talk or do you prefer to learn by interacting with your peers? Chances are you prefer to learn by talking to your peers. The reason peer learning is beneficial is because individuals learn not only through their environment but also through social interaction. Vygotsky (1978) theorized about this interaction and the benefit provided to the learner, and he noted that not only does social interaction promote learning, but it is also inherently cultural. In further explanation of this model, Vygotsky claimed the individual learns best when accompanied by a more knowledgeable person. For example, if a child was to complete a jigsaw puzzle on their own it may take an extremely long time, especially if they had little experience. The child might not think of a variety of strategies that a more experienced person might have when solving a jigsaw puzzle. If an adult with experience solving jigsaw puzzles was to sit next to the child and show them strategies and provide the child support, the student would likely solve the puzzle more efficiently. The idea of a more knowledgeable other is central to Vygotsky's theory of scaffolding. By placing students who are struggling with a more knowledgeable peer, they will most likely be successful in solving or completing a task as a result of the support.

Zone of Proximal Development

Vygotsky's (1973) theory also incorporates a second concept that is integrally related: zone of proximal development (ZPD). The ZPD is the distance between what the student knows and does not know. It is in this space where there are skills too difficult for the student to learn by himself; however, if the student is given guidance and encouragement of a more knowledgeable person, the student can be supported and the learning can be scaffolded. Teachers need to know students' ZPD because it is in that space of unknowing where learning can occur; it is the student's instructional zone. It is also the area in which scaffolding by either a supportive peer, a teacher, or technology can support a student in learning. We often don't think of technology as a scaffold for learning, but it can most certainly be a support for a student to be successful especially if technology is anchored in the students' ZPD. One of the features of technology which students benefit from and enjoy is immediate feedback from computer-based manipulatives (Reimer & Moyer, 2005).

Think About It!

What are some big takeaways that we should consider in our planning and instruction from Vygotsky's Social Cognitive Theory?

_____

_____

Habit 3: Build Understanding

In Chapter 2, we shared how the concrete representational abstract (CRA) model should frame students' exploration and connections to math concepts. Developing conceptual understanding is a tenet of the Common Core Math Standards and often begins with exploration using concrete manipulatives. Another important consideration for designing instruction is based on the work of Lesh et al. (2003) on the five different representations of mathematical ideas. Research has shown that students with flexibility among and between representations have deep understanding and greater retention. Moreover, children who have difficulty translating a concept from one representation to another struggle with solving problems and understanding computations.

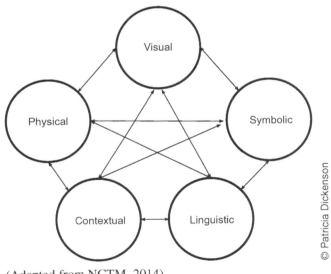

© Patricia Dickenson

(Adapted from NCTM, 2014)

Physical: Concrete models to show and act upon mathematical concepts.
Visual: Diagrams, pictures, illustrations, and other math drawings.
Symbolic: Numbers, variables, tables, and other symbols that are used to record mathematical ideas.
Linguistic: Academic language to defend, discuss, justify, and describe mathematical concepts and strategies.
Contextual: Real-life and situational context is used to support mathematical understanding.

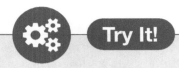

In this Google Slides presentation on ratios, you can see the Five Representations in Action. Which of the Five Representations do you find are most strongly presented and which of the Five Representations will you need to include as an additional task?

Connecting Social Cognitive Theory to Mathematics

Three big takeaways that we must consider from the Social Cognitive Theory are cultural tools, ZPD, and scaffolding. In Chapter 1, we discussed how technology is a "cultural tool" and in this chapter we see the importance of scaffolding and designing tasks within students' ZPD. It is possible to create individualized learning goals for every student, but unrealistic to create 30 different lesson plans for each student in your class. There are a variety of instructional practices that you can incorporate in your math practice that scaffold instruction and work in students' ZPD. Blended learning programs provide you with pathways for providing students with instruction that is adaptive and reflects students' ability. Cloud-based presentation tools provide you with the flexibility to create a variety of tiered activities that students can work through independently until they need additional support and scaffolding. In the following Google Slide presentation for the concept ratios, Dr. Dickenson has created a variety of tasks at an increasing level of cognitive demand.

Even if you do not plan on teaching this concept, you can see how this lesson builds on students' prior knowledge of fractions and creates increasingly challenging questions that requires students to apply what they know in a real-life context.

> **Be sure you reference the Appendix of this book to learn how to "Make a Copy" of all presentations for your instructional use**.

Habit 4: Tools for Teaching and Learning

When it comes to making pedagogical decisions about using technology in the classroom, begin with planning. Decisions about planning not only determine students' actions and outcomes but also directly influence their level of thinking and learning. You can approach planning with a simple question to frame your thinking:

> What do I want my students to learn and how will I ensure they learn it?

Sometimes, our mathematical tasks require a high level of cognitive demand and other times we want to introduce a concept as simple as possible. Knowing the selection of activities and technology will influence our students' levels of thinking and learning is a critical factor when designing instruction.

As we have previously discussed a lesson should begin with activating prior knowledge which provides students with an opportunity to connect with their experiences and what they have already learned. Selecting tasks that build on students' prior knowledge and extend their thinking provides you with an opportunity to take note of students' mathematical thinking including areas for growth, and misconceptions. Providing students with tools to make connections and build on mathematical ideas is paramount to this process.

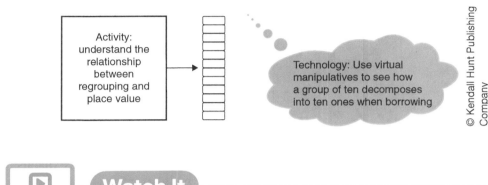

Watch It

https://youtu.be/TlTWjgbZNss

In this video, a first-grade student uses virtual manipulatives to explain how a group of 10 can break apart into 10 ones when borrowing in subtraction. Unlike traditional base ten blocks, a virtual manipulative can actually break apart into 10 ones. This is important for kids to see in order to understand the relationship.

When planning instruction, consider not only the content but also the design of the task so it is aligned with what we know about how our students think and learn. Our goal is to maximize student thinking so what they learn is retained and can be used in the future, perhaps in a different way or across a new context. Not only do we need to plan the lesson carefully, but we also need to consider how to infuse technology across the design to help accomplish the learning objective. Technology should be thought of as a tool to support student learning. Don't begin planning by thinking about what kind of activity will best work with the technology you have in mind; instead, begin planning with your students in mind and what you can do to best support them in understanding and moving toward your learning objective. Chances are you will include multiple ways for your students to become engaged with a concept and include a variety of representation such as hands on manipulatives and virtual tools to support your students in developing understanding. After you have your initial plans in mind, then select the technology tool that will best support your students.

© Patricia Dickenson

We have identified four key ways technology can be infused in your design. As we discuss best pedagogical practices to teach math in Chapters 4 through 8, we also infuse technology in one of these four core ways:

1. **Technology to unpack a concept:** Students use visual representations such as virtual manipulatives, multimedia, presentations, and digital-realia to create a real-world connection.
2. **Technology to explain a process:** Students use virtual tools to demonstrate a procedure, digital media to explore and chunk information, or provide a structure to organize student thinking such as a digital document for recording their notes.
3. **Technology to support student thinking:** Students use a technology tool to digitally record their thoughts and model a mathematical concept or process.
4. **Technology to demonstrate student learning:** Students use technology as an end product to showcase what they have learned about a concept. For example students can create a Kahoot of questions and real world connections related to a math concept.

The four key ways we share with you are focused on **what the teacher does** and what the **students will do**. We believe that teaching and learning is a collaborative process that is both teacher-directed and student-centered. As the teacher, you need to make instructional decisions that support student learning. Sometimes these decisions call for direct instruction where you explicitly teach your students the knowledge and skills they need to be successful, other times your instructional focus is student-centered and your students will be showing you what they know by working collaboratively to problem-solve or engage in a project.

In a student-centered approach you are the guide on the side, providing feedback and asking questions to deepen student understanding. In a teacher-centered approach, you are modeling and demonstrating for your students. You are showing them what they need to do step by step to ensure access to big ideas and procedures.

Think About It!

How does varying your instructional approach support all learners in the classroom? Do you think it is possible to differentiate your instruction and not just your tasks to meet the needs of students who might learn differently?

_____

_____

The process of designing instruction is complex and it will look differently for every teacher and for every learner for which you are designing. Our goal is to give you the tools and big ideas to engage with the process. Throughout your career the way you approach planning will change. The more you develop a mind-set of what your students need the easier this process will be. We know many teachers who plan on their way to work, while they are going for a run, or every Sunday morning when their kids are sleeping. The process is yours, so do what works best for you. Don't worry, we know there is much to teaching and learning in mathematics that is why the chapters 4 through 8 will go deeper into the big five instructional practices highlighted at the end of this chapter to provide you with ideas and structure for infusing technology into each practice.

Habit 5: Mastery Learning

The variety of tasks and ways we engage our learners with a particular concept are the ways we move our students toward mastery. When was the last time you felt like you truly mastered a skill or understood a new concept? Usually this happens after many opportunities of practicing a skill or idea and improvement is the result of some feedback or information on how well you are performing. Mastery learning is a form of learning that requires just that: fixing and then improving from one practice to the next based on feedback. Assessment feedback helps to provide guidance to the student about what was accurate and what needs to be improved. This cycle of assessment, feedback, and adjustment is a constant characteristic of mastery learning as it promotes change and improvement (Bloom, 1971).

Mastery learning is a method of learning that requires regular feedback. Feedback can be peer-to-peer or teacher-to-student. With feedback, students' understanding grows as they can apply new learning to move forward and use self-correction to improve their performance. Ultimately, over time and with regular feedback, students are able to improve practice to the point of having mastery of the learning. In addition to regular feedback, diagnostic assessment at the start of the learning also is used in mastery learning to inform the teacher of what knowledge the students already hold. The teacher can use this at the start of the instruction to target areas of need. Mastery requires individualization in order to be effective as most students are not learning at the same rate. Thus, differentiation is critical to support students. The underlying belief of mastery learning is that students can succeed if they receive specific feedback in which they make an adjustment in their learning until they have reached full mastery.

 Watch It

In this video with high school math teacher Chris Luzniak he shares how to bring math debates into class structures to support students in mastery learning.

https://www.youtube.com/watch?v=IBMnUlOxCbY

© Patricia Dickenson

As teachers, mastery learning informs our work with students. Understanding what knowledge students already have at the start of instruction helps to clarify the next steps in teaching. Students' knowledge gaps are where you want to begin. Oftentimes, skills from previous years may need to be retaught or practiced. Diagnostic instruction, based on the learning progressions we discussed in Chapter 2, gives us a starting place to find out what students should already know at their grade level. Then, unpacking the standard you will teach and identifying the skills and concepts (also discussed in Chapter 2) will target instruction and a give you a place to start with teaching new content. We need to build on what students already know and provide feedback through the learning process. Regular feedback helps students adjust their progress and ultimately gain mastery. Once students gain mastery then the teacher can move forward within the progression of learning.

Stop and Reflect

What are some things you must consider about your learners when it comes to designing instruction?

_____

_____

Getting Started With Design

Now that we've addressed some of the habits of mind of design, let's review the big ideas covered in Chapter 2 that we need to include when designing instruction: (a) unpacking a standard, (b) identifying the Standards for Mathematical Practice, (c) writing a learning objective, and (d) identifying prior knowledge and academic language. These four first steps can help us determine the focus of our instructional design. Now, as classroom teachers we must consider our audience (our students) and who we are designing instruction for.

The four ACTION steps for planning instruction are the following:

   Step 1: Unpack the Math Standard and identify prior knowledge.

   Step 2: Identify the math models and strategies your students will acquire including the academic language and language demand.

   Step 3: Create culturally responsive activities that support, extend and build on students' assets to develop mastery of the learning objective.

   Step 4: Apply technology across activities to support multiple means of engagement, representation, and expression.

Understanding Student Thinking and Learning

In step 3, we can let our creativity flow by designing activities that support student learning. When we anchor tasks in a framework which includes varied levels of student thinking we can plan purposefully to meet the skills and understandings we need to teach to address the content standard. One of the most common taxonomies or classifications of thinking is known as Bloom's taxonomy. Bloom's taxonomy provides a foundation for lesson planning as it directs us in the type of student thinking desired in the design process. Reflecting on objectives and their related activities in light of Bloom's helps us determine at what level we are asking our students to think.

We want to make sure there is a balance of knowledge and facts as well as critical thinking across lessons and units of study. In planning instruction, you must have an idea of where you are going (concepts and skills), plan for how students are going to accomplish the concepts and skills (writing objectives and five practices), and have an eye toward the appropriate task for students to accomplish your learning objective. To begin this process, let's look closer at Bloom's model of thinking.

Bloom's taxonomy is a multi-tiered model classifying levels of thinking and learning. The higher you go, the more complex the thinking gets. The six levels are (a) knowledge, (b) comprehension, (c) application, (d) analysis, (e) synthesis, and (f) evaluation. These levels are often viewed as a pyramid with the first level located at the bottom of the pyramid. Each level indicates a progression of thought and learning, beginning with knowledge and moving up to the next level requiring the learner to engage in more complex mental activity at each step. For example, memorization of addition facts would be an example of knowledge on Bloom's taxonomy for a third-grade student. At this point, a third-grade student should understand addition conceptually and have committed basic addition facts to memory as knowledge that can be recalled. Knowing these basic facts and recalling as memorized discrete knowledge exemplifies the knowledge level of Bloom's taxonomy. However, if students are given a contextualized problem in which they draw on their knowledge of addition and use or *apply* this knowledge in the solving of the problem, they have used application on Bloom's level of higher order thinking. By using this classification model, we can evaluate our methods within the design of our instruction to ensure that students have opportunities across various levels of thinking and learning. We also need to recognize that each level of thinking and learning in Bloom's taxonomy builds on the previous level. In our third-grade basic addition facts example, students take their knowledge that has been learned and then use it when solving problems; thus, earlier knowledge, or understanding, is needed before being able to use that knowledge in the application of that knowledge. Each step builds upon the next step of Bloom's model.

Stop and Reflect

What recent knowledge have you acquired in your class and what have you been asked to do with this knowledge? Where would you place your level of thinking on Bloom's model of thinking?

_____

_____

Anderson et al. (2001) updated Bloom's taxonomy to a more two-dimensional version that puts the learning and thinking into more active terms. For example, in this revised version, the word Remember is changed to Remembering which is more active. Almost all the levels are similar to the original Bloom's levels except for the highest level, which was changed to *Creating* instead of *Evaluate*. The revised six levels of Bloom's taxonomy are described as:

1. **Remembering**: Retrieving, recognizing, and recalling relevant knowledge from long-term memory.

2. **Understanding**: Constructing meaning from oral, written, and graphic messages through interpreting, exemplifying, classifying, summarizing, inferring, comparing, and explaining.
3. **Applying**: Carrying out or using a procedure through executing or implementing.
4. **Analyzing**: Breaking material into constituent parts, determining how the parts relate to one another and to an overall structure or purpose through differentiating, organizing, and attributing.
5. **Evaluating**: Making judgments based on criteria and standards through checking and critiquing.

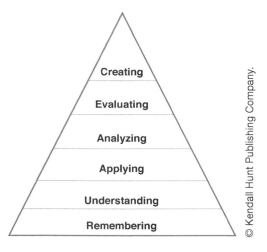

6. **Creating**: Putting elements together to form a coherent or functional whole; reorganizing elements into a new pattern or structure through generating, planning, or producing.

(Anderson et al., 2001, pp. 67–68)

Notice that the bottom foundational level is remembering and the highest level is creating. It is important to note that students need to know specific content as a foundation of their learning, but they can't stop just at understanding and comprehending. They need to use what they know across the levels and be stretched to think at high levels. By doing this, students will have a deeper understanding of the concepts they learn.

Low-Floor High-Ceiling Tasks

In today's heterogeneous classroom, it is highly likely that you have students at various abilities across Bloom's taxonomy when it comes to a particular concept. For example, in a ninth grade class, several students might be struggling to retrieve basic math facts whereas others have achieved automaticity and are able to solve complex problems. Planning for such a diverse range of learners can be overwhelming especially for new teachers. However, teachers who incorporate tasks that have a "low entry and high ceiling" are providing all children with an opportunity to think like a mathematician. Low entry and high ceiling tasks are problems where all students can begin working at their level, and students can be challenged to extend their thinking in multiple ways. As classroom teachers incorporating activities that have a "low entry and high ceiling" is a great way to encourage students to work collaboratively, and create an enriching classroom where students can be challenged and grow cognitively. In Chapter 5, we discuss these types of open-ended tasks in greater detail. You will also find in our tech resource link the category labeled "math tasks" which exemplifies tasks that provide access for all. These types of tasks can move students toward mastery of a concept and push others to continue to develop their understanding; the tasks are easy to understand and visualize but are challenging to solve.

Source: Patricia Dickenson

Watch It

Dr. Dickenson uses a Three Acts math task in this seventh grade class for students to build their understanding of fractions into proportional thinking. She uses the video task to hook students and think about how math is used in the real world. The problem has a low floor and high ceiling and incorporates having students share what they "notice and wonder" about the problem as a way to check their understanding and provide talking points for discussion.

👁 https://youtu.be/FGa0KV8nKfI

Blooming With Technology

The fourth step of planning is purposeful technology connections across the dimensions of Bloom's revised taxonomy. Remember that the technology integration comes after you have decided your activity's learning objectives. Before beginning instruction, it is important to access what students already know, or their *prior knowledge*. For example, if you are planning to teach a geometry unit, it would be good to first find out what your students already know and identify any potential misconceptions they might have. So, in a first lesson in the unit, the learning objective might be to have students demonstrate their prior knowledge of geometric terms (knowledge is the first level on the taxonomy chart), you might consider using an online gaming tool such as Quizlet or Kahoot rather than a traditional paper and pencil assessment to find out how much students know. In a subsequent lesson objective, you might have students explain the geometry terms once they are learned, then you again match the technology to go with your objective and anticipated level of thinking. For this example, you could have students create a video in which they explain the geometry terms they have learned and create a representation (either drawing or with concrete materials) as a part of their demonstration of understanding (understanding is the second level on the taxonomy chart) in a short video using a screencasting tool. Using technology rather than traditional methods will provide students with visual cues to prompt memory (great for English language learners) and create a fun and engaging way to check students' understanding in the process.

The following is a chart with a description of each level of thinking and learning along with useful technology tools for supporting each level of thinking and learning. These are just a few examples of the many technology resources available.

Knowledge Level	Knowledge Level Description (Anderson et al., 2001)	Technology Connection
1. Knowledge	Retrieving, recalling, and remembering	https://quizlet.com https://kahoot.com/mobile-app/ https://www.brainpop.com
2. Understanding	Interpreting, comprehending, exemplifying, classifying, summarizing, inferring, comparing, and explaining	http://www.blogger.com/ (Journaling) https://docs.google.com http://prezi.com/ (Presentations) https://screencast-o-matic.com (Video making)
3. Applying	Executing and implementing	http://blabberize.com/ (make your pictures talk)
4. Analyzing	Differentiating, organizing, and attributing	https://docs.google.com
5. Evaluating	Checking and critiquing	http://voicethread.com http://www.blogger.com/ (blogging) http://docs.google.com
6. Creating	Generating, planning, and producing	http://sketchup.google.com (creating 3-D models) https://vimeo.com (video)

In this 7th Grade Jamboard on Rational Numbers, students classify rational numbers and interpret real world situations.

https://bit.ly/3ztJ3UL

In this 2nd grade Google Jamboard Task on time students differentiate the kinds of activities they engage in throughout the day.

https://bit.ly/3xkJrD1

Cognitive Demand

Think of a job or task that required you to think deeply or work hard mentally. How did it make you feel? Did you feel mentally challenged? Did it stimulate your thinking? Did you feel a sense of accomplishment when it was completed? When we are mentally challenged to think at higher levels, we are being asked to do something that is cognitively demanding.

In math, cognitive demand can be described as the depth of thinking or the cognitive effort required by a mathematical task. According to Stein et al. (2009), when a task is cognitively demanding, it requires students to use conceptual understanding and more complex thinking; this means students must use more cognitive effort than just applying a memorized procedure to solve a problem. Tasks with higher levels of cognitive demand require students to make connections to conceptual understanding, engage in problems that are unpredictable, and experience productive struggle. When we design or select tasks for students, we need to consider the cognitive demand required by the construction of the task and the type of thinking required by the task.

In our design of instruction, we need to examine the tasks given to students in light of what students already know and are able to do. We should also think about the level of thinking that the tasks require. Not only should we consider Bloom's levels of thinking and learning, but we should also recognize that tasks themselves have levels of thinking required just by how they are designed and organized.

In these videos, Dr. Dickenson works with a fifth-grade and second-grade class to identify arrays in their classroom.

Second-Grade Class: https://youtu.be/IslKAeYEW7U

Sixth-Grade Class: https://youtu.be/2UfuRY67LFQ

Grade 2: Operations and Algebraic Thinking

Work with Equal Groups of Objects to Gain Foundations for Multiplication

CCSS.MATH.CONTENT.2.OA.C.4

Use addition to find the total number of objects arranged in rectangular arrays with up to five rows and up to five columns; write an equation to express the total as a sum of equal addends.

 Stop and Reflect

In the second-grade video, how does proposing a problem found in real-life shift student thinking? Does it expand the level of thinking, according to Bloom's taxonomy, rather than if it was presented only in symbolic form? Defend your response.

_____

_____

Grade 6: Expressions and Equations

CCSS.MATH.CONTENT.6.EE.A.2

Write, read, and evaluate expressions in which letters stand for numbers.

 Stop and Reflect

In the sixth-grade video when students are asked to create their own array equation using images, at what level of Bloom's taxonomy were they engaging? Explain your response.

_____

_____

How did the use of technology in these videos shift the learning for students?

_____

_____

Task Design

Mathematical tasks all have inherent levels of cognitive demand; some tasks are more easily completed whereas others are more challenging. When selecting a mathematical task for a lesson, we need to first examine it carefully by asking, *What are the students required to do? To what degree is the task asking students to think? What type of student thinking is required (recall, procedural, or conceptual thinking)?* By asking these questions, we will be able to learn more about the task. In particular, we should ask:

1. Does the task require the student to reproduce previously memorized knowledge?
2. Does the task require the student to apply a procedure that is memorized and disconnected to concepts?
3. Does the task require the student to apply procedures that require conceptual knowledge?
4. Does the task require the student to access previous conceptual knowledge and use it in complex and new ways?

   (Adapted from Stein & Smith, 1998)

The answers to these questions give us clues about the degree of difficulty and complexity required by the task. If the answer is *yes* to the first two questions, it tells us the task does not require much cognitive demand, nor does it draw on students' conceptual understanding. If the answer to questions three and four is *yes*, then the task is connected to students' conceptual understanding and has increased levels of cognitive demand (Stein & Smith, 1998). The differences between the first two questions and the last two questions indicate the level of cognitive demand inherent in the task. Applying a procedure that is already well rehearsed does not require as much cognitive demand as answering a question that is ambiguous, ill defined, and requires the solver to draw on previous conceptual knowledge.

For example, the teacher could ask students to provide a multiplication table and a matching array, which does not require much cognitive effort. Or, as in the sixth-grade video, the teacher could ask students to create their own array using pictures and then to provide an appropriate equation to go along with their images through the use of technology. This second type of task allows students autonomy by giving them room to make mathematical decisions and provides students tools without dictating exactly how they should provide a solution.

There are times when the teacher may decide to use less-demanding tasks, based on the learning objective; regardless, we want students to regularly experience tasks that require challenge and cognitive demand. Therefore, careful consideration is needed when designing tasks or selecting them for instruction. We will discuss more about selecting tasks for lessons in Chapter 5.

As we have articulated in the Chapters 1 and 2, begin by unpacking the standard by identifying the prior knowledge and skills required by the standard. Identify the strategies and models your students will learn, which could be new strategies or strategies that extend previous learning. Creating an anchor chart of the strategies and models will support students in acquiring these new skills. Developing fluency in math requires flexibility in strategies, and the more strategies students acquire, the more flexible their thinking will become.

Content Standard:	
CCSS.MATH.C0NTENT.3.OA.A.1	
Interpret products of whole numbers, e.g., interpret 5×7 as the total number of objects in 5 groups of 7 objects each. *For example, describe a context in which a total number of objects can be expressed as* 5×7.	
CONTENT KNOWLEDGE	SKILLS
products whole numbers Equal groups	Explain a multiplication equation in a context with equal groups of objects and determine the product.
Learning Progression: Prior Knowledge & Skills	
Work with equal groups of objects to gain foundations for multiplication. Students should be able to model and draw equal groups to find how many in all	
Strategies & Models:	
5 groups of 4	**Array**
Number Line: Skip Counting	
Repeated Addition	**Commutative Property**
$4 + 4 + 4 + 4 + 4 = 20$	$5 \times 4 = 20$; $4 \times 5 = 20$

© Patricia Dickenson

Identify ways in which you will incorporate the five mathematical representations into your planning. This process will support you when crafting activities that are aligned with Bloom's taxonomy as well. Notice that the academic rigor increases when students create their own problems and show two or more strategies. Once you have considered activities and representations, the Standards for Mathematical Practice will help you identify the mathematical thinking you want to instill while students are doing the math. The academic language and the language demands of a task can help you attend to students' precision while facilitating a discussion, as well as support your modeling of concepts and skills within your lesson.

Five Representations:

Physical: Use counters to create and solve multiplication expressions to determine the product.
Visual: Students will draw a visual representation for a multiplication expression.
Linguistic: Construct a viable argument about a context for a multiplication expression.
Symbolic: Write multiplication expressions to represent a context.
Contextual: Create a word problem for a multiplication equations.

Learning Objective: Recognize and represent a context for a multiplication expression in order to determine the product and know when multiplication can be used.

Activities:

* Write multiplication expressions to represent a picture.
* Roll two dice and draw a visual multiplication model.
* Use a number line to skip count multiplication problems.
* Create a multiplication problem and show the product using two or more strategies.

Standard for Mathematical Practice
#2 Reason abstractly and quantitatively.
#3 Construct viable arguments and critique reasoning of others.
#6. Attend to precision.

Academic Language:

* Product: answer to multiplication problem.
* Factor: represents the number of equal groups and the number of objects in each groups.
* Multiply: combine equal groups
* Multiplication expression: number of groups x number in each group

Language Demand: Explain a story problem with equal groups of objects and how to determine the product. Utilize academic language while explaining their thinking to peers, engaging in math activities and in assessment. Academic language will be displayed, reviewed and part of daily instruction. Images will be represented with each word to cue recall. Sentence stems will be provided as support.

© Patricia Dickenson

Connecting math to the lives of our students is another way we can support them in developing the belief that math is accessible for all. Creating a positive culture where students feel safe to take risks, make mistakes, and engage in mathematical discussion requires connections and care for our students. When we design instruction that builds on funds of knowledge, we let students know that we care. Assessment is also interwoven throughout our instruction so that students can approach activities with purpose and we can see evidence of learning that is timely and will inform our instruction. As we shared earlier in this chapter, mastery learning requires the intentional use of assessment with feedback, so building in a practice of assessment with feedback also provides our learners with an opportunity to grow and improve. We've also included in this template an opportunity to be intentional with technology integration and ways to consider how you can integrate the math concepts and skills you are teaching across the curriculum.

Cultural Responsiveness	Assessment
I will use pictures that are based on objects that are familiar to my students and their family backgrounds. I will include problem stories that are connected to the funds of knowledge my students bring into the classroom.	When rolling dice, students use a recording sheet to record their multiplication expression and model. Students will work with a partner to create a multiplication problem and engage in math talk to share their strategy and solution. Exit tickets will be used at the end of the lessons to determine if students understand strategies. Students will complete a comprehension check using GoMath digital assessment
Technology Integration	**Across the Curriculum**
Students will use the Toy Theater website to create a visual representation of a multiplication equation. They will use Seesaw to share their image and record their explanation using academic language.	Art: Students will create an tile mosaic using rectangular arrays up to 100. They will record multiplication equations to represent the colors used.

 Try It!

Select a math standard for the grade level of your choice. Unpack the standard and determine what students should know and do. Then, develop two tasks: one that requires lower levels of student thinking and another that requires students to think at the application level of Bloom's or higher. Also incorporate technology. Explain which level you think each task represents on Bloom's taxonomy.

Go to this GoogleDoc and try it: https://bit.ly/3wwA9nC

Planning Learning Experiences

Once we understand what students know, then it is time for us to begin to consider how to design the learning experience. As mentioned in the four action steps, making connections to students' prior knowledge is important for developing students' understanding. As we mentioned in Chapter 2, we also need to consider what the standards say students need to know and do. Once we have identified the concepts and skills to be taught, the next step is to design your plan for instruction. Cultural responsiveness as well as levels of student thinking are important considerations when planning as well as the language demand and strategies that you will be teaching. Technology integration should be used by both you and your students to engage and support students' thinking. We also need to plan with the big five pedagogy practices in mind. As previously mentioned in Chapter 1, these five practices are daily routines, open-ended tasks, project-based learning, problem-based learning, and math centers.

Daily routines are an essential aspect of mathematics instruction, as the repetition and routine allows for repeated practice and the cementing of fundamental learning. Calendar activities are a daily routine that can exist in elementary classrooms, even into the intermediate grades. Calendar activities, as a daily routines, often include activities such as counting days and weeks of school to grouping and regrouping, chanting or counting days of the month aloud, counting the letters in class members' names, daily math problems solved interactively, and mental math problems. These are just a few activities of the many possible.

Open-ended tasks are tasks given for students to solve that have multiple pathways to a solution. This type of task requires students to reason and make decisions about how they want to apply their mathematical knowledge as they take steps toward a solution. These are authentic tasks that require higher levels of thinking and engagement. The tasks generally are authentic because they are interesting to students and because they are relevant and centered in real life and require multiple steps or ways of thinking about a problem. By their very nature, open-ended tasks require students to engage at high levels of thinking and reasoning as they attempt to solve problems for which a solution is not predictable or clearly evident.

Project-based learning is a design for learning requiring more than just basic skills. Students are provided extended time to investigate and respond to a situation or problem in teams. They must determine solutions and make decisions while coming to their own conclusions. This design requires students to be responsible and helps to build confidence by placing the ownership of the outcome or solution on the students' shoulders.

Problem-based learning is an approach to problem-solving that is situated in a real-life context and focused on engaging students in discourse within small groups to determine an appropriate solution. Teachers are facilitators who support students in working through the problem with encouragement and questions to support their thinking. Students share out their solutions and engage in classroom discourse.

Math centers engage students in activities that extend students' mathematical thinking and learning in creative ways. Often, math centers are a collection of varied activities that encourage practice on skills, such as building patterns, creating shapes with tangram blocks, and playing math games and small group instruction. These centers are set up as stations around which students rotate. One of these stations can also include a teacher station where the teacher reviews or teaches a concept in greater depth. Math centers used in this way are an instructional approach; however, math centers can also be a permanent station in the classroom which children can access when they have finished work early or when given as a choice activity. Math centers as a permanent station can offer a variety of manipulatives and materials students can access throughout the day such as tangrams, connecting cubes, counters, dice, tiling cards, game boards, and programs on computers and iPads. Math centers provide students with a myriad of choices in which to engage outside of a traditional basic skills approach; however, math centers often help to practice basic foundational skills. Whatever form, math centers involve the student in a fun and practical way to engage in mathematics.

In Chapters 4 through 8, we will begin to unpack each one of these Big 5 practices so that you better understand how they may be used in your own classroom.

Summary

Students are individuals who learn in multiple ways, so we need to design learning with the learner in mind. In this chapter, we explored how lesson design reflects levels of thinking, and that Bloom's taxonomy helps us to monitor the levels at which we ask students to work and think. We also learned from Vygotsky that students need support or scaffolding when they learn. Mastery learning requires assessment and purposeful targeting of new knowledge, connecting purposefully to students' prior knowledge, and extending students' thinking to new ideas. Social Cognitive Theory tells us that students learn effectively through social interaction. Particularly, teachers should identify students' ZPD, the space between what they know and do not know, and provide social scaffolding to enable student success. Using a more knowledgeable other provides students scaffolding, whether that is human or technological scaffolding. We also examined the ways to challenge students by using cognitively demanding tasks that require higher levels of thinking. Along each level of Bloom's taxonomy, teachers can harness technology in ways that not only engage students but also support higher levels of thinking.

Additional Activities/Discussion Questions

1. Explore one of the technology tools listed under Blooming with Technology. What are the strengths of the tool? How could you see students using this tool to support thinking?
2. Review the learning progressions for the grade level of your choice. How might you capitalize on students' learning and incorporate technology?
3. Identify several math problems found in your math textbook. How could you increase the level of thinking and increase social interaction when problem-solving? How could you engage students in collaboration using a technology tool?
4. Experiment with writing a cognitively demanding math task based on a simple equation. Use the following questions to determine the depth of cognitive demand and then reflect on what was most easy or challenging in crafting a cognitively demanding task. How could you incorporate technology?
   a. Does the task require the student to reproduce previously memorized knowledge?
   b. Does the task require the student to apply a procedure that is memorized and disconnected to concepts?

    c. Does the task require the student to apply procedures that require conceptual knowledge?

    d. Does the task require the student to access previous conceptual knowledge and use it in complex and new ways?

    (Adapted from Stein & Smith, 1998)

Instructor Activities

1. Present your students with several different math tasks that represent various levels of Bloom's taxonomy and various levels of cognitive demand. Ask your students to classify them based on Bloom's levels. Discuss the differences between the tasks.

2. Give your students time to explore the technology tools during class. Ask them to consider a standard at a grade level of their choice and design a lesson incorporating the technology tool.

Chapter 4

Developing Daily Routines in Your Mathematics Practice

Self-Reflection

What skills have you acquired with repetition and practice? How does the structure of routines support you in achieving short- and long-term goals?

It's the beginning of your math period. Your students are sitting on the carpet in anticipation of what they will be doing today. As they wait for you to get started they begin to turn and talk to their neighbor. The manipulatives you have placed on the carpet for demonstration are now being used and distributed by the kids as play toys and a few kids who were once wiggling are now rolling on the carpet. Before you have even begun instruction, you are spending valuable time trying to redirect student behavior rather than teach mathematics.

> A smooth-running classroom is the responsibility of the teacher and the result of the teacher's ability to teach procedures.
>
> —*The First Day of School* by Harry K. Wong and
> Rosemary T. Wong (2009, p. 172)

Daily routines take the anticipation and guessing out of instruction. They add structure to your math period which promotes classroom management. Routines can only be established when the classroom teacher has explicitly taught the procedure for how something should be done and has provided enough practice and corrective feedback to the point where students demonstrate automaticity. For kids who experience unpredictability in their personal life, routines set a tone of consistency and guidance to make good choices. Daily Routines will set the stage for expectations and provide an opportunity to reinforce big ideas, provide practice of key concepts, and develop skills that take time to establish automaticity.

The Purpose of Daily Routines

When teachers want students to have automaticity of skills such as identifying digits and their corresponding value, or developing automaticity of their subtraction facts, this process takes time and practice. Practice needs to take place every day for students to achieve mastery.

In addition to developing automaticity of concepts, daily routines in math also provide students with an opportunity to verbalize their thinking, learn from peers, and self-correct their errors.

In a classroom, where you have students who struggle with math concepts, daily routines spiral curriculum to support students in acquiring the skills they need to be successful. For students who are English language learners, repetitive oral language practice provides multiple opportunities to attend to precision and develop language proficiency.

Daily routines provide language learners repeated opportunities to express ideas and listen to their peers. Teachers can scaffold language with daily routines that can include scripted language for students to rehearse daily which benefits all students.

Stop and Reflect

What math skills or concepts do you think your students will benefit from repetition and daily practice?

_____

_____

Putting Research into Practice

Do you remember how you first struggled to tie your shoes? By rehearsing each step, receiving corrective feedback and daily practice, you soon became independent and could do it on your own. You might also recall peers who could tie their shoes much quicker than you and others who had greater difficulty. Similarly, with procedural knowledge and fluency in mathematics students develop skills at their own pace and with many opportunities to practice. Students need multiple opportunities and continuous practice to reach what the Standards for Mathematical Practice say is to "calculate accurately and efficiently" (NGAC & CCSSO, 2010).

For students to develop competency with a specific skill or concept, Hunter (1982) recommends that teachers utilize both massed and distributed practice over time. Massed practice occurs when new learning develops during time periods that are closely connected, whereas distributed practice occurs when new learning is reviewed over continued periods of time. When practice is repeated over longer periods of time, retention will occur.

Students need multiple opportunities to practice over time and throughout the school year. Mass practice will support students with remembering but learning will decay over time, whereas distributed practice leads to retention. We recommend that you determine what specific skills your students need to develop throughout the school year, and decide which daily routines will best support students toward mastery of skills.

Think About It!

Review the Learning Progression resources as discussed in Chapter 2. Identify the skills that you will need to include in your daily routines for your grade level.

_____

_____

Practice builds efficiency, and students who have computational math skills at their fingertips, can move forward with greater ease. In fact, research shows that students who can retrieve math facts quickly are more likely to do well in math (National Mathematics Advisory Panel, 2008). This is similar to learning to read. When students struggle with decoding words, they have difficulty comprehending the meaning of the text. Students who do not read easily do not have fluency. Similarly, students who struggle in completing basic skills struggle with solving math problems. They might easily lose sight of the purpose or road to the solution, as they have yet to develop mathematical fluency. Students need to acquire the skills to solve math problems and persevere in problem-solving, and that is why practicing procedural knowledge to the point of fluency is essential.

Let's define what we mean by procedural fluency. According to the National Council of Teachers of Mathematics ([NCTM], 2014),

> procedural fluency is the ability to apply processes, techniques, and strategies accurately, efficiently, and flexibly; to transfer these methods to different problems and contexts; to build or modify procedures from other procedures; and to recognize when one strategy or approach is more appropriate to apply than another.

© Rido/Shutterstock.com

For students to be mathematically fluent, they need to have enough practice with various strategies and skills to work efficiently and apply their knowledge flexibly. Students not only need to know their math facts but they also need to know various strategies and select the right strategy needed and apply it to the problem they are solving.

For example, if the question was asked, "What is 12 more than 15?" the mathematically fluent student can identify several strategies to use, such as using a hundreds chart starting at 15, moving down 10 and across two more, applying the standard adding algorithm, visualizing or illustrating a number line starting at 15 and moving forward 12, or they could decompose (break apart) the numbers finding the total using mental math by adding the tens and add the ones and then totaling up how much altogether. Fluency means having the skills to address the mathematics of the problem and the ability to select the best strategies to solve the problem efficiently and accurately. This type of flexibility draws on skills and ways of thinking by applying them broadly and deeply.

👁 **View It:** In this blog post Dr. Dickenson shares recommendations for digital tools to support developing math strategies. http://www.teacherpreptech.com/2018/02/making-multiple-representations-in-math.html

Both procedural and conceptual knowledge are equally essential in mathematics learning, and most experts believe that conceptual knowledge precedes procedural knowledge (NCTM, 2014). According to research, there is a strong link between both conceptual and procedural knowledge; each one contributes to the other. Studies also suggest that procedural knowledge can strengthen conceptual knowledge during practice (Rittle-Johnson, Schneider, & Star, 2015). Thus, there is an important role for practicing procedures and routines to develop fluency (NCTM, 2014; National Mathematics Advisory Panel, 2008).

Major Area of Focus for Fluency:

Grades K-2: Addition and subtraction

Grades 3-5: Multiplication and Division of Whole Numbers Multiplication and Division of Fraction

Grade 6: Ratios and proportional relationship Reason about and solve equations and inequalities. Understand and simplify expressions

Grade 7: Use properties of operations to produce equivalent expressions. Use expressions and equations to solve real world math problems

Grade 8: Analyze and solve linear equations. Define, compare, evaluate and use functions

 Make the Tech Connection: Blended & Gamify

The Gamify and Blended webtools we recommend in our Tech Tool List supports students in developing both procedural and conceptual knowledge through practice and repetition. Many of these webtools are customizable which means that you can select and determine what skills and concepts you want your students to practice. http://www.teacherpreptech.com/p/tech-tools.html

Connecting to Content Knowledge

Mathematics is hierarchical which means that concepts build upon each other and it is difficult to progress in mathematics without the foundational knowledge needed to move forward. The daily routines in this chapter focus on foundational knowledge that students need to develop proficiency. These skills take time and practice which is why routines are so important. Moreover these routines are not restricted to one particular grade or age of students, as we know that a students' age does not represent their level of proficiency. It is important for teachers to know how conceptual understanding develops, as discussed in Chapter 2, the learning progressions are key to identifying what foundational skills students need. For example, with place value students need to understand that a number is made up of one or more digits. If students have difficulty decomposing numbers so that they can represent thirteen as one group of ten and three ones, they will have difficulty with the idea that a number is composed of digits that can be represented by its position in a number.

In this video see what core concepts are needed to be developed in the First Grade. https://www.youtube.com/watch?time_continue=73&v=2ZBtJcKR77Y

Researchers at John Hopkins (2009) have identified five basic building blocks of elementary mathematics: numbers, place value system, whole number operations, fractions and decimals, and problem solving. Elementary schooling is where this foundation begins and as such gaps in these areas can lead to difficulty with math concepts. Teachers need to understand what conceptual understandings are rooted in these five areas so they can develop, extend, and support students with daily routines:

> Mathematics is built level by level. Multi-digit addition and multiplication are built up from single digit operations using the place value system and the basic properties of numbers such as distributivity. The general operations reduce to the single digit number facts. Whatever their level of understanding, students without instant recall of these foundational single digit number facts are severely handicapped as they attempt to pursue the next levels of mathematics. (p.42)

In this video, see how a student puts together his knowledge of multiplying with base ten, place value and partial products to use the area model for two digit multiplication.

https://youtu.be/gMFDqdNm2T0

We've identified eight daily routines to kick-start your math practice. These routines focus on procedural and conceptual knowledge. It is not expected that you use each daily routine every day; rather, you purposefully determine where your students need to grow and which daily routine would best support their development. Later in this chapter, we share how to use each routine and integrate technology to support all learners as well as maximize these pedagogical practices.

Daily Routines	The Focus Is to ...	The Focus Is NOT ...	Technology Resources
Number Talks	Support students in articulating ideas and strategies. Share mental math strategies and solve in multiple ways.	Worksheet driven and independent	Padlet for students to record their strategies or Flip Grid web-based tool for video recording of verbal response.

Daily Routines	The Focus Is to ...	The Focus Is NOT ...	Technology Resources
Data Talks	Data visualization which includes real life data from other disciplines to provide students with an opportunity to interpret data and discuss what they notice, questions they have and connections they can make.	Data disconnected from a real-life context.	Create a Jamboard with a data visualization that can be used as a data talk. Students use sticky notes to post what they notice and wonder. https://jamboard. google.com/d/1B8A j2pkEIJYdqgg0NQ RJNXxVHeFd_ yFy-cSdjPqPFB4/ edit?usp=sharing
Hundred Chart	Develop counting and cardinality skills for numbers 1–100. Identify patterns in hundreds chart. Count on and group by tens. A visual model for problem-solving.	Invented strategies and concrete representations	Interactive Number Chart Math Playground Interactive Number Line for interactivity with hundred chart and number line.
Warm-Ups	Review previously learned math concepts with a short activity that begins at the start of your math block.	Introducing new concepts or summative assessment	Google Forms Woot Math Formative For quick questions data collection and practice.
Calendar Activity	Build number sense with focus on date and patterns in numbers. Reinforce previously taught concepts and spiral instruction.	Introducing new concepts in daily lessons	https://illuminations. nctm.org/activity. aspx?id=3565 To develop fluency and additional practice in calendar routines and practices.

Daily Routines	The Focus Is to ...	The Focus Is NOT ...	Technology Resources
Math Journaling	Record procedural steps of a concept. Solve weekly math problems. Explain your thinking and write. Organize and structure math concepts.	Personal journaling for expression of feelings	Google Docs Digital documents to share collaboratively and assign student work with Google Classroom Learning Management System.
Exit Tickets	Determine what students have learned by the end of a lesson. Include several problems and reflective questions.	Standardized assessment or high stakes test	Google Forms for data collection and Google Drawing for math illustrations. SeeSaw for sharing responses.
Counting Collections	Focus on demonstrating and developing strategies. Support building confidence in using visual representations.	Teacher-driven instruction	Shadow Puppet and Adobe Spark students take a picture of their collection and explain their thinking.

Structure of Daily Routines

When it comes to daily routines, we believe they happen not just within your math block but throughout your day. If you are going to maximize your math instruction with time on task and student attention, you need to determine what works for your students developmentally.

You might start with a daily routine like calendar which emphasizes building number sense by focusing on the patterns and numbers across the days and weeks. While doing this, also include a morning song, class announcements, and weather report. It's okay to integrate subject matter kids really enjoy when the focus is on learning and not just a specific subject. Teaching across disciplines also promotes transfer as students can see how math is applied in other contexts. So go ahead with the morning song, especially if your morning song includes a counting chant and your weather report leads to collecting data and graphing results.

During your math instruction block, you can incorporate a Number Talk as a warm-up and then close your math block with an exit ticket. You might also decide to incorporate math centers toward the end of the school day, when parent volunteers are available and to keep your students on task. During math centers, students can use math journals (another daily routine) to work on the Problem of the Week or class notes from their journal while they work independently. Determining the structure of your math program takes flexibility as well as knowing your students and school schedule. In Chapter 9, we discuss in greater detail strategies for organizing your math block.

Getting Started with Daily Routines

The structure of daily routines is established through explicit modeling, repetition, and practice. In the early grades, chanting by twos, fives, or tens is an example of a daily routine found in the calendar activity. You begin by exploring these concepts during your math instruction and then reinforcing them through practice in a daily routine. When using the calendar routine, for example, use a pointer to point to each of the numbers as you say them, at first. Vary the way you count the numbers. You can skip count, count odd or even numbers, or chant patterns or colors on each day. In time, students should take the responsibility for leading the class in the chant. Then, once students are familiar with the numbers and the routine, you can eliminate the pointer and ask for students to recall the numbers in the chant by memory. You can chant anywhere: lining up at recess, walking to lunch, transitioning between lessons, and, of course, in daily calendar activities. Students know what to do when it comes to these routines because they practice them daily.

Daily routines focus on both procedural knowledge and developing computational fluency, but routines don't just focus on math content. Daily routines also capitalize on students' language. We use language structures as routines to assist students who need support expressing their ideas. Regardless of the daily routine you decide to incorporate, we recommend that you start small and increase the cognitive demand over time. If you try to do too much at once, your students will be overwhelmed and you might decide this approach is not working, when in fact it was just implemented incorrectly. For example, when getting started with a warm-up at the beginning of your math block, focus on the behaviors you want your students to engage in, such as working independently and recording their thinking. Start your math warm-up with only one problem so you can teach the behaviors that are necessary for the daily routine to be successful.

With enough practice and repetition, your students will be leading the classroom routines in no time, and this is true of the kindergarteners as well. First things first, with each daily routine determine the rules and procedures for participation. Create a poster for students to reference and rehearse these rules and procedures each day until they become automatic. You are building young mathematicians with the routines and practices you develop in your students. If you want your students to have proficiency with the Standards of Mathematical Practice, "Attend to Precision," practice through daily routines will get them there. This is true from kindergarten through twelfth grade.

Four steps to starting daily routines:

1. Create a poster or anchor chart for students to reference the rules, procedures, and/or strategies related to the specific routine.
2. Model the routine using think aloud strategies to support what students should be thinking and doing.
3. Rehearse the routine using call and response techniques.
4. Differentiate routines to include student leaders, partner sharing, and opportunities to transfer learning in other contexts.

The Role of the Teacher and Student

Promoting deep learning in mathematics, requires a shift in how mathematics has been traditionally taught. When math instruction is dependent on the teacher, students do not have an opportunity to engage in authentic thinking and the mindset of "not being good at math" is reinforced. While the typical routine of "I do, We do and You do" may produce short term knowledge of procedural skills, research has found it is ineffective for long-term procedural fluency and mathematical reasoning (National Research Council, 2001).

Both the teacher and the student have distinct roles during daily routines. Teachers are responsible for planning the learning and students are responsible for participating and engaging in the challenge. Here are a few other ways that these roles are distinct.

The Role of the Teacher	The Role of the Student
• Plan daily routines to rehearse, extend, or challenge students' thinking. • Focus on one skill at a time during a daily routine, and spend several weeks practicing the same skill until students develop automaticity and ease in responding. • Scaffold language needs through sentence stems and language prompts. • Use open-ended questions with many potential pathways to an answer and many possible solutions. • Keep the focus on student talk and limit teacher talk.	• Participate in chanting, partner sharing, and whole-group explanations. • Listen actively to peers share solutions. • Share actively ideas and responses to questions and prompts. • Attend to precision when responding to questions. • Solve problems using mental math. • Write in journals or on whiteboards responses to group prompts.

 Think About It!

Why is it important to distinguish the roles of the teacher and student during daily routines? How can this help with planning and executing routines in your classroom?

_____

_____

To promote deep learning, teachers must be strategic in how they guide students and engage learners cognitively (Honomitchl & Chen, 2012). We can still be intentional and plan purposefully when presenting a problem, guiding student learning, and fostering reasoning for understanding. Research has found that learning through problem solving allows students to make sense of new concepts and build an understanding of relationships in mathematics (Lester & Cai, 2016).

Assessment and Daily Routines

Daily routines are typically a type of formative assessment to inform you of who's got it and who needs more help. You might start your math block with a calendar activity to reinforce automaticity of the facts, and then take what you have learned about students' knowledge from the assessment and embed it into instruction. You will have just rehearsed the facts as a class and now you can target the instruction to meet the students' needs exactly where they are. If you have a student who is struggling with basic multiplication, you can target instruction to that particular student. If you have students who have mastered their fives, you can push them to the next level and give them challenging problems with sixes. Using what you learn about your students during routines will help direct and adjust the instruction so that it is at students' "just right" level, or zone of proximal development, by providing a cognitive challenge.

Daily routines allow you to analyze how students are progressing. Every time you ask students to respond to a question, you get a window into their minds, and these moments are sources of formative assessment. After a number talk, during which you see a student using a strategy that is more complex than she has been used before, write down your observations. When a student begins to have more confidence sharing his thoughts orally during the calendar activity, record it!

Teachers regularly take anecdotal notes to record information about students. Anecdotal notes are purposeful notes kept as a qualitative record of what a teacher notices about a student's knowledge, skills, attitudes, or behaviors. Anecdotal notes are a form of ongoing assessment. You can record observation notes on any area of student growth or struggle. These notes are extremely helpful when it comes time to set goals for student growth, parent–teacher conferences, or in reporting progress on report cards. Anecdotal notes can be kept in a notebook and organized a few pages per child, or you can write notes on address labels conveniently and place on a clipboard. Teachers often focus on several students (five works well) a day, taking notes on those particular students. Every day, rotate and observe another group of students.

 Make the Tech Connection: Productivity

When it comes to keeping records, technology has a space and place to make record keeping at your fingertips. We both remember when standing file cabinets were a necessity. Nowadays, the best way is to go is paperless. Not only will going paperless save you space, but it will also save you valuable time instead of filing. If your school district is using Google Classroom and Chromebooks, you have a place to get started that is free and already built for student use. If you are without a system to manage student files and share assignments, you can use a learning management system like Seesaw (www.seesaw.com), Canvas (https://www.instructure.com/canvas) or Edmodo (www.edmodo.com) to create digital student files, record assessments, and communicate virtually with students and peers.

👁 View It: http://www.teacherpreptech.com/2018/04/top-two-tips-to-ditch-papertrail.html

Academic Language

Our teaching goal is for students to acquire the language of mathematics by using the associated terms and vocabulary during their discussions with partners or in sharing with a whole group. When students communicate clearly using mathematical language, they are developing communication skills aligned with the Standards for Mathematical Practice. During a Number Talk, listen to your students' responses. Are you hearing them say, "the number in the middle," instead of "the tens place," in a three-digit number? Perhaps you hear "the bottom number," instead of "the denominator?" What students often lack is mathematical academic language.

Being able to use the academic terms and discuss mathematical ideas is what forms the mathematical language, or the academic language of mathematics. Students should be able to use terminology with precision and clarity when explaining ideas, both in written and oral forms. Therefore, providing students with opportunities to develop and practice academic language in mathematics is an important part of teaching math. Daily routines provide opportunities for students to do this practice and, in turn, the daily practice promotes academic language and the confidence students need to hone their linguistic skills.

Research supports developing students' mathematical language by providing student-centered, language-rich learning environments in which students have regular opportunities to use and make sense of math through discussion (Moschkovich, 2013). This is particularly important for English language learners, since research indicates they have limited opportunities to produce orally and often speak academic English less than 2% of their school day (Soto, 2012); therefore, effective teachers should provide many daily experiences to develop talking in math and also provide time to nurture productive oral language. Daily routines encourage such types of discussion and are an excellent way to provide language-rich experiences and reinforce academic language.

For example, let's say you have your third-grade class on the carpet for a Number Talk in which you are exploring the equal sign. You put the following question on the board: $6 + 5 = \_\_\_\_ + 7$

You ask for the students to use mental math to think of the number that should go in the blank. One student says, "11." Since you recognize this as an error, you ask a probing question, "Why do you think that?" The student is then required to defend his answer using more mathematical language to explain the solution. The student might say, "I put together the 6 and 5 and got 11." By requiring the student to defend his answer, the teacher can see if the student is able to use both the mathematics and the mathematical language accurately.

For example in the response given, the student demonstrates ideas with limited use of academic language by saying, "put together," said more accurately, "added" and "got" instead of "sum." Using a technique called revoicing, the teacher can mirror the academic language by responding with the mathematical term properly used. Using revoicing, the teacher would say back to the student, "So you added the 6 and the 5 and the sum was 11." By revoicing, the teacher models the proper use of the academic language (Moschkovich, 1999).

In response to the misconception of "11" as the answer for $6 + 5 = \_\_\_\_ + 7$, the teacher can call on other students to discuss other possible solutions by asking, "Does anyone have a different solution?" The teacher can elicit more answers until an accurate solution is given. If this doesn't happen, the teacher can prompt students' thinking by using drawn representations of the quantities on both sides. As shown in this example, Number Talk serves as a daily routine that not only develops students' academic language but also challenges students' mathematical ideas.

Another beneficial strategy for supporting students' mathematical language development is the use of sentence stems. Sentence stems provide the initial part of the sentence for the students to scaffold their language. This is particularly beneficial for English language learners and students who struggle with writing. Knowing how to start a sentence can be especially challenging for students who are developing language. When the sentence stem is provided, students only focus on filling in the missing information. This reduces the language demand and helps students concentrate on the "meat" of the mathematical response, rather than getting stuck at the start of the sentence.

Prompts for sharing ideas might include the following:

"This is how I solved my problem. First, I _____."

"I agree because _____."

"I disagree because _____."

"I would like to add _____."

Prompts for responding to peers might include the following:

"Why did you _____?"

"How did you _____?"

"How could you _____?"

"Show me how you _____."

"My solution is _____ because _____."

Creating charts with language for students to use during daily routines scaffolds language development for all students. We provide a few examples that teachers can use to support students during daily routines in their production of language (see Figure 4.1).

Notice in the above poster the focus is not just on what the speaker says when sharing ideas, but what the listener says when responding to a peer. The emphasis is on modeling a mathematical discussion with activity not just from students who have the answer but from others who are listening. By explicitly modeling how to respond, the teacher is promoting a discussion and developing students' metacognitive skills.

Math Talk

1. Explain: "This is my solution/strategy..."
   - explain your thinking
   - show your thinkinking

2. "I agree with _____ because _____"
   - explain why you agree with another student

3. "I disagree because..."
   - explain why you disagree with another student, offer a different solution

4. Go Beyond: "This makes me think..."
   - extend the ideas of another student by taking them to other things

5. Ask Good Questions:
   "Why did you ...?"
   "How did you ...?"
   "Could you have ...?"
   "How can that be ...?"
   "What if ...?"

Figure 4.1

In the Appendix, we have included a printout of this bookmark that can be shared with your students as a prompt for engaging in a math discussion. We have found this tool to be highly valuable with all students whether working with a partner, or in the whole group. We also prompt kids who might be reluctant to share by providing them with one of the above sentence starters before our class discussion. We have also seen teachers use these sentence starters as a poster or record on a popsicle stick for students to pick and use during small group work.

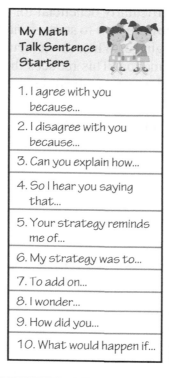

My Math Talk Sentence Starters

1. I agree with you because...
2. I disagree with you because...
3. Can you explain how...
4. So I hear you saying that...
5. Your strategy reminds me of...
6. My strategy was to...
7. To add on...
8. I wonder...
9. How did you...
10. What would happen if...

© Kendall Hunt Publishing Company

 Make the Tech Connection: Connect

Create a poll for students to share ideas and identify students' knowledge and beliefs. Students can respond to surveys via mobile device, computers, or tablets. Poll Everywhere is a webtool that provides you with a code for student to enter and response to a prompt digitally. Poll Everywhere can also be embedded on a Google Slide presentation for live polling to use this tool you will need to download the Poll Everywhere Extension in Google Chrome: https://chrome.google.com/webstore/detail/poll-everywhere-for-googl/jeehnidbmlhpkncbplipfalpjkhlokaa.

Questioning with Daily Routines

Questions are an essential part of daily routines, and questioning yields valuable information about students' thinking, makes learning visible, and adds to formative assessment. How you question your students can either limit or expand their thinking. Open-ended responses provide the most rich and beneficial information that prompt and stimulate student thinking. Using *how* and *why* questions provide a wider range of student responses than *what* questions. When a student provides a solution, you can ask, "How did you solve the problem?" or "Why did you choose to use that strategy?" You can probe for more ways of thinking by asking, "Who did it another way?" or "Does anyone have a different solution?" Asking for various ways of thinking or representing allows for richer discussions and highlights many different ways of thinking. Multiple solutions give students opportunities to critique others' reasoning which is one of the eight standards in the Standards for Mathematical Practice (NGAC & CCSSO, 2010). After a student has shared, a teacher can ask, "Does anyone want to add or build on this idea?" which can add to the complexity of solutions. Questioning throughout daily routines provides valuable formative assessment and helps you know where your students are struggling and what they have learned to mastery.

Questioning in daily routines helps to develop students' academic language. Every time students get a chance to respond orally, they are cementing their own understanding and leveraging the language of mathematics by sharing their ideas. Using technical language and math vocabulary is a critical aspect of being a mathematician, and students need many opportunities to internalize and verbalize their mathematical ideas.

Make the Tech Connection: Collaborate

Flip Grid are digital response systems that promote discussions in the cloud. Create a video question for your students to respond using video to capture their thinking. For example when addressing money concepts, ask students to share all the ways to make 75¢.

Think About It!

Here are a few questions we have found helpful when leading daily routines. Can you determine which Standards for Mathematical practice these questions support?

Can you think of another method that might have worked?

Is there another strategy that might be more efficient?

What do you notice about this method?

Can you describe your method?

Can someone explain why this method works?

Does this answer seem reasonable?

The first three questions above connect to the standard, Reason Abstractly and Quantitatively (NGAC & CCSSO, 2010). When we prompt students to use reasoning in mathematics, we are supporting their ability to consider multiple strategies to a problem and apply the most efficient method. Through questioning students about their reasoning, we can also determine what they understand and what misconceptions they might have.

The last three questions are related to the math practice Attend to Precision (NGAC & CCSSO, 2010). The standard Attend to Precision, promotes active reflection during routines and supports students' use of academic language and vocabulary. When students use symbols and vocabulary to communicate their thinking, we are reinforcing concepts and making math meaningful. We also support students in developing their confidence in mathematics. When students feel confident in math, they are more likely to take risks and engage in more challenging tasks.

In the Appendix of this book we have provided question prompts that are aligned with each Standard for Mathematical Practice.

 Make the Tech Connection: Collaborate

While questioning during a math discussion provides students with an opportunity to share their ideas and listen to others, students who are English language learners need additional time to process their thinking and respond in their second language. A tool that promotes "wait time" can be integrated into a daily routine, providing additional processing time by having students record and share their thinking with a web-based tool.

Two tools to promote processing time are Jamboard (https://www.jamboard.google.com/) and Padlet (www.padlet.com). Both are virtual whiteboards for the teacher to create a prompt and the student to respond using either a tablet, smartphone, or computer. The teacher shares the link and students can respond without having to create a username or password. If you are using Google Classroom or have a class blog or website, all you need to do is post a URL for students to access.

Writing with Daily Routines

Not only do students need to verbalize their ideas but they also need to write them down. According to Kiewra (1987), the act of note-taking is connected to the process of memorization, and leads to the creation of internal storage. Communication is a central feature of the Standards for Mathematical Practice, whether produced orally or in writing. Students are asked to justify their thinking and communicate their reasoning to others. We know from research in language production that oral language precedes written language (California Department of Education [CDE], 2010). With that in mind, orally discussing ideas during a think-pair-share strategy and then writing them down provides support for those students struggling with written language production. Sketchnotes can be used to support students with visual drawings to represent big ideas they are learning about. When it comes time for recall having a visual cue will aid in this process. http://www.teacherpreptech.com/2017/05/to-write-or-not-to-write-that-is.html. Students' written explanations and justifications are helpful in determining students' degree of mastery in learning and can help you gauge their ability to communicate ideas. *Daily Math Journals* is one way to collect students' written explanations and representations. For older students, math journals can be organized with a table of contents, so that students can reference their notebook for ideas and to work independently. We have found in our work with middle school students that organization and note-taking skills leads to greater success in the classroom. Students can also use individual whiteboards to temporarily write their ideas during daily routines.

Make the Tech Connection: Productivity and Collaboration

Going paperless creates an efficient way for students to take notes, organize ideas, communicate with the teacher, and also connect your students to additional web-based resources for remediation and challenge. Teachers can quickly grade student assessments with Google Chrome Add-ons like Flubaroo (https://goo.gl/8UrMJV) which can autograde your math assessments. Students can also collaborate with classmates within the entire suite of Google Tools.

Be sure to watch the videos we have created that will show you how to get started with Google Tools: https://goo.gl/YrY6kt

The screenshot below (see Figure 4.2) is a student-created glossary using Google Docs. Dr. Dickenson created a template for her students to record key math vocabulary terms. The template provides a structure to the routine, but the functionality of a digital document allows

Equivalent Fractions

Definition	Illustration/Drawing
Two or more fractions that name the same amount Equivalent means the same amount. It sounds like equal	I know one fourth is equivalent to two eights

Examples	Non Examples
They have the same amount even though the denominator is different $\frac{1}{2} = \frac{2}{4} = \frac{3}{6} = \frac{4}{8}$	1 whole pizza is not equivalent to one half.

© Kendall Hunt Publishing Company.

Figure 4.2

students to hyper link other ideas and concepts in their definition. Moreover students can quickly insert images to represent concepts which is an efficient way to capture visual representations.

A table of contents was created for organization and students worked collaboratively on this document so that peer editing and revisions were built into this process. You can use this template with your students.

🔖 Snag It: https://goo.gl/kgWM58. This is a Google Docs template for creating a Math Glossary of terms with your students. You can insert images with Google Images instantly. Just select "Insert" then "Image" to search the web, your Google Drive or Desktop.

Let's Explore Daily Routines

Daily Routine No. 1: Number Talks

What's the Goal? Promote Mental Math with Number Talks

This is a teacher-led daily routine that typically occurs at the beginning of your math instructional block to activate prior knowledge of math concepts and spiral instruction. Number Talks are short, no more than 15 minutes, and focused on developing students' computational fluency, as students add, subtract, multiply, and divide without recording on paper. Rules and procedures must be part of your Number Talk routine to support students in having quiet time to think about possible solutions. Students use thumbs up to indicate silently they found a solution and are ready to share, allowing for thinking space.

In the Appendix, you will find the Planning Guide for creating a Number Talk (see Figure 4.3). It is important to think about all possible solutions to the problem as this will help you think about questions you might ask while students are sharing their responses. Furthermore, by identifying the academic language your students will utilize, front-load these words by placing them on the board with an image to help students use the mathematical language with precision.

There are six elements to this planning guide:

1. **Math Concept and Goal:** Identify the math concept you will be teaching and what goal you would like to achieve with your students (e.g., regrouping while subtracting mentally).
2. **Number Talk Type:** Record the math problem you are using and how this will be shared with your students. We will explain each type of Number Talk below.
3. **Academic Language:** Determine the academic language you expect students to use during your math discussion. You can front-load key terms by placing them in a chart for students to access.
4. **Next Steps:** Identify how you will use student data from the math talk to support your students or assess their understanding formally.
5. **Possible Solutions:** Record all the possible ways students might solve the problem. This process will help you think about the kinds of questions you might ask to support student thinking.

Number Talk Planning Guide	
Math Concept & Goal:	Possible Solutions: Record all the ways of showing
Number Talk Type: (Image, Number String, Ten Frame, Other):	
Academic Language:	
Next Steps: Exit ticket, Anchor Chart, Journal or Exit Ticket	Questions To Guide Student Discussion:
NOTES:	

Figure 4.3

6. **Questions to Guide Student Discussion:** Based on student possible solutions, think about what questions you will ask to guide their thinking. For additional question ideas, see the question chart we created in the Appendix that is aligned to each Standard for Mathematical Practice.

What's The Format? Consistency Is Key to Developing Habits of Mind

A routine in Number Talks includes the teacher posing a question, providing thinking time, and then asking students to show if they have a response. The teacher poses the problem orally, shows an image, or writes it on the board or document camera. One way students can show they have a response is by giving a thumbs-up signal. This tells the teacher they have an idea and allows their peers to think of an answer without feeling rushed. Once students have indicated they found an answer, the teacher will call on students to write down their answer without giving input. Then a discussion follows on the answers given. During Number Talks you can elicit more student ideas by posing the question, "Did anyone find a different way?" This type of questioning allows for a variety of student responses and provides a chance to highlight multiple ways of thinking. Before beginning a Number Talk you should review the rules and expectations. We have created a Google Presentation that you can print as a poster or review with your students.

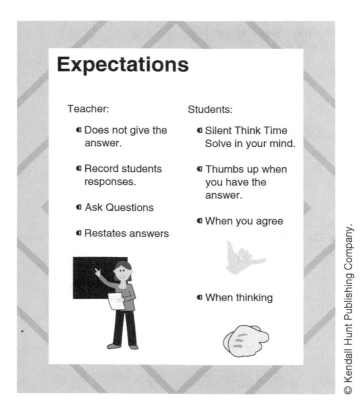

Snag It: https://goo.gl/RYNcPU

Use this presentation to review the rules and expectations for a Number Talk. You can also print out each slide to post and remind students of what they should do during a Number Talk.

Now that we have discussed Number Talks, let's explore the different kinds of Number Talks you can use across the grade span. Then we will provide you an overview of your role as a teacher.

K-2 Number Talks

Dot Cards: To support students in moving toward mental math strategies at a young age, Dot cards are commonly used for a Number Talk as a way to support students' ability to subitize. This means that students can figure out the total without counting.

Hold up one of the three cards below and flash to students for up to 5 seconds. Ask the children, "How many dots did you see?". Give students an opportunity to share out how they recognized the patterns. It is important to start with easy patterns and then move to more complex patterns over time.

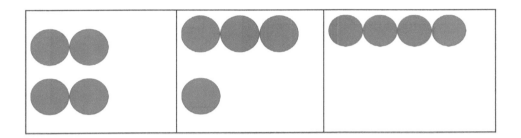

The teacher can either hold up a card, use an overhead projector, or share a virtual presentation for the students to determine the total. Dot cards support students in other related concepts such as "counting on" and "recognizing patterns." We recommend starting with small quantities to build students' confidence. The teacher can lead the students in a discussion on how they determined the amount. Students who are beginning to develop addition concepts might share they saw the first card as "2 + 2." This process will also support students in thinking about the ways to make a number. In future lessons, when students are working toward computational fluency in math they will be more likely to decompose numbers to add mentally.

Rekenrek: For students who need to have a concrete representation, a Rekenrek is a popular arithmetic rack which students can manipulate and is commonly used to develop number sense. This tool can support teachers in providing a hands-on model for building numbers, doubling, counting on, adding, and subtracting. With daily use, this tool can also be incorporated in the context of word problems that involve addition and subtraction. A Rekenrek can be made with beads and string for each student. We've also seen teachers use shoeboxes with rows of beads across to make a three-dimensional (3-D) model. Typically, there are two strings with 10 beads in each row. The beads in each row are broken up into two groups of five red and five white beads. You can also create one row of 10 for students who are working below grade level and five rows of 10 for students who are ready for challenge.

Here are a few ways you can use Rekenreks as a daily activity.

Subitizing: Similar to the strategies with dot cards, the teacher can show the beads and ask students to determine the total. Rekenreks can also be used similar to dot cards where you flash or show the image and ask your students what they see. Using a Rekenrek will help students identify patterns and build their number sense. Furthermore, once students have developed fluency with using this tool, they will have greater comfort understanding place value in which they recognize the number 17 as 10 and 7.

Make a Number: This activity reinforces the idea that the whole is made up of separate parts. In an addition equation the whole is made up of two parts. The beads can be moved so students can build a number. Begin with all beads on the right side of the Rekenrek and move to the left. The first row represents one addend and the bottom row represents the second addend. You might start an activity by asking the students to show you how they can make 6.

4 + 2 = 6

3 + 3 = 6

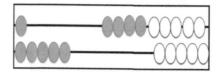

1 + 5 = 6

Once students have developed the idea that a total can be decomposed into different parts you can also reinforce the commutative property in which the numbers can be added in any order but you will still have the same answers, 2 + 3 = 5, 3 + 2 = 5.

Missing Part Concept: An activity that supports students in developing algebraic thinking is where you have students determine an unknown number when given the part and whole. Using the Rekenrek, cover up a part of the beads and have students determine what number is missing.

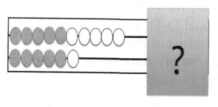

16 + _ = 20

https://youtu.be/Lp_ogl2iH_Q

Make the Tech Connection: Productivity

Once your students have worked with a concrete model for some time, you can use digital tools and presentations to reinforce these math concepts without having to get out the manipulatives and put them away.

We've made a digital presentation for you to use. If you are working with upper elementary students, this is a great way to reinforce basic concepts in a small group or independent setting.

Don't forget to "Make a Copy" and "Save to your Drive" this Google Presentation.

Snag It: https://goo.gl/JAQH8S

Make the Tech Connection Calculate

We love this digital version of a Rekenrek that you can use during a Number Talk. If you have a screen and Internet access, this tool can be used with the above activities. You can move the beads and create additional tens to build larger numbers. You can also hide a portion of the beads for the missing addend activity. Try this with your students as well during computer time with one-to-one devices students can manipulate the Rekenrek based on word problems you create and share with them in a handout to record their answers.

https://apps.mathlearningcenter.org/number-rack/

Ten Frames: Understanding the base-ten structure has become a focal point for early mathematics. In order for students to make sense of what base ten is they need to start with the concrete. Students can prove that 10 ones is equal to 10 by using a ten frame. With enough practice students should be able to recognize that when the ten frame is full that it makes 10.

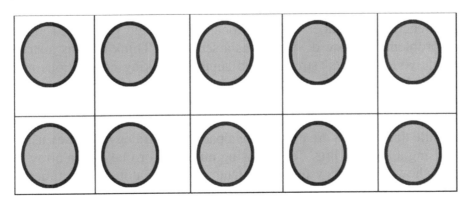

This will help the students count on from 10 when they recognize another digit.

When students see the ten frames full they should start at 10 and add on three more. This process supports students in developing computational fluency. In addition, using ten frames during a Number Talk is a way for students to share strategies that their peers can use in problem-solving. With this foundational skill established, students will have confidence when it comes to their mathematical abilities.

Watch It

This video of a first-grade class shows the entire process of using a Number Talk with a ten frames. https://www.youtube.com/watch?time_continue=12&v=fjCdbSMlxGU

Make the Tech Connection: Gamify

This Greg Tang math game helps students build their understanding of ten frames by creating one with virtual visual models. Play and have some fun. http://gregtangmath.com/tenframemania

3-8 Number Talks

There are a few kinds of Number Talks that are commonly used by upper elementary and middle school teachers. The focus is still on developing students' computational fluency and flexibility while using different strategies but with grade-level content.

Number Strings: Whereas a number talk can focus on a single problem, a number string includes multiple problems that are developed as a sequence. Think of it as a string of math problems that builds your students' strength and supports making connections among problems. According to Callandro (2000), number strings provide students with an opportunity to make connections between conceptual understanding and procedures. A good number string will support students in developing a range of strategies and examine the relationship between these strategies. While the students are explaining a particular strategy that they used to solve a problem, such as using a number line, decomposing numbers, or making an array, the teacher should illustrate or show the strategy for all students to follow along. Sometimes the teacher includes incorrect strategies, too, to promote critical thinking.

Think About It!

Work out the below number string independently and see what strategies you use mentally to solve the following problems.

Number Strings	
Proportional Reasoning	Using both a model and a story context supports students in making connections and deepening their understanding.
	Have students begin by looking at a model and thinking about what the story might be. "Record the students' thinking and statements on the board. Then provide a context, such as "Cecilia attended a 60 minute Zumba class. If she burns 30 calories in the first 12 minutes of class how many calories would she burn after the first 30 minutes and by the end of a 1-hr class?

Multiplication

2×6

4×6

8×6

16×6

32×6

This number string is designed to help students use smaller facts and double their answer to solve additional problems. In this string, the teacher writes the problem and student strategies are modeled. Using a visual model can help students see the relationship between the first factor in the following sequence.

Division

$16 \div 8$

This particular number string helps students understand a relationship among numbers. As the dividend is doubled, the quotient is doubled.

Moreover it is laying a foundation for developing algebraic thinking as students are applying the distributive property in a representation which appears in algebraic form in subsequent grades a(b+c).

$160 \div 8$

$320 \div 8$

$328 \div 8$

$3200 \div 16$

$3216 \div 16$

This string also supports the distributive property in which students already know that $3,200 \div 16 = 200$ and $16 \div 16 = 1$, thus $3,216 \div 16 = 201 (200 + 1)$

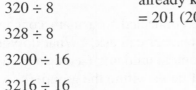

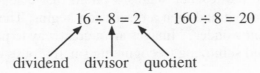

Number Strings

Decimals

6×4

6×40

6×0.40

$.60 \times 0.40$

When working with decimals seeing a string of numbers helps determine how the value changes with a decimal point. Using a context of money helps students see how the value increases/decreases. You can also use a chart to reinforce place value.

Hundred	Tens	Ones	Hundredths	Tenths
	2	4		
2	4	0		
		2•	4	0
		•	2	4

Fraction

$\frac{3}{4} + \frac{1}{2}$

$1/5 + 1/10$

Number lines and money are two models that students develop in relation to fractions.

$\frac{1}{4} = 0.25 \qquad \frac{1}{2} = 0.50$

$$0.75 + 0.50 = 1.25 = 1\ 25/100 = 1\frac{1}{4}$$

$1/5 = 0.20 \qquad 1/10 = 0.10$

$$0.20 + 0.10 = 0.30 = 30/100 = 3/10$$

With the number string, the teacher can also provide a model and context for the student. As noted above, the context helps students see how math is used in the real world and the model helps scaffold instruction by giving students a way to get started. If you ask your students to give you a context for a problem, such as 45 divided by 9, you might hear, "I have 45 pieces of candy and want to share with 9 friends." This is especially important for upper-grade students as more complex math often requires students to recall multistep procedures, so knowing why a problem "makes sense" can help students detect errors and miscalculations. Furthermore, students need to develop an understanding of why a particular strategy makes sense to support retrieval. Using a model within a number string will also help students who struggle with a particular concept to develop strategies within their zone of proximal development.

Number Images: Another approach to Number Talks is called Number Images. Similarly to providing a context for a problem, a number image sets the stage for students to think mathematically about a situation.

With a number image the teacher shares a photo that can be connected to a math concept students are learning about and then a discussion begins. The teacher can ask, "What do you notice, and what do you wonder?" Images are a great way to promote unitizing (seeing a group of objects as 1 unit) and subitizing (recognizing small groups of items within the group).

Think About It!

How can unitizing be used to count the total number of food items in the picture below?

© Patricia Dickenson

Think About It!

What are possible ways students might subitize the image below?

We encourage you to begin to create a collection of Number Talk images that you can use with your class. This is a great way to start off the school year or return from a school break and encourage students to share images and make the math connection.

◉ **View It:** http://makingmathconnection.blogspot. com/p/math-images.html

Dr. Patricia Dickenson connects math images to Common Core math standards.

Three Steps to Number Talks

Step 1. Selecting Problem Types: Your first responsibility is to select the types of problems that will support students in developing computational fluency in your class. Remember when we talked about fluency earlier in this chapter and that students should have the skills but need to develop faster retrieval (speed) to develop fluency? Fluency is developed through practice. The goal of your number talk is to practice strategies that your students have already learned. A good rule of thumb is to identify and practice the skill students are using in their math lessons but need to develop fluency.

Step 2. Present the Problem: Display the problem to the students in a way that all can see and make sense of it. Do not ask any questions, rather provide time for students to work silently on the problem. Once a majority of students display a thumbs-up to show they are ready, record their answers without asking or answering questions, at this point. Record all possible solutions without any comments.

Step 3. Facilitating Discussion: After all answers are recorded, begin your conversation about the answers provided. During the share out, the interaction you have with your students should be more of a conversation than a probing of ideas. Throughout the conversation, you will ask questions to support students in thinking and guide them in sharing their responses. One way you can do this is by recording their name next to their answers. You might say, "Who agrees with Micala's answer and can explain?" You should illustrate the model or record their thinking to provide support and scaffold their ability to share mathematical ideas. Furthermore, by recording students' responses you are also guiding other students to make connections to what their peers are sharing. Using the question chart we provided (see figure), you can further the discussion by having other peers contribute to the discussion.

For example, you pose the following question: "What is ¼ + ½?" If the student responds that she visualized a box with 2/4 and ½ as equivalent and then added ¼ to find the sum of ¾, you would make the following illustration on the board.

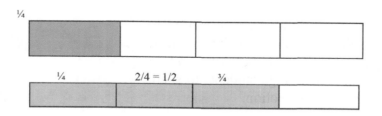

You can continue the conversation with your students by having another peer share a different strategy or share why they agree or disagree with this method.

Watch It

https://www.youtube.com/watch?v=krOIJqwV1YA&feature=youtu.be

Make the Tech Connection: Assess

Using the "Flip Grid" tool, create a mental math challenge (Number Talk) which students respond individually to the prompt.

Watch It

In this video Dr. Dickenson explains how you can go digital with a number talk and shares a virtual number talk with a group of second graders.

https://www.youtube.com/watch?v=UzihGm1Vdf0&t=8s

Snag It: Use the following Google Slide Deck to use for a virtual number talk: https://bit.ly/3wRdMcr

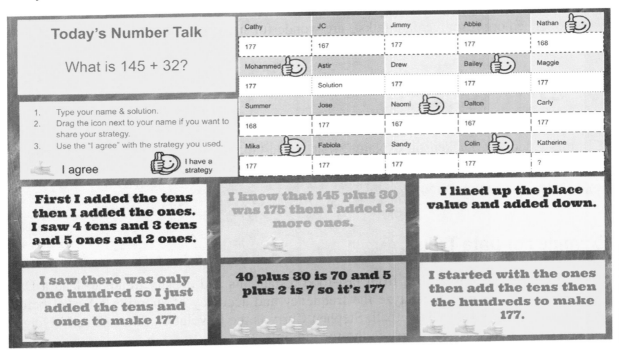

Figure 4.4

Daily Routine No. 2: Data Talk

This routine works across K-12-grade spans and disciplines to support students in making sense of data and engaging in discourse using evidence from visual representations. Students and teachers can connect with problems, situations, and issues using data in a variety of contexts to support data-literate citizens who see mathematics as a sensemaking tool that can ground complex issues. This routine prepares students to be college and career ready as over 50 college majors require a statistics or data science course, and 90% of the world's data have been created in the last two years (YouCubed, 2021). Data science also provides students with the "why" for doing math, and an opportunity to authentically engage with the habits of mind of the Standards for Mathematical Practice as students Make Sense of Problems and Persevere in Solving Them (SMP #1), Construct Viable Arguments, Critique the Reasoning of Others (SMP #3), and Look for and Express Regularity in Repeated Reasoning (SMP # 8).

Similar to a Number Talk routine, a Data Talk begins with sharing a visualization of a data set, and asking students "what they notice" and "what they wonder." As students share their noticing and wonderings, the teacher can record their ideas and ask follow-up questions. Data Talks support quantitative literacy that applies advanced reasoning with basic mathematics to real-world contexts (Steen, 2004). In addition, the Common Core English Language Arts Standards emphasizes a shift from narrative to expository text. In fact, by 12th grade, students are expected to read informational text 70% of the time. Visual representations such as chart, graphs, and tables can hinder students from making inferences and understanding the underlying themes when they lack quantitative literacy. Data Talks can be used across the curriculum and should be used as a tipping point for engaging in a thoughtful conversation. Pew Research Center, (https://www.pewresearch.org), Statica (https://www.statista.com/), and YouCubed Data Talks (https://www.youcubed.org/resource/data-talks/) are wonderful sites to find a rich collection of visual data representations for all grades.

Watch It

In this video, Dr. Dickenson explains what a data talk is and engages a group of fourth graders in a series of data talks using Google Jamboard to record students thinking.

https://youtu.be/tP8UfM79S7s

Examples of Data Talks

1. PE teachers look at data from fast-food restaurants and obesity trends to lead a Data Talk on nutrition or analyze the frequency and accuracy of shooting a basket before leading a lesson in basketball. Stephen Curry is the Revolution: https://fivethirtyeight.com/features/stephen-curry-is-the-revolution/

2. Social Studies and Civics Teachers can use data to discuss the context of a situation, underlying factors, and cause and effect related to events in history. Teachers can lead a Data Talk about how voters learn about political candidates and discuss the role of the media and propaganda: How do Voters First Learn About Candidates? https://www.statista.com/chart/17743/where-voters-learn-about-candidates/

3. English language arts teachers should encourage students to use data to determine whether a claim is supported by reasons and evidence. The ELA framework also

encourages students to integrate information quantitatively to develop understanding of a topic or issue. Data can support students in making content connections to a theme, character motives, and write a persuasive argument using evidence. *The Diary of a Young Girl*, by Anne Frank, is a popular book read in middle school and high school, which highlights the events of the Holocaust, a Data Talk can add to the significance of the author's struggles and the impact across countries. Percentage of Jews Killed During the Holocaust https://qcc.libguides.com/c.php?g=512378&p=3608540

 Make the Tech Connection

Padlet is a wonderful and dynamic tool that can support a data talk with visual images and videos embedded in an interactive space. The teacher can pose a question and encourage students to share their noticings and wonderings.
PE Padlet on Obesity rates: https://padlet.com/thewiredprofessor/7uw9ut60s7mv8clw
Science Padlet on Environmental Issues: https://padlet.com/thewiredprofessor/goupp 34n1iqa

Daily Routine No. 3: Calendar

Keep it Relevant with Calendar

Calendar is an example of a popular daily routine that is connected to students' everyday life. With calendar you are using the context of the date to build computational fluency and reinforce math models. Most of your students have seen and used a calendar in their lives. They organize events and think about planning by using a calendar to guide their thinking. You can introduce the calendar by having students think about dates they celebrate with their family. You can also record special days for your class to celebrate such as student birthdays, school holidays, and class celebrations such as the 100th day of school. With calendar routines, you can spiral the skills that students need to master in math with repetition and practice. We will discuss the routines that you can build for K-2 elementary students and students in the 4 to 8 span.

Getting Started with Calendar

Identify a bulletin board space in your classroom where you can have students sit on the carpet and view the calendar bulletin board activities clearly. The first few weeks and even months (depending on your students' age) will be teacher directed with questions and responses around the selected routines you have chosen for your students. A typical calendar routine begins with identifying "today's date" and asking students a series of questions regarding the date such as:

Is today's date an odd or even number?

What are the ways we can make today's number?

What is one more than today's number?

What is one less than today's number?

Your calendar routines should include skills from previous grade levels for which students need to develop fluency as well as skills they will need to master by the end of the school year. For example, in a first-grade class, the students might be still struggling with the kindergarten skill to know the numbers and the count sequence; therefore, one of your routines would include counting forward from the calendar number and counting back. This is when looking at the end of the year assessment data can be used as a good indicator of the skills students have not achieved mastery in order to inform instruction.

Watch It

In this third-grade classroom, the teacher highlights patterns in the calendar and reinforces mathematic concepts such as arrays and geometric concepts. https://www.youtube.com/watch?v=1YWftMnMfW0

Watch It

In this first-grade class, you will observe how to use Calendar using Google Jamboard for remote instruction.

https://youtu.be/UsUaStMb9N8

Snag It: You can go digital with the Calendar Activity. To create a more interactive experience and have students practice independently https://bit.ly/3zQXN04

Think About It!

Reflect on a time when you learned a new language or developed a skill. What role did consistency and repetition play in your learning?

_____

_____

Here are some ways to use calendar activities.

Calendar Journal: We've included the calendar journal page for you to set up your bulletin board and as a printable for students to complete (see Figure 4.5). You can also place this journal in a clear protective sleeve for students to reuse each day. The calendar journal is also a quick assessment tool to determine what students have mastered and can do independently. At the beginning of the year, we recommend that your focus be on getting students excited about calendar and not focus on the completion and accuracy of the journal page, which will come with time. Initially you might just use the calendar page to use as a teaching scaffold to support you.

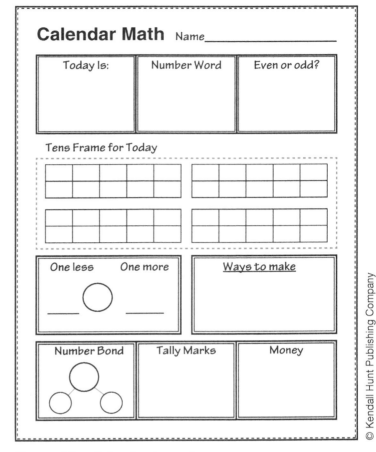

Figure 4.5 Calendar Journal

For many younger students, writing is a struggle and so the focus of this activity should be on recognizing numbers and building confidence in math, not writing. Don't do something your students are not ready for; rather, start off with making them feel that learning is fun and they can be successful. Once you have your bulletin board set up, you can call students to record on your chart. Each section of your calendar should be laminated for reuse each day. Our calendar journal page includes the concepts we want students to record and practice each day. You might not include all the calendar activities on the journal page. See Appendix for a copy of this page.

Today Is: Students record the date. You can also use this as the "Number of the Day" for students who need additional support identifying numbers. The "Number of the day" can be made into a necklace or crown for students to wear. Have students write the word and circle even or odd.

Building Tens and Ones: Use a ten frame and have each day represent one circle in the ten frame as you and your students continue to color or place an object in the tens frame. You might ask students, "How many more to make ten?" and "Can we count by tens to our new total?". Each day will be a new total by creating and adding one to the total from the previous day. This activity reinforces fundamental number concepts. It provides visual practice with these concepts and helps children say numbers and visualize them. For younger students, this routine lays the foundation for place value concepts.

One Less One More: Write the day in the circle and have students record the number that comes before and after the number of the day.

Ways to Make: Students can build their number sense and take the day of the week, such as September 5th, and record all the ways to make 5. The teacher can record the number sentences on the calendar board. A popular center activity for young students is to read the room, and when kids come to the calendar bulletin board they can read the number sentences that were created. You can also use the calendar journal page as one of your math centers for students to record independently.

Money: Connect the concept of money to the number of the day. The teacher can staple a sandwich baggy on the calendar board to hold play money that is added to the bank each day. Counting money each day will help students identify the value of coins and reinforce the idea that there are different values of coins that are equivalent. For example, once the students reach the 10th day of the calendar, they can transfer 10 pennies or two nickels into a dime. In our experience with children, money is a difficult concept for many to grasp; thus, it is an important concept to reinforce and practice daily.

Number Bond: Students need to have a visual representation of the relationship between a number and its part. Students can make connections between addition and subtraction by starting with the whole and one part to find the unknown part. Thus, number bonds help students understand the inverse relationship between subtraction and addition.

Tally Marks: Begin by making tally marks for each day of your calendar activity. This activity reinforces counting by fives. Once students have developed proficiency with counting by fives up to 30, extend tally marks for several months and continue the counting chant.

Weather: Incorporating a "What's the Weather?" component into your calendar is a great way to not only build science into your daily routines, but also integrate math into a science activity. Students can begin to think like a scientist by making observations of the weather and recording data of daily weather patterns. Graphs are a natural way to analyze daily weather and temperature data over time.

Make the Tech Connection: Calculate and Analyze

Once you have collected data for a month, create a digital graph from the National Center for Education Statistics (NCES) site (https://nces.ed.gov/nceskids/) that can be printed out or displayed for your students. You can create questions related to your weather graph that can be used to assess students' understanding of graphs and finding the value. Reading and interpreting graphs appear through the Common Core math standards as Measurement and Data.

View It: http://www.corestandards.org/Math/Content/MD/

Here are some questions you might ask your students after you have graphed the weather data:

- How many sunny days were in April?
- How many more rainy days were there than sunny days?
- What type of weather appeared the most often?
- What type of weather appeared the least often?

Days at School: Recording the days at school builds place value concepts as primary students' progress from the ones, tens, and hundreds. Many primary teachers celebrate the "100th" day of school with their students. The 100th day is also accompanied by a class celebration where students bring in a collection of items to demonstrate their understanding of 100. Within the collection is an opportunity to represent groups of tens in many ways. For example, a student can bring in 10 pennies, 20 paper clips, 30 stickers, and 40 cars to make a collection of 100.

Upper-Grade Concepts: Although "calendar" often appears in primary grades, upper elementary and middle school teachers can use these routines to support students who need to develop fluency in other number concepts such as fractions, decimals, multiplication, and division. Unlike primary students, upper-grade students can record in the calendar journal each day; however, you will not bring them to the carpet if they are in the fifth grade or beyond.

Upper Elementary Template: In the first half of the template, students use the date, which is the number of the day in the month, to determine the factors, multiples, area, and perimeter. Then they use the date out of total days in the month to divide and find the fraction, decimal, and percent. Then the next set of routines include the entire date that is the day, month, and year. It also provides a place to practice writing equations, finding the average, and writing a larger number. Each of these routines are explained below.

Today's Number: Students record the date of the month and determine if the number is prime or composite. For example, 12 is a composite number as it has factors other than one and itself.

Factors and Multiples: Students can then record the factors which are the ways to make the number as the product, and multiples which include the number multiplied by another number. You can also have students reference the previous day's calendar journal to identify the Least Common Multiple between both days.

Area and Perimeter: Students often confuse area with the perimeter and vice versa. If this is the case in your classroom, then your students need more exposure and daily practice until it becomes mastered. Students can build an array that is representative of the date. For example, if the day is the 24th then students can be creative and build a variety of rectangles with different sizes such as 6 by 4 or 2 by 12. You can also have students determine the perimeter and area with smaller numbers. You can ask, "If it's the first day of the month what would each side be?" You might have students who tell you that it's not enough and others who use decimals such as 0.25 for a square or 0.4 for the length of a rectangle and 0.2 for the width. Don't be afraid to let your students struggle and have other students show them their way of figuring it out.

Name_____ Calendar Math

| Today's Number | Factors | Multiples |

Prime or Composite

Ways to Make Area:

Ways to Make Perimeter:

| Division | Fraction | Decimal | Percent |

Daily Big Number
Standard Form:

Expanded Form:

Word Form:

Data Set: _____

Make An Equation

© Kendall Hunt Publishing Company

Multiplication Concepts: For today's day have students identify the multiples and factors of the number. For example, if the day is the 12th the factors are 2×6, 6×2, 12×1, 1×12, 4×3, and 3×4. The multiples are 12, 24, 36, 48, 60, 72, 84, 96, 108, 120, 132, and 144. You can also ask students to identify if 12 is a prime or composite number.

Division Concepts: Using the day as the divisor and the number of days in the month as the dividend. If there are 30 days in the month and the day is the 12th then $30 \div 12 = 2.5$. Once students have developed fluency with division you can challenge your students by using the total number of school days as the dividend or the year.

Fraction Decimal and Percent: Looking at the calendar as a whole is a great way for students to identify the fraction, decimal, and percent. By building this each day, the students will see how all three increase daily and are of equal value. You can also shade parts of the calendar to provide a visual model and help reinforce benchmark fractions. For example, if there are 28 days in the month you can use post-its to cover the calendar in four sections to represent fourths. When there are 30 days, consider using thirds. Getting creative with how students look at these concepts in connection to the real world will help promote transfer. We have also used these concepts when counting of days at school for students to look at larger numbers and we chart this around the room so students can visualize quantity from one corner to the next. In many ways it becomes a virtual number line where we also record equivalent fractions as they are discovered by our students.

The Daily Big Number: Students also need to work with larger numbers and learn how to read these numbers in multiple ways. Use the entire date: so if today is April 15, 2018 (4/15/2018), use these numbers to make one big number in standard form 4,152,018. Students write the number using commas (after a series of three), then write in word form (four million, one-hundred and fifty two thousand, eighteen) and expanded form (4,000,000 + 152,000 + 18). For younger students begin with the day and month and extend to include the entire year (or last two digits) once your students have shown mastery.

Day's Data Set: Use the digits in the Daily Big Number to determine the mean, median, mode, range, outlier, and average. For example, using the date of 4/15/2018, we can break the numbers into the following data set: 4, 15, 20, 18.

Make an Equation: To help build computational fluency and flexibility across concepts take the data set numbers and have students build a math equation. For example, using the numbers we used previously (4, 15, 20, 18) the students might build: $(20 - 15) \times (18 - 4) = 20$.

Tech Connection: Productivity: Create a Google Slide of the calendar activities for quick display and efficiency. Students then complete the daily calendar activity as part of their morning warm-up in Google Slides.

🔖 Snag It: You can go digital with the calendar routine with this Google Jamboard: https://bit.ly/2SOq5Yv

Watch It

In this video Dr. Dickenson demonstrates how to use Calendar routine for Upper Elementary students.

https://youtu.be/wHVWFlTNAlM

Daily Routine No. 4: Hundred Chart and Multiplication Chart

When students are struggling to count with efficiency and fluency, it's time to practice with hundreds charts. The hundreds chart provides a structure for students who need to develop fundamental skills and promote visual patterns to support their development of number sense. With repetition and practice, visual patterns can be established to anchor the strategies you are teaching in your class. Your textbook might have you focus on many strategies for adding or subtracting but without a visual cue these strategies are easily forgotten, as they are often not taught in a meaningful context.

The hundreds chart follows a left to right pattern similar to learning how to read as the numbers are arranged in columns by 10s. Using physical counters such as bingo chips and markers moves students along the math continuum from the concrete to the representational (the

© Patricia Dickenson

hundreds chart) to the abstract (adding and subtracting without any scaffolds). You can have students put clear poker chips on each number to get a visual representation of a number's value and so they make a tactile connection to this activity. Students can count along orally and activate the language part of their brain. Similar to a bingo-type game, the teacher can have students find numbers using clues such as, "The sum of me is three rows of ten and four across, what number am I?"

Here are some additional activities to use that incorporate the hundreds chart.

Find the Date: Use the date similar to the calendar routine within the hundreds chart and ask questions like, "What's one more, one less, ten more, and ten less?", "How many tens and ones in this number?", and "What are the ways we can make this number with numbers before it and after it?"

Skip counting: Start at a number and skip count by five or tens making moves across the number line.

Counting Forward and Counting Backward: Provide students with addition and subtraction facts in which they have to physically move forward and backward to find the sum or difference. For example, if the fact is 32 + 53, students will place a poker chip on 32 then move down five rows (five tens) and across three to reach the sum of 85.

Missing Number: When numbers are missing from the number chart, students use their knowledge of patterns to determine the missing numbers. This helps reinforce the visual model and provides a foundation for place value by looking at digits in the context of having distinct values (tens and ones).

Number Chart Cutouts: Using each square as a cutout of the hundreds chart have students recreate the columns and rows. This process will help cement the mental representation students have been working with in relation to the hundreds chart. We recommend this activity after your students have been working with the hundreds chart for some time. You will know they are ready when they are able to achieve the above activities with greater speed and accuracy.

We have shared a 1–100 chart and a 0–99 chart. These two charts help students see patterns in numbers but the 0–99 chart supports students in understanding the value of zero and the role it plays in place value. As the typical 1–100 chart does not include 0, it is missing a crucial point in students' development of number concepts. There are 10 digits used to make a number and that includes the numbers: 0, 1, 2, 3, 4, 5, 6, 7, 8, 9, and not 10. 10 is composed of 1 and 0.

Hundreds Chart

- View It: https://www.teachingchannel.org/videos/counting-by-ten-lesson

- View It: https://www.teachingchannel.org/videos/visualizing-number-combinations

Hundreds Chart

1	2	3	4	5	6	7	8	9	10
11	12	13	14	15	16	17	18	19	20
21	22	23	24	25	26	27	28	29	30
31	32	33	34	35	36	37	38	39	40
41	42	43	44	45	46	47	48	49	50
51	52	53	54	55	56	57	58	59	60
61	62	63	64	65	66	67	68	69	70
71	72	73	74	75	76	77	78	79	80
81	82	83	84	85	86	87	88	89	90
91	92	93	94	95	96	97	98	99	100

Hundreds Chart

0	1	2	3	4	5	6	7	8	9
10	11	12	13	14	15	16	17	18	19
20	21	22	23	24	25	26	27	28	39
30	31	32	33	34	35	36	37	38	49
40	41	42	43	44	45	46	47	48	59
50	51	52	53	54	55	56	57	58	69
60	61	62	63	64	65	66	67	68	79
70	71	72	73	74	75	76	77	78	89
80	81	82	83	84	85	86	87	88	89
90	91	92	93	94	95	96	97	98	99

 Make the Tech Connection Gamify

Students can work independently on these games by ABCYA to reinforce hundred chart activities. You can also select the type of hundred chart you prefer your students to use.

http://www.abcya.com/one_hundred_number_chart_game.htm

Make the Tech Connection: Collaborate

Display this digital hundreds chart while leading your routines. https://www.mathplayground.com/interactive_hundreds_chart.html

Daily Routine No. 5: Counting Collections

Make it Count with Counting Collections

There are two reasons why we love counting collections. First, students have so much fun counting and arranging objects, and second it is a great way to meet students where they are developmentally in their understanding of number concepts.

Counting Collections provides students with a tactile concrete representation of objects that they manipulate to express their number sense strategies. Students often work with a partner to organize their collection and through this process language is used to communicate and share ideas. Unlike other daily routines that rely on the teacher to transmit information, students take an active role by determining what strategies they will use to count with efficiency. As a result of this active engagement, students naturally work within their zone of proximal development.

This activity provides the teacher with much insight into what strategies students use with ease and where they need to grow developmentally; therefore, the role of the teacher is then to scaffold more sophisticated strategies and promote cognitive struggle. For example, students who are counting with proficiency with one-to-one correspondence can move toward organizing their collection by twos, fives, or tens and using skip-counting strategies to count more efficiently.

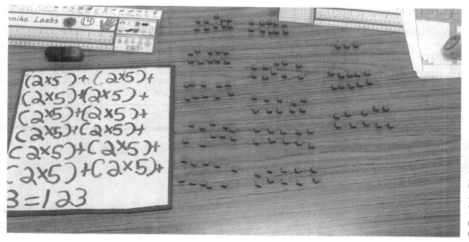

© Patricia Dickenson

In addition to providing an activity that allows students to physically construct their mathematical thinking, Counting Collections reinforces many of the Standards for Mathematical Practice such as "modeling with mathematics" and "look for and make use of structure." Students can also "construct viable arguments and critique the reasoning of others" by providing an opportunity for students to walk around the room and see what their peers have constructed. Students develop more efficient strategies by observing what their peers have done and immediately apply these strategies in the context.

© Patricia Dickenson

 Watch It

In this video a second grader explains how he built an array and counted rows of ten to make his collection. https://www.youtube.com/watch?v=4xpokIjPOdM&feature= youtu.be

With Counting Collections, the role of the teacher shifts from someone who explicitly teaches strategies to one who is making observations of what students have done and questioning students to extend and support their thinking. The types of questions you ask can help students develop more sophisticated strategies. Explicit teaching does happen, but is based on the data you collect and what you know about where students need to develop.

Here are a few activities across the grade span to use with Counting Collections.

Grade	Math Concept	Teaching Idea
K-1	One-to-one correspondence	Have students put objects in a line and count. Students should be able to count each object with a number assigned to it. Start with up to five objects and extend over time to 100.

Grade	Math Concept	Teaching Idea
K-1	Counting & Cardinality	Have students arrange objects in a set and determine how many are in the set by saying the last object in the counting sequence (Quantities up to 120).
K-2	Flexible counting strategies and decomposing numbers	Starting with the total set, students decompose the collection in a variety of ways. Students record their addition sentences and ways to make a number.
K-4	Place value and grouping	Have students arrange objects into different groups and express the place value for each grouping. For example, with a collection of 30 objects students can show three groups of ten or two groups of 15. Have students make illustrations to show their ability to transfer from the concrete to the representational.
2–5	Multiplication	Develop conceptual understanding of multiplication by building on students' understanding of "groups of" twos, fives and tens to record multiplication equations and extend students thinking by adding an object to each group or taking one object away from each group. For example making three groups of five and taking one object away from each group to make three groups of four.
3–8	Division	Use the total number of items in the collections as the dividend. Provide the students with an object such as paper cups that will be the divisor. They must make equal groups to determine the quotient. For example, if there are 138 in the collection this is the dividend. There are six cups (divisor) with 23 items (quotient) in each cup.
3–8	Fraction and Decimals	Use a collection with a variety of attributes that can be arranged by determining the relationship of one part to the whole. For example, if you have a collection of bingo chips (35 in total) students can determine the part (numerator) out of the total (denominator) that is red, white, or blue and record as a fraction.
3–8	Factors and Multiples	Using a large collection, students find the factors that can be arranged to show ways to make equal groups. For example, if the collection contains 30 hearts students can make three rows of 10 or five rows of six and record the factors of 30. With multiples, students create groups of that number.

Watch It

In this video, a second-grade students starts to build an understanding of the relationship between addition and multiplication.

https://youtu.be/aX8c9p2oBh8

Make the Tech Connection: Creation

Have students use their digital devices to take a picture and then record their explanation of the collection they created using a web tool like Seesaw. Using digital tools is a highly effective practice to support students in reflecting metacognitively on their strategies and thinking systematically about what they might do differently. The video above was created by a student who used Seesaw to record his thinking. This was his third video taken as the first two he realized mistakes in his explanation and was able to self-correct by watching his video.

Getting Started with Counting Collections

If you have a penchant for thrift stores, garage sales, or craft stores you will enjoy getting ready for this daily routine. Create baggies of items ranging from 10 to 1,000 items in each bag (depending on the grade level and task) that students can count and easily manipulate into a collection. Typical collections include paper clips, bingo chips, counters, teddy bears, beans, and leftover crafting materials. We strongly recommend that you not use perishable or edible items, as your collection will disappear in no time.

When first introducing Counting Collections to your class, we recommend that you set the norms and expectations for student behavior. Model and provide step-by-step instruction on how to use and take care of the objects that you provide them. Create a poster for student reference and begin with a short activity. Demonstrate the activity as a whole group and model your strategies aloud for students. You can include an anchor chart of strategies for students to reference when they are working with their collections.

Be sure you are collecting anecdotal evidence of student work to inform your instruction. You can provide your students with a handout to record the collection they made or students

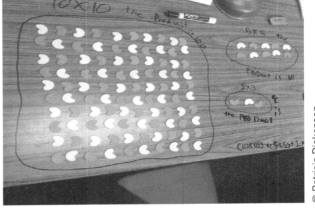

© Patricia Dickenson

can write on their desk with a dry erase marker which will provide you and other students with an explanation when students are looking at their peers' collection. Taking a picture and storing electronic records provides another way to document evidence of students' thinking.

🛍 Snag It: **In this Google slide presentation, Dr. Dickenson and her colleague, Louanne Myers, present to in-service teachers about how to get started with Counting Collections.** https://goo.gl/y6jXC8

Daily Routine No. 6: Math Journals

Write it Out with Math Journals

We have shared earlier about the importance of incorporating writing into your math practice. Journals are one way to capture student thinking but also a powerful tool to support students in moving new information into their long-term memory.

When we learn new information, the way we each process is different. For example, someone might prefer to share their thinking orally with others, whereas others need time to record their ideas and reflect on what they have described. Writing about your thinking is just as important as sharing with peers, as both approaches support metacognition (thinking about your thinking) and this is especially important for supporting students in guiding them through learning tasks, and problem-solving (Verschaffel, 1999). For students who prefer not to share their opinions or ask for help, providing an opportunity to record their thinking is especially important. Writing also lends itself to self-assessment, such as when a teacher purposefully asks questions that help students think about their beliefs and attitude. There is much you can do with math journals and bringing the writing into a digital space using web-based tools allows you to have a digital portfolio to record students' growth and progress throughout the school year.

Whether you decide to go digital or stay with a traditional paper-and-pencil approach, be consistent. Writing is a process, and when it comes to reflecting in math this process may need to be explicitly taught and modeled before it becomes the expectation. You can use any of the sentence stems and prompts we've provided as scaffolds for writing about math.

Other ways we like to use math journals include activating prior knowledge (write about a time where you used fractions in your life), class notes, word problems, planning project-based activities, vocabulary, and practice activities.

For secondary students, we know it is especially important to learn how to take notes and organize their thinking. From our experience working with middle schoolers, students who had strong note-taking skills were more on task and better prepared for assessments. Research also supports this practice as improving student achievement (Marzano, Pickering, & Pollock, 2001). However, providing a structure to math journals is needed along with a process for how your students will take notes. We have included a Table of Contents for upper elementary and middle schoolers to organize their math journal. Since upper elementary students need to know procedural knowledge, having a journal will also help with recall and can be used during independent practice to support students in becoming self-reliant.

Make the Tech Connection: Collaborate

Students can collaborate in small groups or with a partner on a digital notebook. This notebook can be used to support academic language, symbolic and visual representations and recall of conceptual and procedural knowledge. Teachers can assign grades to students digital notebook.

Snag It: https://bit.ly/3gXEbOZ

Daily Routine No. 7: Warm-Up

The Problem with Warm-Ups

In a traditional classroom when it's time to begin math, the teacher usually posts a problem on the board and students work independently. Although the problems are typically used to review previously learned concepts and support students in making connections, this process often becomes perceived by students as "high-stakes." When students feel anxiety and stress about "doing math" learning cannot occur and students become afraid to ask questions and take risks. This might explain why teachers often share with us, "I just taught this yesterday and they already forget." Refrain from beginning your math lesson with a routine that will cause stress and anxiety for your students; instead, start with a way that makes learning math fun.

While there is value in having students complete a "warm-up" at the beginning of math instruction, we argue that this prelude to teaching content, must be high excitement and not high anxiety. Start your class with a digital warm-up that is fun and informal and will encourage more risk taking and collaboration. We have included a table of digital tools and suggestions for engaging and adding excitement to your warm-ups.

Gamify	Kahoot https://create.kahoot.it/ login Quizziz https://quizizz.com/	Create a digital warm-up that can include text or video-based questions. Students work in teams to respond and compete against other teams.
Productivity	Nearpod https://nearpod.com/ Peardeck https://www.peardeck.com	These tools allow you to build in questions into your presentation to collect student responses. Nearpod is a stand-alone tool that is accessed as a stand-alone platform, whereas Peardeck is a tool that you use with Google Slides.

| Collaborate | Google Docs and Google Slides
Padlet
Google Jamboard | These interactive tools allow students to share ideas in real time. You compose a question and students respond and see their peers' responses. |
| Math tasks | YouCubed
https://www.youcubed.org/tasks | Open education resources aligned by grade level and topic. |

Make it Relevant

Don't forget, you can also use any of the creation tools we have shared to create your own video and web-based word problems for a warm-up. In the following video the teacher uses a web tool called Shadow Puppet to capture a picture of her student and then narrate a word problem situation for her students to solve. Trust us, your students will glow when they are featured as your math warm-up word problems.

https://www.youtube.com/watch?v=aVecwCGMZKw

Daily Routine No. 8: Exit Ticket

Save the Best for Last

The last routine that we will share are exit tickets. Exit tickets are commonly used in all subject areas to capture student thinking about a concept and assess student understanding. In math, exit tickets can include both reflective, "How comfortable do you feel about this topic?", and content-specific questions, "List three ways you can write a ratio." In short, exit tickets should capture what you just taught and help you understand two things: (a) Did my students grasp this concept? and (b) Did I do a good job teaching it? We also believe it is important for teachers to assess students' efficacy in math, the more efficacious students feel about math the more likely they are to engage in more demanding math tasks. When it comes to efficacy you might ask, "How confident do you feel in using percent to determine the cost of an item that is 15% off?"

Ways to Go Digital with Exit Tickets: While we believe it is highly valuable for students to record their thinking with paper and pencil, we also see the value of using digital assessment measures to help students transfer their thinking digitally. Online assessment measures are commonly used as high-stakes standardized tests at the end of the year. The more comfortable your students feel with online assessments the more likely assessment results are a true measure and not a reflection of student unfamiliarity with taking a test online. In addition to test preparation, using digital assessment can support you in being more productive in your classroom. Online assessments are easy to grade and often come with built-in grading tools that will save you time and share the results more efficiently.

Make the Tech Connection: Assess

There are a variety of online assessment programs that we share in our Tech Tool List. These tools are labeled "Assess" and feature questions that are aligned by standard and can be searched by grade level. Many of these online programs feature a variety of question types such as multiple, choice, performance-based and video problems. Check out the tech tool list and identify which programs would best suit your students: http://www.teacher preptech.com/p/tech-tools.html

Here are a few recommended tools and ways to go digital.

Google Forms: Use Google Forms to create a variety of question types including open ended, Likert scale, and multiple choice. You can ask students a word problem; have them explain their thinking, steps, and processes. For example, you can challenge, "Record your steps for changing a decimal to a percent using the transition words: First, Next, Then, and Finally." Also you can collect data on students' beliefs, perceptions, and confidence toward math skills and concepts. You can ask, "How confident do you feel about changing a decimal to a percent: Extremely Confident, Confident, Somewhat Confident, and Not at all Confident?" It is just as important to determine how students feel about their ability as it is to assess how they perform academically.

Poll Everywhere: Student polling is extremely popular. An easy way to go digital is to use a tool like Poll Everywhere, as data can be collected on multiple devices such as smartphones, tablets, and computers. All students need to get started is the URL you receive when you make your poll. What makes this digital tool extremely appealing is that students' responses are instantaneously populated in graphs for discussion and sharing. (https://www.polleverywhere.com)

Padlet: Teachers love KWL (Know-Want to Know-Learned) charts and students do, too! But oftentimes we start with what students "know" and "want to know" but misplace the chart when it's time to record "learned." As we shared earlier, reflection is just as important for students as it is for teachers. Using Padlet allows you to keep the chart easily available, just make sure to provide a time and place for students to share what they learned. This tool can help facilitate this final discussion (www.padlet.com).

Google Classroom

One way to easily share Google Forms and documents is with students in Google Classroom. Using this platform, you can assign students tasks and exit tickets you've created.

For teachers who are teaching several math blocks, just one document does it all. Once you create an exit ticket in Google Docs you can share it with every section of your math class and Google will store student data by class.

Twitter

Twitter is a social media platform in which students share their thinking in just 140 characters. What's the significance of just 140 characters? Well, students need to be concise and synthesize their thinking in response to the given prompt. Using a hashtag such as #msgreensclass, students will type the hashtag into their response and then all responses that include this hashtag are collected for review (https://twitter.com/).

Want to see all these tools in action? Be sure you check out our YouTube Channel for Web tool videos in action: https://goo.gl/uyA7q3

Summary

In order to build students' confidence and computational fluency they need practice; however, practice does not equal worksheets through "drill and kill," but rather structured daily routines promote students' ability to communicate and think like mathematicians. Daily routines have roles for both teachers and students. Daily routines are beneficial to include as a part of your daily math block as they develop students' academic oral and written language. We've described just a few commonly used routines such as Number Talks, Hundred Charts, Multiplication Charts, Calendar, Counting Collections, Math Journals, Warm-Ups, Data Talks, and Exit Tickets along with technology tools to infuse your instruction. These are just a few daily routines to get you started as we are sure you will learn many more throughout your teaching career.

The routines in this chapter are structured for daily use and we encourage you to make them your own. In our experiences as classroom teachers, we know the first thing you need to assess is whether the routine is working with your kids or not. When you're trying a new routine, sometimes the first time and even the second time it may not work, but do not give up! Teachers, much like students, need an opportunity to practice and rehearse new skills prior to implementing them in the classroom. In fact, research has shown teachers need at least 20 instances of practice to master a new skill (Joyce & Showers, 2002). We want to encourage you to develop daily practices to benefit both your students' growth and your own.

Additional Activities/Discussion Questions

1. Explore one of the technology tools listed under Exit Tickets or Warm-Ups and create a series of questions that assess students' efficacy and content knowledge in relation to a specific math standard. What are the strengths of the tool? How could you use this tool to support planning?
2. Review the learning progressions for the grade level of your choice. How might you incorporate the calendar activity to support students in developing computational and procedural fluency?

3. Experiment with creating a Number Talk based on a math standard. Identify the different ways students might solve the problem using a variety of strategies.

Instructor Activities

1. Present your students with an opportunity to participate in a Counting Collection activity. Model the instructional choices you would make to support students in recording their thinking and meeting the needs of diverse learners including students with exceptionalities, and second language learners.
2. Have your students select one of the Daily Routines and videotape themselves working with a small group or leading one of these activities in your class.

Chapter 5

Open-Ended Tasks

Engage students in productive struggle and in making connections between mathematical concepts.

—Van de Walle, Karp, and Bay-Williams (2013, p. 103).

You've just begun your math lesson and pose the following problem to your fifth-grade class. "Charlie has two-thirds of his birthday cake left from his party. He wants to share his cake with four of his friends. What fraction of the cake will each friend receive?" Your students appear seemingly ready for action, but as they begin to work, several stop and begin fidgeting in their seats, digging in their desks, and talking to their neighbors. They are off task and not staying focused. One student gets up to sharpen his pencil, while another asks for a drink of water. You know this pattern and begin to check-in with a few disengaged students. They complain, "It's too hard!" You stop and wonder how you might present the problem differently to meet their needs, especially when the task becomes challenging.

The Purpose of Open-Ended Tasks

Regardless of your class size, designing instruction for everyone's ability is a complex endeavor, since students come into the classroom with different funds of knowledge, experiences, and beliefs about themselves as learners. Despite these differences, you must prepare students to meet grade-level standards and access state-adopted curriculum. We often hear from the teachers we work with this is one of the greatest challenges when it comes to planning instruction. One way to address the need for differentiation is to present students with respectful tasks that are reasonably challenging, yet accessible for all learners. These tasks are not pages of endless problems written for one level of learning; rather, they are tasks that respect students' thinking and challenge them to apply their learning at various levels. These types of tasks are not difficult to design, but are highly engaging and require students to use novel ways of thinking. Students certainly know when tasks respectfully challenge their minds. So let's explore the design of creating engaging math tasks.

There are two main types of tasks: *closed-ended* and *open-ended tasks*. Closed-ended tasks are predictable, focus on one way of thinking, and have a single right answer. In contrast, open-ended tasks are unpredictable, provide students with opportunities to explore ideas more broadly, have multiple solutions, and incorporate many ways of thinking and decision-making. There is often ambiguity in open-ended tasks, as such they are frequently referred to as ill-constructed questions or problems. Open-ended tasks require more cognitive effort from students and therefore engage them in higher levels of thinking and learning. Students must draw from their knowledge in broad ways to figure out potential solutions.

Another difference between open-ended and closed-ended tasks lies in the type of thinking required when determining a solution. Closed-ended tasks often draw on narrow ways of thinking that rely on procedure or previously memorized information, while open-ended tasks draw on students' broad conceptual knowledge (Stein et al., 2009). The path to the solution of an open-ended task requires effort, multiple steps, and application of broad conceptual knowledge, rather than rote memorization.

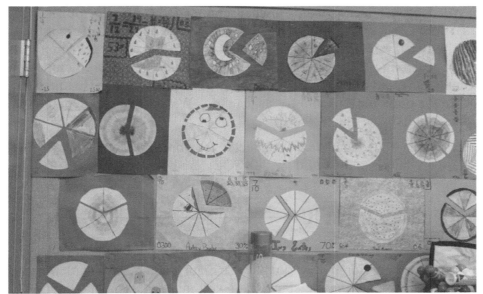

© Patricia Dickenson

Across the Curriculum

Consider the following connections to math concepts and real-world application:

- Exponential growth of viruses.
- Placement of solar panels on a roof for maximum capacity.
- Exchange rate of currency while traveling.
- Developing a business plan for profitability.
- Creating a workout plan to eat healthy and increase fitness.
- Purchasing a home or car for the first time.

An open-ended math tasks can be integrated with art to allow students to show what they know and express themselves creatively. In the picture above, students received a circle to choose how to represent fractional parts and record equivalent fractions as well as decimal and percent conversions.

Putting Research into Practice

When you were in school, do you remember completing pages upon pages of math practice problems? Interestingly enough, research suggests that students who spend most of their time practicing isolated procedural skills with single, closed-ended questions have difficulty transferring math knowledge to real-world situations. Moreover, students who have a procedural orientation to mathematics believe that to solve any math problem they have to follow a rule or procedure. This interferes with students' ability to apply their knowledge and therefore they do not consider reasoning when challenged by math in everyday situations (Boaler, 1998). Studies show that students who regularly use open-ended cognitively demanding tasks have higher levels of conceptual understanding, increased academic achievement, possess stronger reasoning skills, and use novel strategies to solve problems (Boaler, 1998; Carpenter, Fennema, Franke, Levi, & Empson, 1999; Stein, Smith, Henningsen, & Silver, 2009). These are the outcomes we aim for as teachers. We want our students to transfer math learning to their real lives!

🛍 **Snag It:** These open-ended math tasks connect to the popular Roblox game Adopt me where kids purchase digital pets. https://bit.ly/3h0sEQc

Think About It!

In your observations of children, how do they use math when playing with friends, games, toys, or in conversations? What are some ways you might ground and connect the math concepts you teach to students' lives?

_____

_____

The more you know about your students and their thinking, the more students learn. Research shows a direct connection between teachers' knowledge of students' thinking and students' achievement levels (Carpenter et al., 1999). This means that *you* matter in the equation of student learning. In fact, you need many ways to make your students' thinking visible to know what is going on in their minds. Visible thinking means asking your students to record or share their thoughts in ways that you can see and hear. You do this by having your students use math journals, create representations (concrete and illustrated), write and orally justify answers, and share solutions in front of the class, in groups, and in pairs. This can be done in traditional ways or by using online tools; we recommend that you do both. By incorporating these methods, you make students' thinking visible allowing you to assess students' knowledge and progress, which should then guide your next instructional steps.

Structure of Open-Ended Tasks

Let's explore an example of an open-ended task that we call The Pattern Task. In Ms. Brown's first-grade class, students have been examining patterns, a concept at the heart of the mathematical practice of understanding structure. They have spent time practicing making patterns and developing conceptual understanding of patterns in various forms and complexities. In this lesson, Ms. Brown challenges her students to apply their knowledge of patterns. She begins by providing each student a different colored patterned fabric square. They are instructed to identify the pattern they see, such as in the following examples (see Figure 5.1).

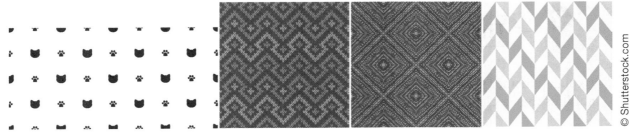

Figure 5.1 Patterned Fabric Squares.

Students are next challenged by Ms. Brown to search for patterns around their classroom. They record their patterns by taking a picture using Adobe Spark (https://adobespark.com) a digital tool where they can annotate and share their discoveries with classmates. They are encouraged to find as many patterns as possible and move around the room. Some students move to the calendar corner, others to the book baskets, and a few students look at the backpacks lined up on the wall. While students are examining patterns around the room, Ms. Brown begins to observe and question particular students about their findings. She does this purposefully to assess students' thinking and check their justifications. This informal conferencing gives insight into the decisions students are making as they search for and examine the structure in patterns.

How is The Pattern Task challenging, open-ended, and cognitively demanding? As presented, students must find a pattern in the classroom which is the first challenge. Then students must record the pattern using digital tools. This also requires cognitive effort and attention to precision which is one of the Standards for Mathematical Practice (SMP #6). Since there are multiple solutions, this problem can also be characterized as open-ended. Students can come up with a myriad of answers, based on the classroom context. Of course, the teacher must evaluate students' responses to make sure they are accurate, but the teacher gets the benefit of seeing if students can independently identify patterns which is a high-level cognitive activity. The patterns students find include the colors of the carpet or patterns in the decorative bulletin border. There are many possibilities, which is precisely why this type of task is classified as open-ended.

Not only does The Pattern Task allow for many solutions, but it allows students to work at their own level. Your middle-range student may find three or four patterns. Your struggling student may find one pattern, and your advanced student may find seven or more! Every student can be successful and work at their own level. The added benefit is that all students can engage in The Pattern Task, unlike a task where there is only one problem, at one level, with one way of solving, and one solution. With an open-ended task, struggling students can initiate ideas at whatever level they can engage, while advanced students can find complex patterns and multiple solutions, keeping them continuously challenged. All students are challenged to think deeply and broadly, and the task is open-ended, relevant, and cognitively demanding. When students are presented with an open-ended task, you are less likely to hear, "It's too hard!".

Think About It!

Explain whether you think an open-ended task may be more accessible to a wider range of abilities than a closed-ended task.

_____

_____

Watch It

In this video, Dr. Dickenson works with a second-grade class to identify arrays in their classroom. An array is a group of objects or pictures that are arranged in columns and rows to represent a model for multiplication. This standard is introduced in second grade and developed as a foundation for multiplication.

Part 1: Introducing the task: https://goo.gl/TnwH3n

Stop and Reflect

Dr. Dickenson introduces the Array Scavenger Hunt task by sharing pictures of objects from her home and asks the students to determine if the pictures represent an array. How does this approach to instruction engage learners?

_____

_____

Now that Dr. Dickenson has introduced the task and the students have had the opportunity to activate knowledge related to the task, the students are able to move around the room and decide where they see an array in the classroom. The students are provided with a graphic organizer to record their findings. The graphic organizer will help to plan future instruction and evaluate students' ability to transfer concepts into a real-life task. Remember, the role of the teacher is to observe the students and ask questions to support their understanding.

© Patricia Dickenson

🔖 **Snag It:** A copy of this graphic organizer is included in the Appendix.

Name	Date

Counting Collections: Scavenger Hunt:
Identify arrays in your class and record a number sentence to represent each array.

1.	2.
3.	4.

Think About It!

Later on in this chapter we will talk specifically about how to assess student work with open-ended tasks, but for now, what do you notice about student learning from the Array Scavenger Hunt Task? How might open-ended tasks support various levels of understanding?

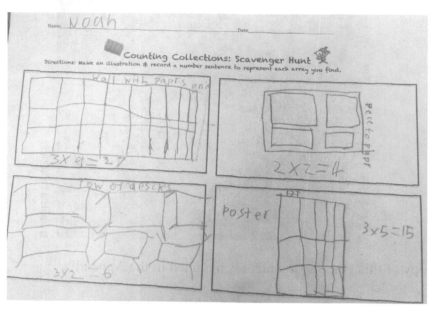

© Patricia Dickenson

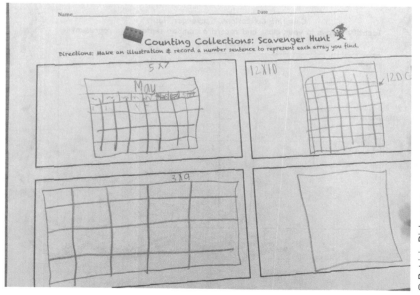

© Patricia Dickenson

In the two examples of student graphic organizers above, the teacher can determine what students are able to do independently and what understandings students have about multiplication. In the first example, the student identified several examples of multiplication arrays with groups of twos and threes. This finding suggests the student has made the connection between multiplication and repeated addition and can identify and illustrate a model that supports this finding. In the second example, the student selected more complex multiplication arrays. The student may be exploring if their understanding of an array can be extended beyond groupings of twos, fives and tens. Sharing these student examples in a group discussion would help students deepen their conceptual understanding of multiplication.

Watch It

In this video, Dr. Dickenson questions the students about their understanding of arrays they identified in the classroom. Notice how when students struggle with explaining their ideas rather than providing an answer, she asks another question to prompt thinking about the task at hand. https://youtu.be/byUX3DIn_EA

Think About It!

What questions might you ask students as they look for arrays in your classroom?

_____

_____

Routines and Open-Ended Tasks

Recall in Chapter 4 Daily Routines, we introduced Counting Collections as a routine that will introduce and reinforce modeling with multiplication by having students use objects to build an array. Now that students have experienced constructing an array, an open-ended task is used that allows students to identify arrays in their classroom. This extends student thinking by applying arrays in a real-life context. Notice how this progression of math tasks moves students from the concrete to the representational and then symbolic stages of thinking.

Daily routines and open-ended tasks support each other by having students apply information in multiple contexts. These pedagogical approaches support both procedural fluency and conceptual understanding. In Chapter 6, project-based learning will take students deeper into the math by transferring the strategies and procedures they have learned in a real-life context, as in our example of the Array Scavenger Hunt. For example, students might apply their knowledge of an array to create a school garden with certain constraints. These pedagogical approaches to designing instruction are at the heart of Universal Design for Learning (UDL) in which students are given multiple means of representation, action and expression, and engagement.

Tech for One and Tech for All

In Ms. Brown's class, students use the digital tool Adobe Spark to capture patterns they found during a scavenger hunt. In Dr. Dickenson's class, students illustrated the arrays they identified using a graphic organizer. Creating illustrations and annotating pictures with digital tools provides students with opportunities to express and represent their knowledge in multiple ways showing their understanding. For Ms. Brown's first-grade class, capturing photos is a better way to assess students' understanding than making illustrations, as several students in her class have yet to refine their fine motor skills to make intricate patterns. Technology can be extremely beneficial in primary classes as the process of showing what students know may interfere with their ability to express their mathematical thinking. Writing or illustrating can be a challenge for young learners, whereas technology can provide an opportunity to express their ideas. In Dr. Dickenson's class, the Common Core math standard explicitly calls for students to create multiplication models, in which case students need to be able to illustrate a model for multiplication, as shown in the graphic organizer. Selecting technology tools is not a one-size fits all approach. As the classroom teacher, you must decide which tool will best support your learners in meeting the goals and standards.

Furthermore, we want to recognize that technology may not be as accessible to all students and teachers in a particular school. For example, in Dr. Dickenson's class during the Array Scavenger Hunt she had several devices but not enough for every learner. Due to this limitation, Dr. Dickenson placed devices at math centers for students to take pictures of their illustrations and annotate their photos as part of their digital portfolios in the SeeSaw platform (www.seesaw.com). To teach for mastery, students need to see that concepts are connected in multiple ways to deepen their understanding. Remember, our young learners are building their schema for concepts in math, so the more they can experience math in positive ways and connect curriculum to what they already know the deeper they will understand math concepts.

 Make the Tech Connection: Creation Tools

As a way to extend students' thinking and make the home–school connection, have students take photos of objects in their home that represent an array. This might include a bookshelf, window frame, or countertop. Students should label each picture and record an equation to express the total.

👁 **View It:** See a student example here using Google Slides to create a slideshow about arrays in his home: https://goo.gl/a46h9N

Attributes of Open-Ended Tasks

The math tasks that we have discussed so far are robust and can be easily applied across math concepts. Whether you teach first grade or eighth grade, the world provides many opportunities for students to discover the math in their lives. In our discussion of math tasks, we have identified six attributes of open-ended tasks:

1. Open-ended with multiple solutions
2. Multiple entry points at differing levels
3. Various student learning levels possible
4. Engage and interest students
5. Conceptually-based
6. Increased levels of cognitive demand

These attributes are important to think about as we move forward in our discussion of designing and creating open-ended math tasks. We want to remind you that the knowledge you gain from learning how to create, assess, and facilitate an open-ended math task can easily be incorporated into the curriculum you are given by your school or district. We think this is important because no curriculum will be designed for your learners, unless it is designed by you. We believe this is important for several reasons:

- Open-ended tasks support all learners in your classroom from the gifted and talented, to students who are working below grade level, to second-language learners.
- Open-ended tasks provide you with an opportunity to make mathematics culturally relevant and highly contextualized in the lives of your students.
- Open-ended tasks are a powerful assessment tool that can show you what students know and where they need to grow.

Gummy Bear Task	**Chairs Task**

There are six bags of fruit gummy bears in each box of gummies. Each bag of gummies contains 12 gummies bears. If the student store wants to have a supply of 400 gummy bears, how many boxes should they order?

Catherine needs to set up chairs for 145 people to attend the school talent show. What are the possible ways she can arrange the chairs?

Figure 5.2 Third Grade Tasks

Although the two Tasks in Figure 5.2 might be engaging and provide students with a challenge, only the Chairs Task lends itself to multiple solutions. With the Gummy Bear Task there is only one right answer, although students may arrive at the answer in different ways. The Chairs Task not only allows multiple solutions but it also provides additional insight into how students use and think about the relationship of multiplication and division to problem-solving with mathematical modeling. This task could include additional challenge with constraints, such as "each chair is 2 feet and each row must not extend beyond the stage view of 20 feet." Differentiation provides challenge for students who are working above average, by providing increased opportunities to think and apply their skills.

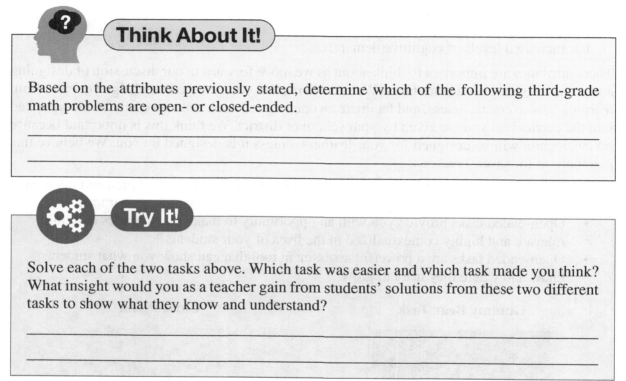

Think About It!

Based on the attributes previously stated, determine which of the following third-grade math problems are open- or closed-ended.

_____

_____

Try It!

Solve each of the two tasks above. Which task was easier and which task made you think? What insight would you as a teacher gain from students' solutions from these two different tasks to show what they know and understand?

_____

_____

The Role of the Teacher and Role of the Student

Open-ended tasks have different purposes for both the teacher and the students. For the teacher, open-ended tasks provide a true sense of what students know. Through open-ended tasks, a teacher can see various ways in which students respond, since the tasks make student thinking visible and support varying degrees of response. Generally, teachers require students to complete fewer tasks when using open-ended tasks versus closed-ended tasks. This allows teachers to easily analyze students' skill development and conceptual understanding. Open-ended tasks provide a greater degree of challenge, more solutions, and multiple concepts embedded in a single task; thus, teachers can do more with less tasks for students to complete.

For students, open-ended tasks are inherently interesting and are more appealing and engaging since they require an inquiry approach to learning (Sullivan, Warren, & White, 2000). Students may find open-ended tasks to be more relevant, meaningful, and connected to real life., Teachers find open-ended tasks to naturally connect with students and make mathematics more enjoyable because of their engaging characteristics. Tasks that are open-ended are also inherently differentiated which means that every student (evn those who struggle) can respond and find success.

Across the Curriculum

The concept of "Open-ended tasks" can be applied in other content specific areas. Consider in a Physical education or Music class where students have the choice of creating a dance or composing a piece of music based on criteria that students should be familiar with. This approach would provide the teacher with rich data on what the students has learned and can elaborate on without the teachers' guidance.

Thinking and Open-Ended Tasks

Open-ended tasks allow students many ways to enter the problem and many solutions. In the two examples of the Gummy Bear Task and the Chairs Task, you can see the difference between closed-ended and open-ended tasks. The closed-ended task has one solution and provides given quantities, even though students have a certain degree of challenge figuring out the quantities and establishing a solution. The open-ended task allows for a broader range of thinking, includes multiple solutions, and requires students to access their conceptual understanding of numbers and operations to arrive at a solution. A somewhat simple task of arranging chairs requires students to think flexibly about grouping quantities in multiple ways.

In Chapter 3, we discussed how cognitively demanding tasks require greater levels of mental effort. Which one of the two tasks, the Gummy Bear Task or the Chairs Task, do you think requires more mental effort to solve? Both tasks require different types of thinking and could be considered mathematically challenging. The Gummy Bear Task requires students to conceptualize the task and apply knowledge about quantities, but the Chairs Task, which is open-ended, requires students to think more flexibly and in broader ways since students must establish the parameters of the grouping of chairs and determine the many possible outcomes, while still managing the quantities. Even when adding constraints, the Chairs Task still requires broader ways of thinking and applying mathematical knowledge.

Try It!

Identify a problem from the math task category of the Google Sheet and share why you believe it is an open-ended task. Think about how you might support students in accessing the task in multiple ways by incorporating a webtool. http://bit.ly/2ws8INT

_____

_____

Questioning with Open-Ended Tasks

Questioning is a common and effective tool teachers use to monitor students' thinking and promote learning. Questioning is used by teachers for different purposes. Sometimes questions help to probe students' reasoning and higher levels of thinking, whereas other times questioning can support divergent student thinking about a situation or activate prior knowledge. This draws us back to our discussion in Chapter 3 about the revised Bloom's taxonomy (for a reminder, see Figure 5.3). Lower level questions tend to focus on recall of information and fall into Bloom's *knowledge* and *understanding* categories. These types of questions ask for students to recall basic facts at the comprehension level. However, higher-level questions ask students to move beyond general recall and instead *apply*, *analyze*, *evaluate*, and even *create*. Higher-level questions target students' reasoning and evaluation skills. To respond to these types of questions, students must use information in deeper and broader ways. Teachers must ask students to answer by making connections between ideas and providing explanations. To gain higher levels of thinking, students must also respond and evaluate their peers' ideas. Oftentimes, students have to respond to an idea by creating their own responses in ways that are original. These actions are prompted by teacher questioning which pushes students to higher levels of thinking.

Teachers use a variety of questions at various levels; however, research shows that approximately 80% of teacher-initiated questions are at lower cognitive levels (Marzano, Pickering, & Pollock, 2001). Is that a bad thing? At times, your questioning should be at a basic level as

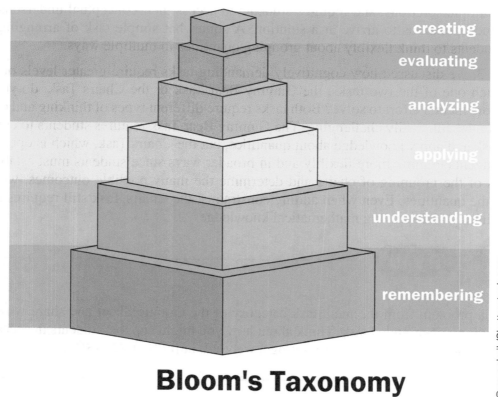

Bloom's Taxonomy

Figure 5.3　Revised Bloom's Taxonomy (Anderson et al., 2001)

you check for recall of newly learned information; however, if questioning remains at lower cognitive levels on a regular basis students' thinking will also remain at these lower cognitive levels. If this is the case, your students will have difficulty with tasks that require rigor and higher-level demand. We want our students to struggle productively so that they can persevere in problem-solving and become critical math thinkers.

Let's take a look at possible teacher questions at various levels of Bloom's taxonomy based on the following Pancake Task.

Pancake Task

The school is having a pancake breakfast and expect over 250 people to attend. To make 14 pancakes, you will need 3 cups of pancake mix, 1½ cups of milk, and 2 eggs. Determine how many pancakes you expect each person to eat and the amount of ingredients that should be purchased if there are 10 cups of pancake mix per box, 16 cups of milk per gallon, and a dozen eggs in a carton. Solve and draw a representation to illustrate your solution. Write an explanation for your reasoning and the decisions that you make (Table 5.1).

Table 5.1 Pancake Task

Levels of Thinking	Teacher Questions
Creating	Is there an equation that we can write to generalize our solution?
Evaluating	Does your solution make sense?
	Did you solve for all parts of the problem?
	Does your representation make sense?
	Did you clearly label your representation?
Analyzing	Look at the parts of the problem and your solution, did you find all the information necessary?
	What information can vary between you and your partner's solutions?
Applying	What steps are you going to use to solve your problem?
	How are you going to organize your data or representation?
	Can you think of a previously learned strategy that you can use to solve this problem?
Understanding	What is the question asking?
	What information do you know?
	What information do you need to find or determine?
Knowledge	What is the task telling you?
	What quantities are you given?

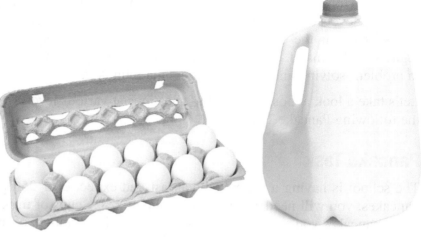

Images © Shutterstock.com

Stop and Reflect

Would you consider the Pancake Task to be an open-ended or closed-ended task? What changes in the teacher question chart above do you notice across the levels of thinking?

_____

_____

Questioning is an integral part of your work with students especially as they engage with problem-solving. The types of questions you ask can support your students in understanding the task, extending their thinking, and applying different strategies. For many teachers, asking questions in mathematics is difficult. You may have experienced a math teacher who believed their role was to disperse information rather than ask questions to support student learning. We know this approach might support some students but not all; moreover, if we want our students to own their learning, we need to give them the chance to do so. Questioning puts the onus of learning on the student which has been linked to increased student understanding, an awareness of misconceptions, and lack of understanding (Chi, 2000).

As you begin to plan instruction, include the questions you will ask students to support their thinking. As we demonstrated in the Pancake Task, you can ask questions at varying levels of Bloom's taxonomy to differentiate instruction for your diverse learners. Let's take a look at how the types of questions we ask can facilitate or hinder learning. In the Chairs Task, we share both open- and closed-ended questions. Notice how you might respond to these types of questions and what kinds of questions might be most helpful to support students' thinking.

Catherine needs to set up chairs for 145 people to attend the school talent show. What are the possible ways she can arrange the chairs?

Open-ended questions:
- How are you thinking about this task?
- In what possible ways can you arrange 145 chairs?
- Can you draw an arrangement or use concrete materials to make a visual representation?
- How can the chairs be arranged?
- How can you represent your solution?
- How could you explain your solution?

Closed-ended Questions:
- What are the factors of 145?
- What is the question asking?
- What is the event?
- What are you arranging?
- How many people are attending the school talent show?
- What are you being asked to find?

 Try It!

We've changed the Gummy Bear Task into an open-ended task. Develop as many open-ended and closed-ended questions as you think possible.

The student store wants to order 400 gummy bears but they are not sure how many boxes to order because it is unknown how many bags of gummy bears will be in each box. What are some possible combinations of boxes that might be ordered if each box has a number of bags?

Open-ended questions: Closed-ended Questions:

 Think About It!

How did this process get you to reframe your thinking about how to support students in an open-ended task to a closed-ended task?

_____

_____

Planning Questions for Open-Ended Tasks

A way to be alert to your questioning practices is to analyze the questions you ask before teaching the lesson. In preparation, plan your target questions in advance. This ensures a variety of questions are included at different levels. You should anticipate the types of questions you might ask from the start to the end of the lesson.

Here is a checklist of questions you can ask yourself before, during, and after instruction.

Before instruction while planning:

- How do I connect to and access students' prior knowledge?
- How am I giving students opportunities for concrete or representational understanding through manipulatives and/or use of models or pictures?
- How do I support students' conceptual understanding of the topic?
- How do I support students' fluency in relationship to the topic?
- How do I anticipate struggles students might have with the task?
- How do I plan to differentiate for the needs of my struggling/at risk students?
- How do I plan to differentiate for the needs of my advanced students?
- How do I support students' linguistic demands throughout the lesson?
- How am I engaging students in productive work around the math concept?
- What questions can I ask that require critical, high-level thinking?
- How am I assessing what students learn?
- What evidence am I going to collect of student learning and thinking?

During instruction:

- Am I challenging students with high-level questions?
- Do my questions include a range of thinking across the revised Bloom's taxonomy?
- Am I providing enough support for student thinking?
- Am I giving students enough time to work on challenging ideas?
- Am I removing the cognitive challenge by giving students too many hints or providing the answer too quickly?
- Am I supporting students who may be struggling significantly with the content?
- Am I giving students time to talk to each other and use their academic language?
- Am I challenging students to use the academic language skills when responding to peers and whole group?
- Am I revoicing, or mirroring back students' language with academic language, to build their language skills?
- Am I using wait time to allow students to process and think before responding?

After instruction:

- How does the evidence/product demonstrate student learning?
- How precise were students' solutions?
- In what ways might I need to reteach skills or concepts?
- How well did I scaffold learning for struggling students?

- How well did I extend the learning for high-performing students?
- In what ways did the students use their academic language successfully?
- In what ways did students struggle when using their academic language?
- How should I support students' language during the next lesson?
- How did students think about their own work or apply their ideas to new or novel situations?
- How did students analyze or evaluate their own work or other students' work?
- How engaging was the learning experience or task?
- How rigorous or cognitively demanding was the student task?
- How did my questions challenge students' mathematical thinking?
- If I were to teach the lesson again, how would I teach it differently? How would I keep it the same?

Reflection is a critical part of becoming a thoughtful practitioner. Be aware of your questions, student responses, and make adjustments. This process will help you to meet students' needs, improve your instruction, and develop reflective skills.

During our work with teachers we developed various strategies to monitor and improve teachers' levels of questioning, such as recording questions on an anchor chart for reference, posting questions on a card, or placing them on a ring. Question-rings were kept at hand and used at various points during lessons. They became prompts for teachers when posing questions to guarantee students were challenged to think at higher levels. What we found was questioning on the spot without these extra supports, did not naturally move teachers to higher-level questions.

Another extremely helpful strategy teachers shared was to preplan and have questions written in advance of lessons. Just the act of writing out higher-level questions purposefully ahead of time made them more likely to occur during instruction. Regardless of your method, find ways to prompt yourself by using a question-ring, preplanning, or even inserting questions in the notes section of your presentation. The key is to find the method that works best for you.

Not only should you consider questions in the development of your practice, but questioning should also be considered in the development of your students' metacognitive skills. Since open-ended tasks require students to consider multiple strategies and produce multiple solutions through various pathways, your questioning should elicit students' thinking in many different ways. The following are examples of questions you might use to develop students' metacognition. Consider placing these questions on a question-ring to use during instruction.

- How did you approach the task?
- How did you decide what to do?
- How many solutions did you find?
- Why do you think your solution is accurate or true?
- How does your representation show your ideas?
- How is your solution the same as your partner's?
- How is your solution different than your partner's?

- After seeing your partner's solution, would you change anything in your solution?
- Do you have any questions after seeing your partner's solution?
- Do you agree with _____'s solution? Justify why or why not.
- Do you disagree with _____'s solution? Justify why or why not.
- Can you create another question like the one you just solved?

These types of questions require higher levels of thinking and develop students' reflective skills. Some questions ask students what they did in the process of solving an open-ended question at the application level. Other questions ask for comparison of ideas which causes students to think at the analysis level. Questions that ask for justification or explanation of thinking, push students thinking to the evaluation level of Bloom's taxonomy. When asking students to create their own questions using the same concept, you are asking them to work at the highest cognitive level: create. Questioning develops students' metacognition and leads to greater self-awareness and self-regulation by directing students' thinking.

Make the Tech Connection

For remote teaching consider using a water fall technique where you pose a question to the class and then when prompted by the word "waterfall" all students press enter and share their questions into the chat.

Writing Open-Ended Tasks

There are a few different approaches to writing open-ended tasks. One of the first ways is to write a closed-ended question. Think about what you are asking of students and then rewrite the question to use the same skill, but make the question wider. When you take this approach to developing open-ended tasks you are "working backwards" (Sullivan & Lilburn, 2004).

Let's try writing a task by working backward. For example, we may traditionally give our students a question for multi-number addition, such as 356 + 245 = ___. In the process of making an open-ended task, examine the traditional answer. Ask yourself, "What I am asking students to do or know at the core of this question?" and "What are the characteristics of the answer?" Once you have the characteristics isolated, begin to develop a task that not only asks students to provide a response with the same skill and the same general type of answer, but does not limit the response to one single answer. A multi-answer problem with a wide variety of pathways becomes much more attainable, interesting, and requires significant cognitive effort. Instead of asking students to do the single traditional problem, you can ask students a more open-ended problem, such as, "What two, three-digit numbers added together have a sum between 500 and 600?"

To rewrite a task using the backward approach, use the following steps:

1. Identify the task as it would traditionally be asked (closed-ended).
2. Determine the characteristics of the task. What skills/knowledge am I asking students to practice?
3. Rewrite the task so that it allows for more solutions and is broader in nature (open-ended).

The second approach to moving a task from closed-ended to open-ended is to adapt the task (Sullivan & Lilburn, 2004). For example, the task, "A girl brought 12 cookies to give to her three friends. How many cookies did each friend get?" can be adapted slightly by changing the amounts. This task can become, "A girl brought a bag of cookies to give to her three friends. How many cookies did she bring and how many did each friend get?"

To rewrite a task using the adaptive approach, use the following steps:

1. Identify the closed-ended task.
2. Identify the parts of the task that can be rewritten to be open-ended.
3. Rewrite the task so that it is open-ended.

Identify a math task for students to complete, then select either the backward or adaptive approach and write both a closed-ended and open-ended task. Make sure to align the task with the grade-level concepts and skills of your choosing. Work out potential responses to the question.

Grade   **Concept and Skill(s)**

Closed-ended Task   **Open-ended Task**

Share your task with a colleague and evaluate each other's task to see if is open-ended task or not:

1. Open-ended with multiple solutions
2. Multiple entry points at differing levels
3. Various student learning levels possible

4. Engage and interest students
5. Conceptually-based
6. Increased levels of cognitive demand

👁 **View It:** In this video Dr. Dickenson uses an open-ended task from the website Open-Middle for 2nd grade students to craft solutions related to fractions and percent.

https://youtu.be/HEbGHAhN0t0

Prompting Classroom Discourse

You have planned your open-ended math task, thought about potential solutions, and created questions to support students in developing their ideas and assess their learning. You have even included several ways to integrate technology throughout this process, but it's not over just yet. The final act of your math task, is extremely beneficial to student learning and growth, it happens when you share solutions and strategies to solve the math task in a classroom discussion. At the end of your math task comes one of the most important aspects of advancing student understanding of math: classroom discourse. Classroom discourse does not happen in a silo where one student is sharing with you what they did and how they did it. Discourse evolves in a whole-group setting where multiple students share their solution with their peers and critique the reasoning of others. According to the National Council of Teachers of Mathematics:

> Effective mathematics teaching engages students in discourse to advance the mathematical learning of the whole class. Mathematical discourse includes the purposeful exchange of ideas through classroom discussion, as well as through other forms of verbal, visual, and written communication. The discourse in the mathematics classroom gives students opportunities to share ideas and clarify understanding, construct convincing arguments regarding why and how things work, develop a language for expressing mathematical ideas, and learn to see things from others perspectives. (2014, p. 29)

 Stop and Reflect

After reviewing the above statement from National Council of Teachers of Mathematics (NCTM), what do you believe to be the importance of supporting discourse across the grade span?

_____

_____

This powerful statement is a call to engage all learners in mathematical discourse. Remember, just like we ask open-ended and higher-order questions to support students in doing the math, we should take a similar stance when leading students in a class discussion of math. This call to action may come easily to some learners, but others may have difficulty in this process. Just like we plan for our questioning process, we should also anticipate what will occur during classroom discourse.

Stein and Smith (2011) identified five practices that support classroom discourse.

1. **Anticipating:** Identify how students in your class will tackle the problem, and what errors and misconceptions you might anticipate.
2. **Monitoring:** As students work through the task observe how they approach the problem, what strategies they use or did not use, and identify misconceptions and errors they make.
3. **Selecting:** Review students' solutions and determine which particular students should share their work to the class. You might select a student who approached and solved the problem differently as a way to make connections and examine a variety of solutions.
4. **Sequencing:** Determine the order for students to share their solutions as a means to promote discourse and engage the learners in discovery. You can decide to share incorrect answers first as a way to identify common errors and then present correct answer so students can see a trajectory of how to get to the correct solution. Likewise, you can share complex strategies first to promote discourse and create disequilibrium before sharing a simplified approach.
5. **Connecting:** Once the solutions have been shared, lead the students in a discussion on how these strategies and approaches are connected to the mathematical concepts and ways of thinking.

Let's see this in action:

https://www.youtube.com/watch?v=1cqrQFXwLLA

What do you notice about the sequencing of solutions and how ideas are connected to support student learning?

_____

_____

Make the Tech Connection: Create

Flip Grid (https://flipgrid.com) is a video response tool that can enhance your ability to ask good math questions and promote classroom discourse among all learners, not just a select few. This tool will help you prepare in advance the kinds of higher-level questions you want to ask your students about their solutions. Moreover, as classroom discourse typically occurs at the end of the math task, you might find yourself short on time to engage in a meaningful discussion. This tool can help capture students' thinking and solutions and share their responses for future discussion. You can use this tool with Google Classroom to organize your students' workflow or share a link on your class website. Students only need either the URL for the question or a class code that you share. Login is not required.

Try It!

We've created a question on Flip Grid about Open-Ended Tasks. Share your response with other readers and create a community of math teachers who are sharing ideas for implementation. https://flipgrid.com/26f994

Math Talk Moves

The talk we engage in around mathematics with students is an essential part of our teaching and student learning. Whether questioning or responding, both teacher and student play a role in classroom discourse. The most common form of questioning in the classroom typically takes place in the form of an IRE pattern, known as Initiate, Respond, and Evaluate. In this pattern, the teacher asks a question, a student responds with expected information, and then the teacher evaluates the student's response as either correct or incorrect. Classroom-based research has shown us this type of discussion does not effectively expand student thinking and has limited effectiveness. Current research supports active discussions during which the teacher purposefully leads students by using a practice called "talk moves" in order to lead a discussion forward (Chapin, O'connor, & Anderson, 2009; Kazemi & Hintz, 2014). Several of these talk moves are listed with examples in Figure 5.4. Students can use these moves as they agree, disagree, or revise their way of thinking. When students know how to respond to ideas and to each other, the discussions become more productive. These talk moves are a strategy to use and even teach students as they engage in math discussions. Teachers, as always, must teach students what this sounds like and looks like and give students many opportunities to practice as they learn each of these math talk moves. A copy of this poster is included in the Appendix.

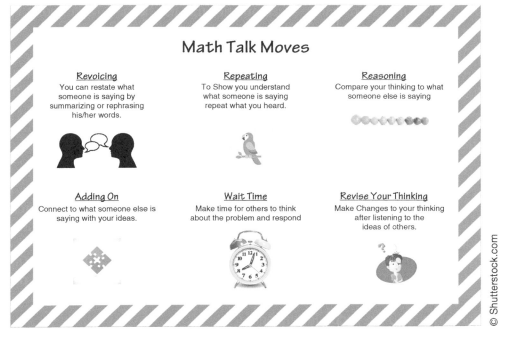

Figure 5.4   Math Talk Moves

Across the Curriculum

Talk moves can be a positive practice across disciplines. Consider a Social Studies class engaged in a discussion on the fall of the Roman Empire or an English language arts class critiquing a poem to explore the author's intent, having a protocol in place can frame the discussion and provide students with a scaffold to actively listen and engage with intent.

Assessment of Open-Ended Tasks

Assessment of open-ended tasks can take multiple forms. Observation of students' oral and written responses is one way to reflect on student learning during instruction and practice. When students work on their own, in pairs, or small groups, you can listen to their language and ideas. Conferencing with students and recording anecdotal notes is another way to gather assessment data. A more formal way of assessing is to gather students' work and use a rubric to evaluate student progress. Rubrics are used to evaluate work based on multiple levels of criteria. See the criteria in the rubric in Table 5.2. This type of rubric can be used or adapted when using open-ended tasks.

When assessing student performance in open-ended tasks, you can use a rubric to set the expectation and monitor students' progress toward meeting goals. Having a consistent and clear rubric across tasks will help students work toward mastery as they self-reflect on their performance and set goals. Goal setting is a research-based practice that has been shown to positively impact student achievement (Marzano et al., 2001).

Rubrics are valuable tools that provide specific criteria for evaluating student work. The criteria is important for the teacher and the student to review prior to starting a task. The teacher must know how to consistently and clearly evaluate students' work products. Whereas the student must know how they are being evaluated and what the criteria means. It is also extremely important for students to understand the criteria before they begin a task, as it will guide their behavior as they formulate ideas, draw representations, and organize their solution.

In the below rubric, there are four categories and four levels of evaluation. Each of the categories (solution, strategy, organization, and quality of evidence) are critical aspects of any final solution. Students' final solutions should be descriptive along with reasoning and evidence, such as pictures, words, or symbols, illustrated on paper or described through digital resources. Representations of this nature show students' thinking and the strategies they have applied. How the students organize information and the degree of explanation through drawings (or digital images) and written explanations aids in determining the quality level of the work.

Table 5.2 Upper Grades Open-Ended Task Rubric

	3	2	1	0
Solution	Correct solution that includes an accurate explanation with a supportive and purposefully connected representation.	Partially correct solution with minor errors in reasoning or computation, connected representation.	Incorrect solution with errors in reasoning or computation, representation may or may not connect.	No attempt to provide a solution, reasoning, or computation. May or may not include a representation.
Strategy	Selection and application of strategy is effective and connected.	Generally correct selection and application of strategy.	Inaccurate selection and application of strategy.	No attempt to select or apply a strategy.
Organization	Clearly organized showing complete mathematical thinking.	Generally organized showing mathematical thinking.	Limited organization of mathematical thinking.	No attempt to organize mathematical thinking.
Quality of Evidence	Sufficient evidence to show thorough understanding of the problem.	General evidence to show understanding of the problem.	Limited evidence showing little understanding of the problem.	No evidence to show understanding of the problem.

Rubrics allow for evaluation at many different levels. The teacher is one level of evaluation, however, the teacher should not be the only evaluator of students' work. Students should also critique peers' thinking and apply the rubric at the peer level. When students evaluate their peers' solutions, they are working at the "evaluating" level of Bloom's taxonomy, which means they are engaging in high-level thinking. When students evaluate other's thinking they also begin to think metacognitively about their own work, naturally encouraging self-analysis and evaluation. While students should engage in peer evaluation, students should also engage regularly in self-assessment. This means literally taking the rubric and using it against their own solutions.

To use the rubric at different grade levels you will need to make some adjustments. Clearly, young children in the early primary years may not be able to read and use this rubric; however, you can make a simple rubric with a sample of student work to demonstrate what it should generally look like at each level. Using "I" statements can also help student with understanding the criteria. Students can still rate their work with an Emoji representing different emotions for each of the levels (Table 5.3).

Table 5.3   Sample Primary Grades Open-Ended Task Rubric

	3	2	1	0
Solution	My ideas are correct and I explain my thinking. I made a picture that clearly shows what I know.	Some of my ideas are correct and I made a picture to show what I know.	I made a picture to show my thinking but my answer is not correct.	I did not give an answer and I did not make a picture to show what I know.
Strategy	My strategy is strongly connected to my solution. It is clear how I applied my strategy to my solution.	I selected a strategy and it is mostly correct and connected to my solution.	I did select a strategy but it is not correctly used.	I did not select a strategy and use it to solve the math task.
Organization	My understanding of the math task is clearly organized and labeled.	I organized my thinking and it is showing my understanding of the math task.	I tried to organize my thinking but it is not very clear.	I did not try to organize my thinking.

	3	2	1	0
Quality of Evidence	I have more than two ways to show my understanding of the math task.	I have one way to show my understanding of the math task.	I have some ideas but not a complete way to show my understanding of the math task.	I did not share any ideas to show my understanding of the math task.

Images © Shutterstock.com

Types of Open-Ended Tasks

Now that we have discussed the attributes of open-ended tasks and what you will need to include in your design, let's explore some variations of open-ended tasks that can be used throughout your math practice. Open-ended tasks can be implemented and used as an assessment tool, for practice and remediation as well as for homework.

Tiered Activities: Creating Challenge for Every Learner

Teachers often teach to the "middle," or the average student, but must also include the needs of advanced or struggling students, too. As classroom teachers, every student should be considered, which means a one-size-fits-all approach doesn't work. Since we know students learn at varying rates and levels, we also need a variety of ways to meet the needs. To do this, we can use tiered activities to build differentiation into our instruction.

Think about how a ladder is constructed. Every step of the ladder requires a bit more effort to climb. Tiered activities are like steps on a ladder; each step represents an added level of challenge. Students access the steps appropriate to their knowledge and skill level. This meets varied students' needs at the basic, average, and advanced levels. Tiers can be leveled by knowledge and skill, student interest, or learning style. The tiers make the learning accessible with varied levels of entry and output, allowing students at all levels to be challenged. What is important to note, however, is that tiered activities of this nature are NOT the same as tiers in Response to Intervention, a system of intervention and support for struggling students.

Before you can assign students to the appropriate tier, you must know where your students are in their development of knowledge and skills. Once this is known, then you match the students' needs to the appropriate tier. Ultimately, you want students to learn within their zone of proximal development (see Chapter 3). Students should be challenged just enough to be interested, engaged, and challenged, but not to the point where learning becomes too difficult or frustrating.

Let's take a look at some tiered task examples. Within this task, three levels of activity based on the three levels are described. Students at each level are challenged based on the skills they possess. In these tasks, the teacher would assign the students the tier that best meets the individual student's need.

Advanced Tier: (Challenge)

At this level, students meet the standards and objectives along with increased challenge and complexity. Students demonstrate competence in concepts and skills.

Moderate Tier: (Intermediate)

At this level, students meet the standards and objectives along with increased challenge. Students demonstrate growing skills and conceptual understanding.

Basic Tier: (Warm-Up)

At this level, students meet the expected standards and objectives. Students demonstrate developing skills and conceptual understanding. Some students may need additional scaffolds and accommodations for support.

Primary Grade Example

Standard: CCSS.K.G.B.4 Analyze and compare two- and three-dimensional shapes, in different sizes and orientations, using informal language to describe their similarities, differences, parts (e.g., number of sides and vertices/"corners"), and other attributes (e.g., having sides of equal length).

Basic Tier Activity: Students are given an envelope with shapes of varying sizes including circles, triangles, and squares. The students are to organize the shapes into like groups.

Moderate Tier Activity: Students are given an envelope with shapes of varying sizes, including circles, triangles, squares, rectangles, and diamonds. The students are to organize the shapes into groups based on attributes.

Advanced Tier Activity: Students are given an envelope with shapes of varying sizes and colors including circles, ovals, triangles, squares, rectangles, diamonds, and pentagons. Students are to organize the shapes by attributes. They can make as many different organizations as possible.

Upper Grade Example

Standard: CCSS.Math.6.RP.A.2

Understand the concept of a unit rate a/b associated with a ratio a:b with b ≠ 0, and use rate language in the context of a ratio relationship.

Basic Tier Activity: Students evaluate two different cell phone plans to determine which one offers the best rate package. In a monthly package, students must consider the price, data, and number of lines offered.

Moderate Tier Activity: Students evaluate three different cell phone plans to determine which one offers the best rate package. In a monthly package, students must consider the price, data, number of lines, and any additional features such as cost of phone.

Advanced Tier Activity: Students evaluate four or more cell phone plans to determine which one offers the best rate package. In a monthly package, students must consider the price, data, and number of lines, cost of phone, and international rates.

Think About It!

How do the tiers influence the type of thinking required by students? How do tiered activities provide differentiation? How might you support students who are working below the basic tier?

_____

_____

Make the Tech Connection: Productivity

Teachers can craft tiered tasks using Google Jamboard. Create three slides on the Jamboard for each task. Visuals can be added to provide a visual cue or context. Students can use the shape tool to create a visual model or use the text tool to explain their thinking. Check out this Jamboard for engaging students in Open-Ended Tasks on Rational Numbers.

🔖 **Snag It:** Rational Number Open-Ended Tasks https://bit.ly/3ztJ3UL

Watch It

In this video Dr. Dickenson engages 7th graders in an series of open-ended tasks on Rational Numbers with Google Jamboard.

https://youtu.be/_VhMqTJPCac

🔖 **Snag It:** Unpacking Ratios: https://docs.google.com/presentation/d/1htzlaaU8Gf2zD 6aSihI9sOFchS5rl2RHCyiUZvKNk04/edit?usp=sharing

---

Getting Started with Tiered Activities

Before introducing tiered activities, you must create a classroom where students understand and appreciate learner differences. According to Roberts and Inman (2007), the first step to develop this type of environment is provide time for students to recognize their own strengths and weaknesses through self-assessment. Once students recognize their strengths and weaknesses they become more accepting of others' differences. Recognizing others' strengths and weaknesses helps to establish an atmosphere of understanding diverse ways of learning. Self-assessments and reflection enable students to gain self-knowledge (another form of metacognition) by exploring strengths, weaknesses, personal learning preferences, and intelligences (Armstrong, 1999; Wiggins & McTighe, 2005). This type of self-awareness enhances students' metacognition and awareness of their own learning and is a perfect foundation for introducing tiered activities.

 Make the Tech Connection: Productivity

You can collect self-assessment data using a variety of web-based tools for students to share their ideas and responses with you. For younger students we recommend tools that allow students to record their thinking and beliefs. This might include a tool such as SeeSaw (https://web.seesaw.me) which is a digital student portfolio system. For older students we recommend creating a survey on Google Forms (https://www.google.com/forms/about/) as this tool allows you to save your survey measures.

Implementing Tiered Activities

Tiered activities can be introduced during any mode of instruction at the beginning of a unit to determine students' prior knowledge, in the middle of a unit to understand what strategies students have acquired and what you might reteach, or at the end of your unit to assess student learning. You should determine the needed skills and concepts of the task prior to implementing and identify students' levels of skill and knowledge so they can be grouped according to their tier. These are flexible tiered groups that are in place just for the task at hand. Regardless of the groupings, students can work at the various tiered levels, whether in small group settings, whole-group settings, or during warm-ups at the start of a lesson. Whatever the instruction, the teacher can provide levels, or tiers, of challenge. Remember, the goal of tiered instruction is to provide support for all students at whatever level of learning and increase their cognitive challenge to keep them engaged. It is a "win-win" for everyone. Students are still getting access to the content standard and you are differentiating instruction to meet students where they are and not where the textbook wants them to be.

When we "teach outside the box" we are designing for our students and being flexible in our approach to instruction. This approach to instruction might require you to modify your curriculum so that students have the ability to access content information. With technology, you have a way to support and engage all learners so differentiation is built into what you do, rather than isolated at various points throughout the instruction.

 Make the Tech Connection: Blended Learning

While we recognize the need to differentiate instruction for math tasks, we also recognize that students need personalized learning that can adapt to their needs and abilities. Blended learning is when students learn in both face-to-face classroom instruction along with online instruction in an adaptive program. We have found that when students are given additional resources to understand and deepen their understanding of concepts and skills through an online math program, their efficacy for doing math and working with their peers will increased dramatically. Online curriculum can give students immediate feedback, remediation, and additional challenge to meet a wide range of learners in your class. Strong blended learning programs determine students' ability and provides curriculum that is within their zone of proximal development. We've included a list of blended learning programs in our Math tech list (see Appendix).

Developing Habits of Mind: Struggle

We hope you realize by this point in the chapter that engaging, facilitating, and designing open-ended tasks requires a shift in the teacher's role from "sage on the stage" to a "guide on the side." In our work with students and open-ended tasks, we have found the best part of using these tasks are the discussions and teachable moments that emerge when students are "doing the math." You don't need to mull over hours of assessment data to know where students are, because with open-ended tasks understanding and areas for growth emerge organically. We can see where students struggle whether it is in the solutions they provide or the activities they select to complete.

Struggle also provides the teacher with opportunities to reframe student learning. For example, when working with students on a series of tiered activities on fractions, Dr. Dickenson noticed students were comfortable with benchmark fractions (1/2, 1/4, 1/3, 1/8) but had difficulty visualizing less common fractions such as 1/5. To address this difficulty, she created a minilesson to build on students' understanding of fractions with money. She asked students to make the connection to coins they were familiar with and extended their thinking to determine the value of 1/5 in a dollar. Students knew that ¼ represents 1 out of 4 quarters in a dollar so what could 1/5 represent? The students' discussion led to a visual model in which $1.00 could be seen visually as having five parts. Students were then able to make the connection between a dime (1/10) to 1/5 being two dimes 2/10 and equivalent to 1/5. Students used Google Drawing to share their visual models with the class (see below drawing).

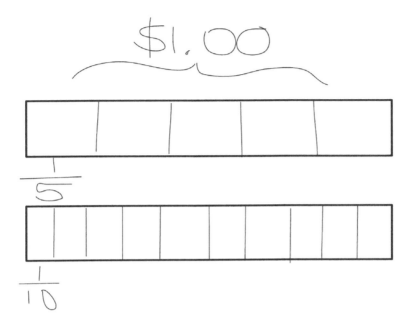

 Make the Tech Connection: Create

The above image was created with Google Drawing to provide a quick visual model for students to reference. When working in Google Docs on a specific math task, students can choose "insert" and then select "Drawing" to include a visual representation of their work.

We recommend that math tasks include writing, reading, listening, drawing, and technology. Writing can take place when students record their ideas or explain their solutions.

Reading is part of making sense of a task and when students read the explanations of their peers. Listening occurs when there is a mathematical discussion that students must make sense of and connect students' explanations to their ideas. Drawing is the visual representation students create to explain their thinking, and technology can be used to support or enhance any of these stated components. Technology is a tool, just like a ruler or a pencil, which will support students in understanding, explaining, and demonstrating what they know.

Games

Math games are oftentimes open-ended tasks with multiple entry points for students to share their knowledge and skills. For example, you can have students work with a partner to roll two die and create a fraction with one dice being the numerator and the other the denominator.

Think About It!

Examine the image of a fraction dice game in Figure 5.5. What attributes of this game supports open-ended tasks? How might you modify this math game to practice other skills, such as decimals, percent, and addition?

_____

_____

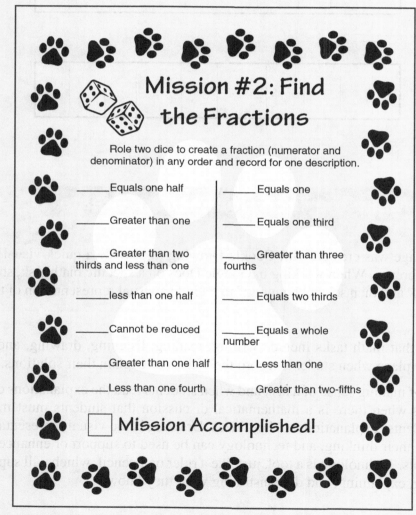

Figure 5.5 Fraction Game

Students then match their fraction with a description such as "equals one half," or you can have students create their own description of the fraction they rolled. Remember, you know your students best so make sure to adjust games and tasks according to their ability and interest. Consider how the task below is open-ended. Earlier in this chapter, we identified six attributes of an open-ended task:

1. Open-ended with multiple solutions
2. Multiple entry points at differing levels
3. Various student learning levels possible
4. Engage and interest students
5. Conceptually-based
6. Increased levels of cognitive demand

We've included a copy of this game and other fraction tasks for you in the Appendix of this book.

For younger learners, another whole class game that supports open-ended thinking is, "What Two Numbers?" In this game, the teacher writes a number on the board. The goal for the students is to find as many number combinations as possible using any operations to make the number. This is a wonderful game because it is as simple or as complex as students make it to be, based on their conceptual knowledge. For example, the teacher can give a second-grade class the number 35 and ask students to generate as many true number combinations that equal that amount. Students generate on their own paper as many combinations as possible. For second graders, this may be numbers such as $30 + 5$, $25 + 10$, and $34 + 1$. However, some students may also think about combinations with other types of operations such as $45 - 10$, 7×5, or $70 \div 2$. For kindergarteners or first graders, students can use linking cubes to find the two numbers by composing and decomposing the cubes to make number combinations around a lower number such as 10 or 15. With a younger group, make sure students all have the number of cubes to start. Then they break apart and put back together as many combinations as possible, keeping record on an individual chart or class chart. As with all games, it is important to create a climate of enjoyment that emphasizes thinking rather than competition.

🔖 Snag It: Check out this Jamboard that we crafted for students to play a digital version of the game target number where students create an equation with the numbers in the number bank.

🔖 Snag It: https://bit.ly/3dsfCsA

Student-Created Open-Ended Tasks

Another approach to working with open-ended tasks is to have your students create them. We find this approach to resonate strongly with students as they are familiar with the context in which mathematics is part of their lives. Students also have an opportunity to exercise 21st century skills, collaboration, creativity, critical thinking, and communication, when they work with a group of peers to create an open-ended task. You can set constraints on the task such as what operation they should use and a range of numbers to work within; however, students should have the freedom to create a problem situation in which they apply math. This is also a great way for students to integrate English Language Arts into mathematics. Students will be familiar with basic plot structure and now they can think about this format in the context of a math problem. As math is everywhere in our lives, this kind of activity will help students see the connections.

The final product of this task is a video-based word problem, created by each group of students, that is shared with the class and then solved. Even if the process or problem has misconceptions, this too can become a teachable moment for students to learn and grow.

 Watch It

https://youtu.be/aVecwCGMZKw

This video-based word problem was created with Shadow Puppet (https://itunes.apple.com/us/app/shadow-puppet-edu/id888504640?mt=8) which is an application for device. Students can take pictures, record audio, and narrate their word problems.

 Make the Tech Connection: Math Tasks

Students can use a phone to record a video of themselves performing the word problem. These videos can be included on a web tool like Edupuzzle (https://edpuzzle.com/) where questions can be asked after viewing the video. If you want to gamify this activity then upload the videos to YouTube then use a web tool like Kahoot (http://kahoot.it) to incorporate all student videos in a game response format.

Virtual Tools and Open-Ended Tasks

Virtual tools have found a place and a space in our adult lives. From tracking the number of steps we've accumulated during a walk, to managing our household budget with online banking. There are many ways we use digital tools to support and mediate the decisions we make. Digital tools have the potential to make our lives more productive. When it comes to math instruction, however digital tools are seldomly used to support student learning and create meaningful experiences. If we want our students to be college and career ready, we need to create opportunities for students to utilize web-based tools and develop digital literacy.

Have you used web-based tools to determine the distance between two locations and the time it will take you to travel? How about shopping for airfare online and determining the best time and route to travel? These experiences are in many ways open-ended tasks supported with virtual tools, as you plan and problem-solve in creative ways.

There is much potential for using online tools to facilitate and support math tasks. Give students a budget to create their dream bedroom with items from an online website or research data from the basketball season to determine which player on their favorite team should be selected as the most valuable player. The Internet not only includes a variety of web-based tools to support students learning but includes a wealth of data that students can access at their fingertips to make learning relevant.

Here are some ideas of open-ended tasks which can be paired with digital tools across the grades to support learning of math concepts.

K-2	Open-Ended Task	Technology Integration
Counting and Cardinality	Provide students with problem situations to model with mathematics.	Use a digital tool such as Glenco Virtual Manipulatives or Harcourt Counters for students to solve the problem situation and illustrate their thinking. Students can select the setting and types of manipulatives they will use. You can take a screen shot and print the picture for students to record their equation.
Numbers and Operations in Base Ten	Students create virtual arrays and show what they know using virtual manipulatives created in Google Slides.	Use Google Slides to create a ten frame for students to move objects and solve a variety of problem situations.
Data and Graphing	Students are asked to collect data about their favorite pet, activity, or holiday.	Once data is collected students can include their results in a NLVM tool or using a iPad app such as Teaching Graphs.

3–5	Open-Ended Task	Technology Integration
Decimals	Give students open-ended tasks with money to make connections to decimals. For example, "What coin combinations can you represent for $1.00?"	Add the chrome extension Money pieces to your web browser which can be used on or offline. Students can drag and drop money pieces. Students can create a virtual graphic organizer using Popplet to represent their knowledge of decimals.
Fractions	Ask students to use virtual fraction pieces to find equivalent fractions. Post student discoveries on a class number line for discussion.	There are several types of fraction representations in the NLVM web tool. Have students compare pieces and place on a number line.
Division & Multiplication	Construct problems using number pieces to illustrate a situation, such as beginning with the dividend and determining the divisor and quotient.	The number pieces tool from the Math Learning Center enables students to construct models and annotate using writing tools.

6–12	Open-Ended Task	Technology Integration
Variety 3-Act Math Task	Select content specific open-ended tasks from Dan Meyer's 3-Act Math task	Students watch a video-based problem related to a real-life situation and determine what information they need to know and then share their solution. Use the student video graphic organizer above for students to create their own video problem.
Ratio	Create a slideshow of a product review using data from Amazon and ratings from product reviews.	Google slides of Ratio word problems that are open-ended and support students in expressing understanding in a variety of ways.
Equations/ Graphing	Solve open-ended tasks that are tiered and allow for student collaboration.	Desmos tools allow student using an online graphing calculator that includes a variety of virtual pen colors and displays.

The Internet is rich with virtual manipulatives that can be utilized through a variety of devices. These tools support open-ended tasks as students drag and drop pieces in ways to represent their thinking. In our list of Math Tools you will see a list of resources that are free and available to use.

In addition to web-based tools, handheld devices offer much flexibility for teachers to create learning opportunities outside of the classroom. This can be a powerful experience to connect to the lives of students. For example, students can use their personal phones to take photos of objects that represent geometric shapes or when learning about decimals participate in relay races to record their time in a sprint.

It is important in your exploration of digital tools and apps to be flexible in your thinking and "think outside the box." If you want to know what will be most meaningful to your students, observe them throughout the day and find out about their interests. Recall the scavenger hunts we referenced earlier can easily incorporate technology with digital devices to capture images and objects. Sometimes technology use is that simple but a powerful way to engage young learners and capture their thinking.

Google Slides can also be used to make virtual manipulatives that are connected to the lives of your students. On our YouTube channel, we have shared a video on how you can create open-ended tasks with virtual manipulatives in Google Slides. When creating a series of open-ended tasks with virtual manipulatives, Dr. Dickenson first found out about the lives of her students. She created scenarios that would be familiar to her students such as going to the park or gardening. In another example, she made virtual base ten blocks for students to model two digit multiplication. In each example, she made sure to create opportunities for students to demonstrate their understanding using both the representational and symbolic model. These activities can be used across the grade span at varying levels to support students in either writing an equation or using a visual model to represent multiplication.

🛍 Snag It: **TWO-DIGIT MULTIPLICATION**

🛍 Snag It: Building Arrays

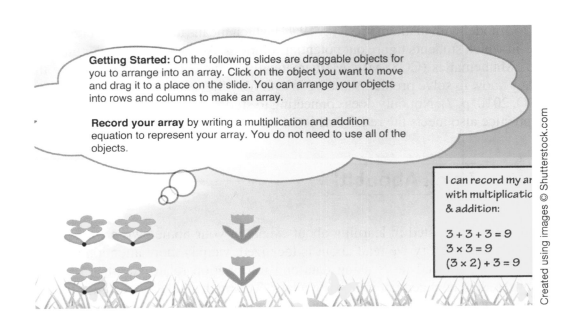

Getting Started: On the following slides are draggable objects for you to arrange into an array. Click on the object you want to move and drag it to a place on the slide. You can arrange your objects into rows and columns to make an array.

Record your array by writing a multiplication and addition equation to represent your array. You do not need to use all of the objects.

I can record my ar
with multiplicatio
& addition:

$3 + 3 + 3 = 9$
$3 \times 3 = 9$
$(3 \times 2) + 3 = 9$

Created using images © Shutterstock.com

Watch It

In this video, Dr. Dickenson works with fourth-grade students to demonstrate how to use the Virtual manipulatives she created in Google Slides https://www.youtube.com/watch?v=MFd94KSQB-c&list=PL7zSfM_BeFCvWGXEPXA2uSYTTwi1QqCB4&index=6

 Stop and Reflect

What virtual tools do you use in your life to help you "do the math"? How do the visual aspects of these digital tools support you in making decisions?

_____

_____

Open-Ended Tasks and Online Data

Remember how we mentioned that open-ended tasks should be culturally relevant and connected to students' everyday lives? Well, the tasks you create can include online data and information to make math more meaningful. In fact, this is an important aspect of mathematical modeling which requires students to examine important issues and use math as a tool to figure out situations (Lesh & Doerr, 2003). The Standards for Mathematical Practice also requires students to "model with mathematics" (SMP #4) which means teachers must present real-world problems in which students figure out potential solutions. According to the Common Core State Standards Mathematics (CCSSM), "Mathematically proficient students can apply the mathematics they know to solve problems arising in everyday life, society, and the workplace" (NGA & CCSSO, 2010, p. 7). Not only does connecting to students' lives create relevance for learning but this practice also meets the requirements of the new standards.

 Think About It!

Are you more interested in learning about events in your hometown or in another place far away? When a story we read about is localized, we pay more attention and are more interested. Open-ended tasks using data and information related to students' lives can motivate student engagement in solving a task. The math suddenly becomes important as it is contextualized in things they know and have experienced.

You can use data and information from the Internet to create open-ended tasks in two ways.

1. Share data with your students as an open-ended task for them to interpret. For example, if students examine the cost of a used car in two different dealerships, they can make a comparison of which store offers the better deal and what might influence a higher cost in a different neighborhood. Students will need to use reasoning to determine what factors may impact the cost, but more importantly they need to do the math.

2. Share data with students to tell a story. The question posed to students uses the data to contextualize the situation, by asking, "What does the data represent and what does it tell you about a context or situation?" For example, looking at the data from a recent local election, what might the data tell you about the beliefs of voters in their county? In this way, the teacher has the students use the data to tell the story. This type of task requires high-level thinking skills that not only engages students but also provides them with a starting point for launching into a math task.

https://youtu.be/u-K2DZXaiVM

In this video, Dr. Dickenson has students review prices of homes for sale in the students' neighborhood. They need to determine the average cost where they live and identify outliers in a particular data set for an upcoming project-based learning task.

Getting Started with Using Data in Your Class

1. The first step in this process is to take a real-life situation and make the connection to a mathematical problem. Ensure that the situation is interesting to your students and connected to their lives.

2. Next, after you present the situation, provide your students with an opportunity to ask questions and reflect. You can create a T-Chart with the word "Notice and Wonder" to record students' thinking about the situation or use the Padlet tool (www.padlet.com) to create a virtual whiteboard where students can share ideas instantaneously. Student questions typically emerge when they are asked to "wonder" about a situation. These questions can serve as a launching point into the task.

3. Then, identify any constraints and assumptions about the task. In the car example given above, you can ask students to describe what they must assume when comparing these two cars. For example, the cars may be the same model with similar mileage and students might assume they are both in excellent condition. You might also have students share some constraints that they identify within the situation. A constraint might be not knowing how the price is impacted by the local sales tax of the town.

4. Determine how to make sense of the problem and provide choice in determining the solution. This is the point where students determine the strategies they will use to solve the problem.

5. Finally, the last stage of this process is sharing solutions. In this stage, students exercise SMP #3, when they "construct viable arguments and critique the reasoning of others." This is a powerful process that can impact student learning. We have our students record their findings using Google Classroom so they can be shared with peers and others can post comments or questions. If laptops are not available, use a poster and conduct a carousel activity where students record comments and questions on a post-it note for their peers to review.

Across the Curriculum

We love engaging our high school students with Data Talks on current events and trends. The Pew Research Center has a variety of Social Trends charts that can be used in a data talk with your students to discuss anything from politics to issues related to health and pop culture.

https://www.pewresearch.org/

Putting it into Practice: Planning Guide

We know that planning is an essential part of your practice, so we've created a planning guide to help you remember all of the aspects we have discussed for creating an open-ended task.

Mathematical Goals: Identify the goals of your math task and what you would like to achieve by having your students work through the task. Is your goal to determine students' prior knowledge before beginning a new unit, determine what strategies students are able to apply independently, or assess their understanding at the end of a unit?

Standard/Practice Standard: Identify the mathematics standard you are working on and the standard of mathematical practice that you will address in this lesson (see Chapter 2).

The Task: Record the task that you will present to your class.

The Hook: Determine how you will present the task in a way to engage and support students.

🛍 Snag It: A copy of this planner is included in the Appendix.

Anticipated Strategies and Misconceptions: Share what strategies you anticipate students will use and the misconceptions they may have when working through the task.

Open-Ended Task Planner

Mathematical Goals:　　　　　　　Standard/Practice Standards:

The Task:

How will you present the task and hook the learner?

Anticipated strategies and misconceptions:　　Questions to support student thinking:

Approach for class sharing/discourse:　　Questions to support student sharing:

Learner Outcomes and Plan to Integration Technology:

Questions to Support Student Thinking: Record what questions you might ask your students while they are working through the task based on the strategies they may use and the misconceptions they might have.

Approach for Class Sharing/Discourse: Describe how you will approach having a discussion in your class, which might include using technology to share out or recording solutions on a poster for critique in a student gallery.

Questions to Support Student Discussion: Determine what questions you might ask to support students in explaining their ideas and critiquing the reasoning of others.

Learner Outcome and Plan to Integrate Technology: Share what you hope students will achieve as a result of engaging in this math task and how you plan to utilize technology to support the learner outcomes.

Summary

Open-ended tasks support students in growing cognitively in their math development. We believe these kinds of tasks should happen regularly in your classroom. This chapter illustrates the process of creating, evaluating, and determining the kinds of open-ended tasks that support all learners in engaging in math. Questioning is an essential part of this process that requires you to work through the tasks to determine how you can best support you learners. The kinds of questions you ask students should lead to productive struggle and not just the solution. What is most important about open-ended tasks is the sense-making that occurs and not the answer-getting. It is important to remember that your questions should support student learning and not push them toward an answer. Think like a scientist and determine what insight you can gain about your students' knowledge and understanding of math as they work through open-ended tasks.

Additional Activities/Discussion Questions

1. Reflect on the questions provided for you to consider before, during, and after instruction. Determine what skills or areas you need to improve in your own teaching practice.
2. Identify technology tools from this chapter that you are excited to try in your class and create a plan for implementation.
3. Join a Twitter discussion with fellow math teachers by using the hashtag #mtbos and find a math task that meets the attributes of an open-ended task.

Instructor Activities

1. An important aspect of planning for math instruction is spiraling content to support both procedural fluency and conceptual understanding. Challenge your students to make this connection by designing an open-ended task that is connected to a daily routine and discuss how the two are connected and support students with developing procedural fluency and conceptual understanding.
2. Provide your students with several learner profiles such as a student with learning challenges, a gifted student, and a second-language learner. Have them create a tiered activity based on a grade-level content standard for a lesson they might teach.

Chapter 6

Project-Based Learning

Self-Reflection

What kind of learning activities captivate your interest for a long period of time?

"Tell me and I'll forget. Show me and I may remember. Involve me and I learn."

—Benjamin Franklin

What if you were asked to design a classroom of the future and determine the floor plan, technology, and futuristic features? Perhaps you were given a budget to plan your grandmother's 90th birthday party at her favorite location, Disneyland. When tasks are brought together with both students' interests and math skills in real-life projects, the result is called project-based learning (PjBL).

© Gorodenkoff/Shutterstock.com

PjBL is a student-centered approach known to provide students with cognitive challenge in response to questions or problems for which students design solutions. In PjBL, students engage in extended investigations in which they work autonomously using problem-solving and decision-making skills. Oftentimes, students produce realistic products or presentations as an outcome of these investigations (Jones, Rasmussen, & Moffitt, 1997).

The Purpose of PjBL

When kids say they "don't like math," don't be surprised; most likely they think math is boring and not important to their lives. Chances are they've probably experienced a traditional approach to math instruction, one with worksheets and problem-solving tasks that were devoid of relevancy to their lives. Lack of interesting and relevant material are two main reasons why students claim they are bored in school (Yazzie-Mintz, 2007), but when students are engaged in meaningful tasks they are more likely to learn more effectively (Hancock & Betts, 2002).

> PjBL puts the meaning into the task, and shakes-up the traditional approach of math instruction by engaging students in a real-life project that allows them to develop and use their knowledge and skills in a meaningful way.

The purpose of the project is not to supplement the curriculum, but rather it *is* the curriculum; all knowledge and skills are taught through the project itself. As a result, students not only experience purposeful learning of skills and knowledge but they also learn to apply the knowledge and skills while engaging in solving a problem. The purpose of PjBL is to learn knowledge and skills within the context of something larger: the project.

Convincingly, PjBL meets the requirements of the 21st century skills, as outlined by the Common Core State Standards. Using PjBL means that students engage in the four Cs: critical thinking, communication, collaboration, and creativity (The Partnership for 21st Century Learning, 2015). Many argue for PjBL as an instructional choice since it promotes deep learning of content through application, a requirement of the Standards for Mathematical Practice. Also, PjBL is an approach that uses skills and knowledge in authentic ways and is often integrated across other content areas. An added benefit of PjBL is that it addresses students' motivational needs through cognitive challenge and choice in the process of learning valuable skills and concepts (Barron et al., 1998; Bell, 2010).

Technology integration is a natural and valuable aspect of PjBL as students search, gather, record, and produce their findings in response to their investigations. PjBL enhances students' digital literacy as they discriminate the usefulness and reliability of sources. They also use technology to record information and display their knowledge (Bell, 2010).

Putting Research Into Practice

At the core of PjBL is the belief that children must engage in meaningful activity. This notion of learning and engagement can be traced back to Dewey (1938) who believed students need to find meaning in learning. Researchers have found Project based activities do just that—provide meaning. Because students find the learning to be meaningful in PjBL, motivation is increased. In fact, PjBL is so effective in engaging students in prolonged and deep investigation that this approach has grown in popularity (Blumenfeld et al., 1991). Studies have shown students who engaged in PjBL out-performed students taught in traditional ways. Additionally, PjBL was identified as improving students' responsibility, independence, and discipline (Bell, 2010). Overall, there is a high regard for PjBL as a method that sparks students' interest and creativity while simultaneously developing independence and problem-solving skills.

Though the benefits for students are great, using PjBL also provides benefits for teachers. PjBL gives teachers a way to integrate content across the disciplines. Integration across disciplines is when content from more than one discipline is present in the learning experience. As PjBL situations are often set in real-life contexts, content integration occurs naturally. Math can be integrated with science, English language arts, music, art, social studies, physical education, and technology.

Putting Ideas Into Action

Let's say you are planning an upcoming unit for your fourth grade class to address the following math standard:

Apply the area and perimeter formulas for rectangles in real-world and mathematical problems. In third grade, students developed an understanding of area and learned how to measure area by counting unit squares ([CCSS.MATH.CONTENT.4.MD.A.3](#)). Now you must extend students' thinking about area in a real-world context. In your science block, students are learning about ecosystems and there was much interest among students when it came to endangered animals. Is it possible to build on students' interest in science to extend their thinking and promote mastery in mathematics?

Absolutely. Designing a PjBL activity is a great opportunity for students to transfer learning and apply the concepts of area and perimeter into a meaningful project. Students can apply these concepts with an investigation to create a zoo for endangered animals. This project could integrate curriculum across content areas as a way to support students in making meaningful connections and applying learning in the context of a real-life situation. As a way to set the stage for the project you pose the following driving question to your students:

How can I design a zoo that will most resemble endangered animals' natural habitat and protect them from extinction?

© Sukpaiboonwat/Shutterstock.com

Here are some ways you can integrate other subjects into this project to meet the driving question:

Science Connection: Research the living needs of endangered animals such as elephants, tigers, and bears, and create recommendations to meet the animals' needs.

Engineering Design: Design a 3D model of a zoo based on the animals' needs to be healthy and thrive.

Math Connection: Determine the area and perimeter of the zoo design and make scale representations of the habitats.

Writing Connection: Write a proposal to city council that shares rationale for the habitats selected with reasoning for the design. Create a web page for the public to share information about the zoo and the kinds of animals that reside there.

Art Connection: Use watercolor or clay to create a work of art for the zoo design and include on a website.

Technology Connection: Research animals on National Geographic website for kids (https://kids.nationalgeographic.com/animals/) and create a website promoting zoo on Kidblog (https://kidblog.org/home/). Play a math game to practice the skill of constructing area and perimeter with immediate feedback (http://mrnussbaum.com/zoo/).

Reading Connection: Read informational text about one endangered animal. Highlight facts related to why this animal is endangered and include in the proposal why the city council should fund your project.

These tasks require students to apply skills in math, science, technology, and art, as well as work together cooperatively while listening and speaking with purpose. As you can see, there are many life skills and disciplinary content areas integrated in PjBL tasks like this one. Content integration is a natural benefit of using PjBL because real-life contexts are interconnected and naturally intertwine subject matter.

Meeting the Needs of All Learners

Another benefit for teachers when using PjBL is that differentiation happens quite seamlessly. There is much space in these types of activities to shift the cognitive demand, have students work collaboratively, incorporate technology to assist and support students with special needs, and have opportunities to work one-on-one with students.

In the Zoo Design activity, students can begin by working in small groups to investigate the habitat of three endangered animals. Students and groups who are ready to take on an additional challenge may complete an advanced task such as writing questions to interview a zoologist or emailing the staff at the local zoo to learn more about a particular animal. Once they have completed this task, they can share their findings with their peers.

With PjBL, students work at their own levels providing natural differentiation in which students are stretched cognitively. PjBL provides formative assessment as teachers observe their students applying concepts and skills in the context of problem-solving and investigations. Using technology, students can access leveled readers and watch videos to support understanding of concepts. Students who struggle with writing can access assistive technology using voice recognition to complete a writing assignment or have text read to them using a Google Chrome extension such as Read Aloud (https://chrome.google.com/webstore/detail/read-aloud-a-text-to-spee/hdhinadidafjejdhmfkjgnolgimiaplp?hl=en).

Since PjBL is personalized, differentiation can occur naturally within the choices and decisions made (Bell, 2010; Grant, 2002). As shown in Table 6.1, the roles of the student and teacher are quite distinct. Unlike Chapter 1 Daily Routines, which are highly structured and teacher-directed activities, PjBL is driven by the students' questions and explorations.

Table 6.1 Roles in PjBL

Teacher's Role	Student's Role
• Presents an introduction to set the stage for the question or investigation • Sets clear expectations and provides reminders and guidelines for completing the project • Provides driving question or assists students in developing their own driving question • Acts as facilitator and mentor • Supports students in learning key skills and concepts throughout the investigation • Oversees student decision-making and provides guidance in the investigation • Provides accommodations and modifications for students with academic challenges • Acts as audience for the final solution or presentation	• Explores a driving question or real-life problem • Collaborates with peers • Applies skills and knowledge to solve question or problem • Learns skills and knowledge necessary while solving question or problem • Uses the Internet and resources (texts or subject-matter experts) to gain information • Conferences with the teacher regularly about choices and decisions • Documents progress and reflects on the learning outcomes • Defends final solution or presents final product for critique and evaluation

 Think About It!

After reviewing the roles of the student and teacher for PjBL, how might you provide appropriate accommodations and modifications for the Zoo Design project?

_____

_____

Structure of PjBL

In our experience working with students and teachers to develop and execute project-based learning activities, having a structure to support students' progress throughout the project is essential for success. This is especially important for younger students who are just getting started with working on projects and need guidance to self-regulate and monitor their learning. As you begin to develop ideas for a project consider how you can organize and chunk tasks to support student learning. There are many ways you can facilitate student learning in the structure of PjBL. For example, you can share or even create with students a criteria chart (like a to-do list) to organize the flow of the project, provide graphic organizers for students to record ideas or collect research, and connect students with online activities to develop fluency with skills needed throughout the task. Remember, the structure of the project will guide your students toward success but also provide you with critical evidence to evaluate your students' learning.

Just like any goal in your life that you want to complete, it all starts with creating a list and identifying the tasks, then working through each task until you've completed the project. You might even give yourself reminders, rewards, and peer motivation to stay focused and move toward your goal. We've identified six steps that will help you think about how to structure and support students in PjBL tasks:

1. **Identify tasks:** In your project create scaffolds to support all students. Even the brightest kid in your class will need help managing the task. Don't assume students can go it alone. Provide opportunities for students to collaborate and share ideas.

2. **Block Time for Project Work:** Project based tasks won't get finished if you don't make time to complete them. Consider the tasks you have created in your project and how much time your students will need. Set time each week for students to work individually and collaboratively as well as conference with you.

3. **Utilize Technology:** Creating a digital space for students to get organized and manage their work is essential. Limit the number of sites your students visit to stay on task. Create folders on your desktop or in Google Drive for quick access to documents that will help students work efficiently.

4. **Review and Reflect Students' Progress:** Students not only need feedback from you but they need to develop the skills to reflect on their work critically and make changes. Be sure you are modeling this process and thinking aloud as a strategy to support students in developing self-reflection and metacognition.

5. **Connect to the Driving Question:** The driving question is the focal point of your project. When students get off-task or spend too much time on one activity, bring them back to the driving question to redirect their work and focus on what they need to achieve.

6. **Celebrate Success:** The end of the project does not mean students simply turn it in and get a grade. Be sure you prepare an end-of-the project celebration where you invite other grades, the principal, parents, and experts from the community to showcase your student work and receive some recognition.

Beginning PjBL with a Driving Question

What does a police officer investigating a crime, a scientist testing out a new idea, and a teacher creating a PjBL activity all have in common? They focus their work on a driving question to guide what they do and how they do it. Creating a driving question is essential for hooking students into a task and keeping their focus throughout the project.

In the Zoo Design task, we created the driving question, *"How can I design a zoo that will most resemble endangered animals' natural habitat and protect them from extinction?"* This question was posed to our students to investigate a problem or issue. While students engage in the process of exploring the question or problem, they work on key standards that are either introduced or practiced as part of the investigation.

The driving questions can be created by you or with your students to focus students' learning and allow them to examine a situation from different perspectives. That means no two projects should be exactly alike as students are working from their own frame of reference. Moreover, the driving question should engage students in an investigation before they reach a solution to the question.

Driving Questions Should:	Driving Questions Should Not:
• Be the focal point for everything that students do throughout the project • Require student investigations • Be based on evidence • Have multiple responses and final products • Excite students about learning • Give students a voice and a choice • Provide students with a focus and direction throughout the project	• Be just an introductory topic to get students engaged • Give students all the information they need to solve a problem • Be subjective • Have only one answer and solution • Be geared as practice for high-stakes tests • Be limited and linear • Make students confused or unsure in their task

Now It's Your Turn!

Let's say you are teaching third grade and the next unit is in Numbers and Operations in Base Ten with a focus on: "Fluently add and subtract within 1000 using strategies and algorithms based on place value, properties of operations, and/or the relationship between addition and subtraction (CCSS.Math.Content.3.NBTA.2)." You are thinking this would be a great time to implement a PjBL activity as your students have skills with adding and subtracting but need more practice in a real-life context to support fluency. Your initial idea for the project is to have students plan a trip with a budget and determine the cost and expenses for their family. What might you consider for the driving question and what interdisciplinary connections could you make?

What might your driving question be for a PjBL activity where students are planning a trip and developing fluency adding and subtracting within 1,000? How can you integrate other subject areas and technology into your project?

The Task: Students will plan a trip to develop fluency adding and subtracting within 1,000.

Driving Question: Ideas for Integration: Technology Connection:

Now that you have had an opportunity to practice creating a driving question, ideas for technology, and cross subject integration, we will discuss how you can create tasks for your project. Feel free to extend your thinking of the Planning a Trip project with tasks you might create. In our experience with students, creating a family trip always peaks students' interest because kids love to travel and talk about places they have visited with their family. You might decide to have your students plan a trip to a new place they would like to visit, a place they have already been to, or a place they are learning about in their social studies standards.

Here are a few tasks our student have done with this driving question: create a travel brochure based on your selected destination, write a review of a place you will stay, plan your trip with a fixed budget and select at least three excursions to take during your trip, and calculating the distance between your home and your destination. There are also many ways to include technology in this project such as using word processing tools to create a brochure, digital posters such as Canva, Google Maps and Google Tours to determine the distance and create a travel plan, and compare costs of actual vacations through a website such as Trip Advisor (https://www.tripadvisor.com) or Travelocity (https://www.travelocity.com).

We find that students are much more motivated to "do the math" when they are working with actual data. How students collect and organize data and information is important to consider and that is why creating tasks are an essential aspect for a successful project.

👁 View It: Get Going with Google Tours http://www.teacherpreptech.com/2018/07/the-idea-of-bringing-outside-world-of.html

🔒 Snag It: See the appendix for a copy of this activity.

Creating PjBL Tasks

In our Zoo Design project we set the stage for creating a design of a zoo by investigating about a particular endangered animal. In a highly structured PjBL task, the teacher begins the initial investigation as a whole group using direct instruction to review how to research and record ideas about an animal. This style of instruction best addresses the needs of students with learning disabilities. By taking the time to provide this initial guidance, including where to find information and record ideas, students understand the requirements and then can work independently. Below is an example of criteria you might require students to find as part of their investigations. Even though this might seem like just a science activity, there is math that is explicitly used in their investigations.

Task *1: Investigating Endangered Animals Habitats.
In the first task, investigate three endangered animals that will reside in your zoo. It is important to learn about the kind of habitat you will need to create for each animal to thrive in their new home. Click here to go digital with this document.

© Shutterstock.com

Let's learn about your animal (click here). Complete the below criteria and include additional information that will support you in designing a zoo.

Animal Name & Scientific Name	Polar Bear Ursus Maritimus which means "maritime bear"
Describe location, climate & area:	The polar bear lives in the arctic. The arctic is a region that is located in the northern part of the earth. It is extremely cold with temperatures ranging from -29 to -32 F and in the winter can drop to below -58 F.
Life span:	15 to 18 years
Size	Up to ten feet tall
Weight:	Up to 1700 lbs
Date:	Seals, whales, and walruses
Life Style & Behaviours	Born on land but spend most of their time in sea. Spend their time hunting, mating, and denning.
Interesting Math Facts:	Can swim 100 miles at a stretch; Only 25,000 left from changing temperatures and global warming.
Additional Information:	The polar bear is an endangered animal because of a loss of sea ice from global warming and changing temperatures.

🛍 Snag It: **https://bit.ly/2G7A4vq**

We're sharing with you a Google Doc to copy and use with your students. As this is yours to keep, feel free to modify to best support your students' learning needs. There are also hyperlinks embedded in the document to National Geographic Kids page for students to quickly access information about their animal and stay on task with web browsing.

You can also use this format for other PjBL activities you plan in the future.

Think About It!

https://bit.ly/2G7A4vq

After reviewing the task we created for Zoo Design, how might you use this format for students who are planning a trip?

_____

_____

You might modify this table into a T-chart and have students compare the cost of two different ways to vacation in Alaska, one that would require five nights stay at a hotel versus a 5-day cruise with all costs included. Having students make comparisons is a great way to promote higher order thinking in mathematics.

Going Digital with PjBL Tasks

The best thing you can do to keep your students organized and working cooperatively throughout the project is to go digital with your tasks. Digital tools allow you the flexibility to push out information to your students instantaneously, from including where to go search on the web to providing instantaneous feedback in a web-based tool.

Depending on your learners, you might decide that students are ready to work with Google Docs or Google Slides to organize their work and create a presentation to share. We typically see these platforms being used at about the second-grade level once students have developed the fine motor skills to type and are ready to work efficiently with technology. The best part of using a tool like Google Docs is you are able to provide feedback directly in the margins of students' papers. It is also very typical throughout a project to make changes to best meet the needs of your learners, and with digital tools you can make "on the spot" changes to your document without having to run-off 30 more copies from your copy machine. Think about all the trees you are saving!

Supporting Students with Digital Tools

If you are worried that typing will be extremely labor intensive and time consuming, Google Docs allows your students to work collaboratively on a document through sharing—both students can see and work on the document each on their own computer or tablet. Google Docs also includes a voice-to-type feature by selecting Tools and then Voice Typing. This opens a microphone icon for students to speak their ideas that are then directly typed out on the page. A bonus feature for second-language learners is that they can narrate their ideas in their primary language and the tool will translate the document into English.

Don't believe me, watch this second grader explain the voice typing feature. **https://bit .ly/2FVQ3N0**

Another benefit of using a web-based tool is the expandability of text boxes. Unlike a print-out worksheet that has students writing in a limited space, students can write endlessly with a digital document. They can easily import videos, include hyperlinks to resources, and, if they are using Google Slides, they can embed videos to make their presentation more robust. Moreover, you will likely witness students who take their motivation for learning well beyond the classroom walls. Students can work from home and receive additional support from parents when using a web-based platform to organize their writing. You no longer have to worry about finding students' lost work or wondering who forgot to write their name since it is all in one place.

Putting Tasks All Together

If you've been reading this book from the start, you have probably recognized how much we love tables to organize student and teacher learning. This is especially important when it comes to PjBL as completing tasks are essential to moving forward in a project. In our Zoo Design example, we created a table for students to use to support their learning. There are five activities they must complete, and each activity will help students move forward in the project. This is also a digital document that is shared with the students and includes a place for the teacher (who is the Mayor) to provide feedback. The To-Do section and tasks include hyperlinks to online sites and other digital documents that the students will use to complete their project. Students check off the box when they are done which lets the teacher know they have completed the task and are ready for feedback.

To-Do	Tasks	Mayor's Feedback
☐ <u>Research</u>	Identify at least three animals that you will learn more about and create a habitat for in your new zoo design. Complete at least three <u>Animal Investigations</u>	Great job identifying three endangered animals. Include descriptive detail about their homes for your zoo.
☐ <u>Certify</u>	Complete the online activity for calculating area and perimeter. Take a snapshot of your completion and include here as evidence you are ready to build.	Great job demonstrating mastery of this skill you are ready to move on to the next task!

To-Do	Tasks	Mayor's Feedback
☐ **Sketch It**	Use graph paper to create an initial sketch of your new zoo. Be sure your sketch includes the Zoo Criteria. Upload your photo to Adobe Spark and provide a narration which explains your drawing.	Your initial sketch includes area of each exhibit however you will also need to include the perimeter to ensure your visitors can walk around the space.
☐ **Design It:**	Design a model of your zoo by making a poster, 3-D model, or diorama. This will be on display and shared during our walking tours.	Your poster includes all the required criteria. Include color to your sketches for the audience.
☐ **Create**	Make a digital brochure of your zoo which features a map and description of the animals that can be shared with the public.	The map you created is drawn to scale but should also include a legend to let the reader know what each icon represents.

⬛ Snag It: **https://bit.ly/2KcnHk3**

This type of chart can be used to help you organize the PjBL tasks you design for your students.

Creating a Hook

You might have a great PjBL activity with tasks, graphic organizers, and technology integrated throughout, but without an enticing hook your project may experience a "failure to launch." Think about how you can connect students to the moment and get them excited about launching their PjBL activity. Here are a few ways to create an exciting hook:

1. Show a short and funny movie clip that gets students excited about the task. For example, in our Trip Planning activity we showed a funny movie clip where the family gets lost.
2. Dress up to match the occupation with the PjBL activity. For the Home Design activity, Dr. Dickenson dressed up as an engineer with blueprints, hard hat, and safety vest.
3. Invite an expert to share their expertise. This could be a parent who works in the industry your project is connected to or someone from the local community who can share what they do and get kids excited about learning.
4. Tell or read a compelling story that will set the stage for a driving question.
5. Make it a mystery that students need to solve.
6. Create an emotional connection to the project; once students started learning about endangered animals we knew the Zoo Design activity would be a success.
7. Root the problem/situation in actual data that will compel and motivate students.
8. Create competition by having a PjBL activity in which teams compete against each other for titles such as "Best Project Design," "Most Creative Project," and "Best Product to Meet the Clients' Needs." Your titles can emerge based on the criteria of your project.

In our planning template, you will record how you will "hook" your students, and this might just take more than one strategy. If your first take does not work, you can always give it another go. What works for one group might not work for another. You'll know when your students are "hooked" when they keep asking you when they can work on their project again!

Watch It

https://bit.ly/2wCfC6q

In this video, Dr. Dickenson introduces a PjBL activity to her sixth-grade students. What do you notice about how she introduces the activity and creates a hook for students to engage in the project?

_____

_____

🔖 **Snag It: https://bit.ly/2I7nJx4**

This PjBL activity has students designing a home based on criteria. How might you modify this task for lower grades? What support and scaffolds might younger children need to get started?

Across the Curriculum

Make a Stem connection and have students construct a kite and apply math skills to attend to precision and reflect on their design for future iterations.

High school students who are learning about Trigonometric ratios can explore the relationship in right triangles by constructing a clinometer. This tool will allow students to determine the height of an item not in their reach, such as a rooftop or the top of a tree. To ground students' investigation and integrate geometry standards, begin by constructing a kite with tetrahedrons and connecting to surface area and volume. This exploration allows students to connect math with their personal lives and see math as a tool. To extend the project have students use Google Earth and look for structures that include right triangles such as the Great Pyramids. Students can construct a scale model of the structures they find of interest in the real world and integrate Social Studies and English standards with the option to learn more about the selected structure, why it is famous, how it was constructed, and more interesting facts.

🔖 **Snag It:** Check out this High School Digtial Project

https://bit.ly/362sLEM

Review and Reflect

Providing students with feedback and an opportunity to reflect is a critical component of developing a growth mindset in students' learning. If you want students to attribute their success to their effort and not just their intelligence, be sure to provide students with specific measurable feedback that can be used to deepen their learning and effort. With PjBL, the focus is not just on students' intelligence but on their effort. We have seen tremendous effort from some of our lowest students in math during PjBL activities, positively impacting their efforts during traditional math instruction as well. When students accomplish a project they move from a mind-set of "this is too hard" to "this is achievable with effort." Furthermore, when students are interested in a topic and see the relevance to their lives, they are more likely to make mistakes and take risks which is essential to developing a growth mind-set.

Reflecting and reviewing work is not something that comes automatically to students, especially young learners. You must provide time for students to actively reflect on their progress and think about what they can do differently. Oftentimes, this happens when students have a chance to learn from their peers either through observation or peer feedback. These two skills need to be explicitly taught and modeled for students. You can provide some of the sentence frames we have shared in Chapter 4 to help students in this process.

With technology tools such as Google Docs you can also use the "Add Comments" feature to have students share their feedback on a document. The most important aspect of receiving feedback is the chance to revise one's thinking. Be sure your students have time to make revisions and use peers' feedback constructively.

Assigning Groups: Group Work

Group work in the PjBL approach is grounded in the theory of social constructivism (Vygotsky, 1978). According to this theory, it is through group process that learning occurs; thus, group work is vital to developing meaning. In groups, students negotiate their role and together work toward a solution. They also co-learn with the teacher who acts as a facilitator. Since the investigation may take students in various directions and is not prescribed with specific outcomes, the research recommends you not assign roles but instead allow them to evolve (Marx, Blumenfeld, Kracjik, & Soloway, 1997).

When students work collaboratively in PjBL, heterogeneous grouping is recommended (Cheng, Lam, & Chan, 2008). This means that you, the teacher, predetermine the groups by strategically placing students who learn at high, middle, and low levels in the same group. One way to do this is to organize a class list, by placing your students from low to high based on achievement. Using the list, select a low, middle, and then high student and assign these to a group. Continue this process until you have placed all your students in a group. These groups then become the heterogeneous groups in which the students work throughout their investigation. We recommend creating new groups for future tasks so that students learn to work with many different classmates over time. Research also recommends that groups not exceed four students per group or they become too large and students do not share the load of responsibility (Marzano et al., 2001).

Two key things you must consider for group work is students must be taught how to listen to each other and to think before they respond (Palinscar & Brown, 1984). Explicitly plan for ways to encourage active listening and engagement in discussions with their peers. This might consist of a quick check-in and share-out before students get started with their projects. You might also have students provide peer feedback and encourage students to incorporate their peers' ideas into their projects. Creating a community of students who learn from one another takes time and practice, but these are behaviors you can establish with your students which will last a lifetime. With PjBL you are really setting the stage for students to be college and career ready. In your planning sheet, we have included a section that addresses the 4Cs of 21st Century Skills: collaboration, communication, critical thinking, and creativity. Think about which skills you will address that best support your students to thrive in the real world.

 Stop and Reflect

The 4Cs of 21st Century Skills, collaboration, communication, critical thinking, and creativity are identified as skills students will need to be college and career ready. How might you address these areas in a PjBL activity?

_____

_____

The Challenge of Group Work

Most students have not been given such freedom and autonomy in their work and will be challenged at first managing, pacing, and organizing their ideas and strategies in a PjBL activity. Thus, it is critical you anticipate these challenges and provide scaffolds for students. It may also be beneficial to start with smaller problems first and then build students' experience with complexity over time as a scaffold for independent learning. The following graphic organizer may be helpful as a planning page for students as they go through their investigation with their group.

Require that student groups complete the following record:

1. Identify **what we know**. Students examine the driving question and pull out pieces of information and list what they know from the question and supporting materials.
2. Identify **what we need to know**. Students examine the driving question for the unknown information both explicit and implicit in the prompt and make a record.
3. Identify **where to look for information** (beyond the teacher!).
4. Students **assign specific jobs** to members of the team. The teacher can be a part of this, especially for students with learning difficulties to ensure they are given an appropriate challenge and necessary support.

5. Record **what we found**. Students record the steps taken.
6. Identify **next steps** in the investigation. Students ask themselves what they should plan to do the next day.

This PjBL Organizer should be completed every day students work on the project as they move themselves through their self-identified steps. Filling out the steps every day helps students see that they are going through a cycle of problem-solving. They must constantly assess and reassess what they need to pursue and what tasks are at hand. Using a graphic organizer provides a tangible method for organizing, self-regulating, and collaboratively tackling each of the steps in problem-solving. The graphic organizer also acts as a tool for reflection and goal setting, two necessary metacognitive strategies for those who engage in any sustained problem-solving task.

🛍 Snag It: **shorturl.at/gKOY2**

A digital copy is provided of the PjBL Organizer for students to record their planning and data.

PjBL Organizer—Date _____

1. What we know	2. What we need to know

3. Where to look for or gather information	4. Assigned jobs
	1. _____ 2. _____ 3. _____ 4. _____

5. What we found	6. Next steps

Connecting the Standards for Mathematical Practice to PjBL

We think the SMPs fit nicely with this approach to instruction. Throughout the stages of a project, students have many opportunities to connect to the SMPs. In the first stage of the project your students are likely to "make sense of problems and persevere in solving them" (SMP #1). This is essential for students to think about the task and how they will approach it. In the next stage, students are working on task in a group, and these tasks should provide students with an opportunity to "model with mathematics" (SMP #4) and "use appropriate tools strategically" (SMP #5). When students are in the final stage of the project and are sharing their final products with peers and other people, they most certainly will have an opportunity to "attend to precision" (SMP #6) and "construct viable arguments and critique the reasoning of others" (SMP #3).

The chart below provides a description of how you might consider the SMPs in your planning of a PjBL activity. (NGA & CCSSO, 2010)

Standards for Mathematical Practice	Description
1. Make sense of problems and persevere in solving them	Students explain the meaning of a problem by identifying its parts, a point of entry, and work toward a solution, making changes as necessary. They should persist with solving even when the problem is difficult.
2. Reason abstractly and quantitatively	Students are to deconstruct a given situation by identifying quantities using symbolic representations or pictures. In addition, students should make sense of the quantities and units.
3. Construct viable arguments and critique the reasoning of others	Students are to justify their solutions and present their reasoned statements to others. They should also listen to other's mathematical arguments, ask questions, and critique their validity.
4. Model with mathematics	Students are to solve problems in real life by using illustrations, diagrams, or objects to show their understanding. They may also include equations to demonstrate their understanding of a given situation.
5. Use appropriate tools strategically	Students are to select the appropriate tools and apply them to a given task. Tools may include concrete models, paper, pencil, rulers, protractors, and calculators.

Standards for Mathematical Practice	Description
6. Attend to precision	Students are to clearly discuss and articulate their own reasoning using mathematically accurate language. As well, students are to attend to precision in their accuracy in solving problems, specifying units, and labeling solutions.
7. Look for and make use of structure	Students are to find patterns and structure in numbers, equations, and collections of objects.
8. Look for and express regularity in repeated reasoning	Students are to look for numbers or calculations that are repeated to find methods and shortcuts when solving problems.

Planning PjBL Activities

Designing your own PjBL activity means you are taking into consideration your students' interests and funds of knowledge. Funds of knowledge are your students' experiences outside of school and home knowledge that they can draw on and apply to their academic learning (Moll, Amanti, Neff, & Gonzalez, 1992). There are many PjBL activities available online, but nothing will match your students' interests and abilities unless it comes from you. It is important to know the steps to designing your own activities since it will meet your students' developmental and curricular needs, and highlight their interests as you know your students best.

We have identified three stages to successfully plan a PjBL activity:

Stage 1: Setting the scope

Stage 2: Goals and targets to support all learners

Stage 3: Assessing and reflecting

In the first stage of planning, determine the driving question, what students will accomplish in the project, what standards the project will meet, and how you will present the project to your class. In stage two, identify goals and targets for students to achieve as they work throughout the task, including modifications or adaptations to support students who are second-language learners and/or have academic or social-emotional challenges. In the third stage, determine how you will assess student work, both as a final product and throughout the project while working in small groups, with a partner, or individually. Similarly, determine how students will reflect throughout the project, such as by asking questions or engaging in classroom discourse. Be sure you include how this evidence will be recorded and shared.

Stage 1: Setting the Scope

Project-Based Learning Planning Template

Teacher Name: **Grade Level:**   **Project Title:**

Content Standards Addressed: (National Math Standards or Common Core/NGSS)

Cross-Curriculum Connections: (other standards and subjects you will address in this project)

<u>Driving Question</u>: (the question that drives the work)		
Project Summary: (what students will do, learn, and accomplish by the end of the project)		
<u>21st Century Skills</u>: (what will be taught and assessed—based on 4Cs framework)	Creativity:	Critical Thinking:
	Collaboration:	Communication:

1. **Content Standards and Cross Curricular Concepts:** Identify the math concepts and skills your students need to learn or that they can use in review (see Chapter 2). Include how cross-disciplinary concepts will be incorporated to reinforce the math concepts and apply them meaningfully.
2. **Driving Question:** Identify a question or problem that fits your students' interests and developmental needs and incorporates the concepts and skills in your standards.
3. **Project Summary:** What do you want students to do, learn, and accomplish by the end of the project?

4. **21st Century Skills:** Determine how the project can include the four Cs throughout the scope and sequence of the project. How might technology be included as a means to support students in achieving the 21st century skills?

Stage 2: Goals and Targets to Support All Learners

Stage 2: Goals and Targets to Support All Learners

Learning Outcomes and Targets: (what targets students will meet to be able to complete the project)

Instructional Strategies: (what you will provide to support student learning, scaffolding information with materials and lessons aligned to learning outcomes and assessment)

Checkpoint: (how you will ensure all students are on track and moving toward the learning goal)

Learning Outcomes and Targets: Identify what learning outcomes you want students to achieve throughout the project. This might consist of more than just math, such as the ability to communicate ideas effectively in their group and critique each other's project by attending to precision with mathematical language. The targets you set should be how you chunk the project to meet checkpoints along the way. Your project might be to create a vegetable stand for a class farmers' market, but your students will need to first investigate seasonal fruit in the area, determine a cost point, and work with a budget to make a profit. There are three targets for this particular activity.

Instructional Strategies: Review the target, outcomes, what your students will be doing throughout the project, and determine appropriate scaffolds that you will utilize to support student learning. This might include criteria charts, graphic organizers, student groupings, video presentations, and one-on-one and team meetings throughout the project.

Checkpoint: Set the stage for how you will frequently provide both group and individual feedback throughout the project. Determine what kinds of technology you might consider using to provide you with the power to assess students both formally and informally.

Stage 3: Assessing and Reflecting

Stage 3: Assess and Reflect

Assessment Products:	Individual:	Specific Evidence and Completion:
	Group:	Specific Evidence and Completion:
Reflection Methods: (how students will capture their thinking across the scope of the project)	Individual: (graphic organizer/journal)	Group/Team:
	Whole Class:	Other:

Assessment Products

Individual: How will you assess students individually? Provide ideas for specific evidence and completion of product. If students are creating a final product as a group, what else might you consider as an individual assessment such as a journal log, quiz, or writing sample?

Group: Determine how you will assess students as a group. This should be shared with students before the beginning of group work. The assessment might include a group evaluation as part of their final presentation or a peer evaluation in which members of the group evaluate each other.

Reflection Methods

Individual: What methods will you use to support students in reflecting individually on their own work and effort? You might include an exit ticket at the end of each day or a journal entry that is shared only with the teacher.

Group/Team: How will you encourage reflection as a group? What specific strategies might you implement such as having students' groups respond to prompts or share areas of challenge and ways to grow within their group members?

Whole Class: How will you take time throughout the group project to reflect on what is working and what is not working? You might consider having a bulletin board space as an ongoing space for reflection where students can record their questions and what they have learned throughout the project.

Other: What other people and ways might you include as a reflective way to share students' growth and progress on the activity? Will you use social media tools such as SeeSaw or Edmodo, a school website to share photos of students collaborating, or email updates on students' progress?

The following is a fourth-grade PjBL Planning Template example:

Project-Based Learning Planning Template		
Teacher Name:	**Grade Level:**	**Project Title:**
Dr. Coddington	4th–5th	Playground Planning

Content Standards Addressed: (National Math Standards or Common Core)

Solve problems involving measurement and conversion of measurements.

CCSS.MATH.CONTENT.4.MD.A.1

Know relative sizes of measurement units within one system of units including km, m, cm; kg, g; lb, oz.; L, mL; and hr, min, sec. Within a single system of measurement, express measurements in a larger unit in terms of a smaller unit. Record measurement equivalents in a two-column table. For example, know that 1 foot is 12 times as long as 1 inch and the length of a 4-foot snake is 48 inches. Generate a conversion table for feet and inches listing the number pairs (1, 12), (2, 24), (3, 36).

CCSS.MATH.CONTENT.4.MD.A.3

Apply the area and perimeter formulas for rectangles in real world and mathematical problems. For example, find the width of a rectangular room given the area of the flooring and the length by viewing the area formula as a multiplication equation with an unknown factor.

Cross-Curriculum Connections: (other standards and subjects you will address in this project)

CCSS.ELA-LITERACY.W.4.1

Write opinion pieces on topics or texts supporting a point of view with reasons and information.

CCSS.ELA-LITERACY.SL.5.4

Report on a topic or text or present an opinion, sequencing ideas logically and using appropriate facts and relevant, descriptive details to support main ideas or themes; speak clearly at an understandable pace.

CCSS.ELA-LITERACY.SL.5.5

Include multimedia components (e.g., graphics, sound) and visual displays in presentations when appropriate to enhance the development of main ideas or themes.

VA:Cr1.1.4a

Brainstorm multiple approaches to a creative art or design problem.

STAGE 1: PLANNING:

<u>**Driving Question:**</u> **(the question that drives the work)**	How can you organize the playground to include a new piece(s) of equipment? Where would you place the new equipment so it is safe for kids?
Project Summary: **(what students will do, learn and accomplish by the end of the project)**	The playground is getting new equipment! In this task, you have been asked by the principal to give a recommendation for additional playground equipment to add to the playground. In order to proceed, you need to research the following: a. How big is the existing playground? b. What already exists on the playground? (Create a scale model on a grid of the playground and existing equipment.) c. What additional equipment do you want to add and how can it be added safely? Determine the cost. d. Plan where you would put the new equipment on the scale model. Make sure it fits safely! e. Create a proposal for your meeting with the principal using Google Slides. Show on your model where the new equipment should be placed and why. Use the model to defend your idea. Write and record your defense of the plan detailing why your model is safe and reasonable.
<u>**21st Century Skills:**</u> **(what will be taught and assessed based on 4Cs framework)**	**Creativity:** Students decide which equipment they want added to the playground and where it is to be placed. They also must develop a scale model of the playground. **Collaboration:** Students will work together to determine the size of playground, develop a model of the playground with the new equipment, and defend their idea. **Critical Thinking:** Students must determine the cost of the playground additions, develop a scale model of the playground, and decide where the equipment should be placed. Students must provide rationale for the safety of the placement. **Communication:** Students will use Google Docs to present their idea to the principal along with a written plan and model.

Opening Event: (how you will engage the students and spark their interest)	I will create a short iMovie to pitch the idea. The movie will feature our playground, focusing in on various pieces of equipment. At the end of the video, the students will be challenged with the scenario and the driving question.
Question to Lead the Discussion	• What actions helped you in the development of your project? • In what way was your team successful? • How could your team have worked more effectively or efficiently? • What was the greatest challenge? How did you overcome it? • What did you learn as a result of this investigation?
Resources and Materials	**Material/Equipment:** TV or monitor for video viewing Builder's measuring tapes Rulers Example scale drawings Graph paper List of playground equipment with given dimensions Math textbooks **Technology:** Hardware - Chrome Book or iPad Software - Google Slides **Community/Onsite people:** Principal

Think About It!

How does this type of activity meet the demands of the Standards for Mathematical Practice discussed in Chapter 2?

_____

_____

_____

Integrating Technology with PjBL

Throughout this chapter, we have highlighted best practices to integrate technology throughout your PjBL activity. Let's recap some of the best practices on how you can seamlessly integrate technology into your activities.

Tech to Research: Throughout this chapter, we have shared ways that you can use technology to have students research concepts (such as the animal investigation) or get data (prices of homes). We think getting and retrieving information is much more efficient with technology, especially when technology is at students' fingertips. The key for teachers is to make this information accessible. Creating documents with hyperlinks to trusted websites will ensure your students' browser will land safely on a desired page.

Tech to Organize: The success of your students' projects resides in part in the way you organize and guide their learning throughout the project. Creating digital templates with criteria charts and templates keeps students on task and goal directed. Watching a how-to video on Khan Academy, recording research information, and collaborating with peers can be quite overwhelming and confusing to students if the organization and plan is not clear. There are numerous sites out there that will manage your weblinks and organize your files, but instead of looking for the latest gadget to hit the web, focus on the simplest one that will fit the need. We find that organizing everything with Google Classroom keeps all of our work under one umbrella and provides a safety net for our students to explore without getting overwhelmed.

Tech to Practice: Let's face it, sometimes math students just need practice in order to develop fluency. When it comes to developing students' computational fluency, technology games and adaptive learning can provide instruction that best matches your students' abilities. We strongly encourage providing such opportunities in your PjBL tasks. This will boost your students' confidence and make them feel more competent when working with their peers. Math Playground (https://www.mathplayground.com/) and Academic skill builder (https://www.arcademics.com/) are two fun websites that will support building computational fluency.

Technology to Create: Students' products of learning should be driven by choice (from the student) and not necessarily what works best with the rubric. Although some students might enjoy the process of creating a website to showcase the virtual playground they created, other students might enjoy building a real model with legos. Products of learning should be student-centered and based on their preference. Technology can capture what students create with screencasts to record their explanations to images and digital models that provide an accurate representation. The aesthetic of what students create should not be more important than the math that represents what they create.

There are many possible types of activities around which to plan a PjBL task. Here are some other suggestions:

K-2: Driving Question	PjBL Tasks	Technology Integration
Counting and Cardinality Create a board game that will help your classmates practice counting objects and identifying the number.	Create a board game for your friends to play. Determine the number of spaces and layout of the board. Write directions for how to play and how to win the game.	Have students explore and play online board games to record features of a game. Create a digital game using Quizziz (https://quizizz.com/) or Kahoot (https://create.kahoot.it/) based on math content and have students create a board game using these web-based tools. Students can also create a game on Scratch (https://scratch.mit.edu/).
Addition and Subtraction With Money How can we design a better lunch menu for our school with healthier food options?	Decide what changes you can make to the current lunch menu and create a new menu with different options and prices. Determine the difference between the items you are exchanging.	Practice exchanging money game. Use Google Chrome Extension Money Pieces by Math Learning Center to create scenarios for students to solve.
Data and Graphing What kinds of questions can we ask to learn more about our classmates?	Create an all about our class book using data from student polls to share connections. Examine patterns in students' interests.	Students can use NCES Create a Graph https://nces.ed.gov/nceskids/createagraph/ to create a visual representation of their data. Once their data is created have students use the tool Book Creator (https://bookcreator.com/) to share their data and explain their findings.

3–5: Driving Question	PjBL Tasks	Technology Integration
Decimals You're opening an online store to showcase your favorite collectibles. What's the best way to sell your products?	Design an online store using your knowledge of decimals and current prices of products you would like to sell. Design a website to showcase your products. Determine the cost, tax, and price of shipping.	Investigate online products you are familiar with for your store. You can choose to create a website using Blogger or Kidblog. https://kidblog.org/home/
Adding and Subtracting Fractions It's Back to School night and you and your team are managing the pizza booth. Create at least four pizzas to sell. Each pizza must be the same size but represent different fraction values. Use fractions to create recipes for each pizza you create.	During a school family activity, students are managing a pizza food booth where they will sell by the slice. Students must anticipate how many pizzas they must preorder based on anticipated consumption. They must also calculate anticipated sales and earnings.	Use the National Library of Virtual Manipulatives app to practice creating equivalent fractions using circles. Use Google Drawings to illustrate and create pizzas. Determine different fractional pieces and equivalency for pizza slices and costs. Have students include their images in a Google Slide presentation and teach another class about equivalent fractions.
Geometry and Graphing It's Spring Break and you have 4 days to go camping with your family. Determine the best location where you can enjoy the beach and your family.	Plan a camping trip determine the distance, price for meals and entry to state park and additional excursions. Supplies and menus for each night and what size food portion each person in your family will receive.	Use Google Maps to plot points for the field trip and create an audio narration of the trip with Adobe Spark Determine the classification of animals, trees, birds, and flowers that are native to the area. Create a park brochure with Canva (https://www.canva.com/).
6–8	**PjBL TASK**	**Technology Integration**
Fraction, Decimal, Percent Your job is a dietician and creates healthy food plans for clients.	Plan a daily or weekly menu based on recommended calories per day using a given list of foods and calories.	Use Popplet to plan menu. https://www.choosemyplate.gov/MyPlatePlan Gather information from National Food Activity https://ndb.nal.usda.gov/ndb/search/list

Expressions and Equations

Your job as a stock market analyst is to make recommendations for clients to purchase company stock. Determine which stocks to purchase and monitor your gains and losses.

Create a stock market analysis briefing for a stock you are following. Create an equation to determine growth or loss over time for five different stocks. Given a budget of 10,000 determine which stocks to purchase and the price. Create line graphs to monitor loss and profits for your clients.

Use Excel or Google Sheets to calculate price points including purchase, selling, profit, and loss. Use digital tools to track stocks https://finance.yahoo.com/

http://news.morningstar.com/briefnet/marketupdate.aspx?page=StockMarket Update

Graph results using Desmos. https://www.desmos.com/

Statistics and Probability

You work for a fashion magazine and need to write an article on current teenage trends.

Write an e-zine with your group to be distributed at our school. Collect data and analyze findings.

Use Google Forms to create a survey for students to create digital data. Share question set on Twitter or Facebook to get a bigger data set.

Geogebra to graph results https://www.geogebra.org/

Students can use the webtool Flipsnack to create a digital ezine (https://www.flipsnack.com/ezine/)

9–12 Driving Question	Project-based Learning Task	Technology Integration
Geometry You are crafting a kite for Kite Flying Day. Your kite should contain two-dimensional triangles to form a tetrahedral.	Construct a kite and determine the surface area and volume. How many two-dimensional triangles will you need to form a kite?	Use Tinkercad to create a digital model of your kite. (https://www.tinkercad.com/).
Trigonometric Ratio You are a geologist and need to determine the height of a tree and the proximity to a home. The tree is no longer alive and the owner is afraid if it falls, it will land on her house.	Build a clinometer to determine the height of the tall tree and the proximity to the home.	Students use Flipgrid to share their report and demonstrate the use of their clinometer.

Systems of Linear Equations	Use a cartesian plane to graph equations and plan a unique community. Utilize systems of equations to map streets.	Students use EquatIO to graph equations and plan their community (https://www.texthelp.com/products/equatio/).
You are a city planner and need to determine how to support the growth of a community. You will need to develop a plan in place to ensure the community will be efficient and continue to grow.		

Additional Ideas:

- Plan a holiday party in which students must plan a menu and activities with a given budget and criteria. Create an electronic invitation for the party.
- Plan a school garden in which students design the dimensions of the garden beds and select plants within a given budget. Determine a schedule for planting and harvesting crops that are best grown in your geographical region.
- Create an event for students to participate in at a school Olympics. Write the rules and demonstrate the procedures. Collect event data and summarize data distribution among age groups, grade levels, and gender.
- Design an amusement park in which you must create a map of the area with rides and height requirements for riders. Determine what concession booths your park will have and costs for tickets.

 Watch It

https://youtu.be/Jcq1OYuXRzE

In this video, second- and third-grade students explain a math game they created and how to win the game.

 Try It!

Now it is your turn to try your hand at writing a prompt for a PjBL driving question. Select a grade level and examine the standards for concepts and skills. Go through these steps:

1. Identify specific concepts and skills your students need to learn or that they can use in review (see Chapter 2).
2. Identify a topic that fits your students' interests and developmental needs that also incorporates the concepts and skills to be learned.

3. Write a driving question that outlines the investigation for students.

_____

_____

_____

_____

Assessing PjBL Tasks

Anytime you use a task that is nontraditional, open ended, and performance based the assessment must match the task. Obviously, using a multiple choice assessment to evaluate students' scale models of the playground plan would not make sense! Therefore, when evaluating students' progress, you need to identify your criteria and develop a rubric to match.

Typically, we develop rubrics with several categories, each with specific requirements, or criteria to be met at various levels. Providing a rubric allows students to see the criteria that will evaluate their work. A rubric makes clear the expectations students must meet and takes away the "got you" kind of evaluation that happens when expectations are unclear or poorly communicated.

In the following Playground Task Rubric, notice the categories on the left. These categories identify the specific areas in which students are to be evaluated. The numbers represent levels of accomplishment based on the criteria. You want to identify the categories that fit your specific task question. What are you expecting students to research? How will they present and defend their ideas? What evidence do you expect students to provide for their thinking and solution? You may also want to include students' ongoing record of their steps and thinking as a part of the evaluation. You may also have students submit for evaluation their graphic organizers or journals showing their thoughts and progress.

Playground Task Rubric

Categories	3	2	1	0
Playground Plan	Playground plan is accurate and includes an appropriate scale model of the playground with the new equipment added; shows accurate area, perimeter, dimensions, and scale.	Playground plan includes a mostly accurate model of the playground with the new equipment; shows somewhat accurate area, perimeter, dimensions, and scale.	Playground plan includes a model of the playground with the new equipment that is limited in accuracy; includes area, perimeter, dimensions, and scale that are not accurate.	Does not include a model of the playground with the new equipment; no area, perimeter, dimensions, or scale included.

Categories	3	2	1	0
Critical Thinking	Written response to the driving question is accurate and provides a thoughtful, critical defense showing strong mathematical reasoning.	Written response to the driving question is somewhat accurate and provides a defense with mathematical reasoning.	Written response to the driving question is provided but may not be accurate or provide mathematical reasoning.	No written explanation or mathematical reasoning is provided in response to the driving question.
Documentation and/or Journal	Project documentation/journal is complete and reflects a detailed record of the investigation.	Project documentation/journal is somewhat complete and reflects a record of the investigation.	Project documentation/journal is missing data and parts of the investigation.	Project documentation/journal is missing most information.
Teamwork and Communication	The group worked effectively and strategically to investigate the driving question.	The group worked together with some effectiveness to investigate the driving question.	The group struggled to work effectively while investigating the driving question.	The group required significant assistance to work together.
Organization and Neatness	Final products have clear and coherent organization and are neatly presented.	Final products demonstrate organization and are somewhat neatly presented.	Final products have limited organization and neatness.	Final products are lacking organization and neatness.

Summary

If the goal of education is to prepare students to be college and career ready, then PjBL is the way to go. With this approach to instruction, you can design projects that best captures students' interests and provides the individualized support they need to be successful. The process is not always linear and there is much preparation to do, but when it comes to student engagement, kids love PjBL and they learn so much! For many students this is the first time math actually makes sense because it is rooted in their lives and experiences. PjBL is the perfect place to go digital. When Dr. Dickenson first began teaching middle school, one of the most challenging aspects of PjBL was organizing seven classes with 49 different projects. Using digital tools and resources, students manage their own projects and teachers can provide feedback and suggestions instantaneously.

Additional Activities/Discussion Questions

1. Review the framework for 21st Century Learning (http://www.p21.org/about-us/p21-framework) and determine which skills are your strengths and some areas for growth.
2. Select one of the activities shared and create a rubric to evaluate students' final products.
3. Design a digital to-do list for a project-based activity. Create hyperlinks to tasks that students must complete for their project.

Instructor Activities

1. Use one of the project-based activities we have shared with you to have students experience what it is like to work on a project in a group. Remember, teachers tend to teach the way they were taught; this is especially important if your students have never experienced working on a group project. You will need to be very explicit with your expectations.
2. Have students create a PjBL activity in a grade-level group. Create folders for each group to share their project with other groups and provide feedback.

Chapter 7

Problem-Based Learning

Self-Reflection

What kinds of problems do you like to solve and what strategies do you use? What kinds of problems do you solve in everyday life? How do you rate your problem-solving skills?

There are two versions of math in the lives of many Americans: the strange and boring subject that they encountered in classrooms and an interesting set of ideas that is the math of the world, and is curiously different and surprisingly engaging. Our task is to introduce this second version to today's students, get them excited about math, and prepare them for the future.

—Jo Boaler

Timmy and Anna play the popular video game Minecraft for hours after school. In the game, they are building dwellings, constructing roadways, and approximating the distance between two points. But when it comes to applying the strategies they are using in this popular game to solving problems in their classroom, they are unable to do so. Despite having informal math strategies, which they apply intuitively during game play, transfer to formal mathematics does not occur.

From playing games, counting objects, and constructing figures with toys children naturally possess mathematical strategies, problem-solving, and reasoning. However, when students come into the classroom their intuitive knowledge is often disconnected from the formal math lesson. A connection between the informal strategies students bring into the classroom and the formal strategies they are learning about must be made to make mathematics meaningful. Formal strategies are aligned with grade-level standards and are often explicitly taught by the classroom teacher. Informal strategies are situated in the lives of students and are intuitive. According to the National Math Council (2004), classroom teachers should design instructional activities that incorporate students' preconceptions and allow students to use their informal problem-solving strategies toward deeper math thinking and more effective strategies.

Making a connection between students' informal and formal math strategies means you know the lives of the students you teach.

From the prior knowledge students bring into the classroom, to how they spend their time after school, the more you understand the lives of the students you teach the better you can build this bridge so that students are engaged and connected to the math.

© Patricia Dickenson

Think About It!

How is problem-solving and mathematical reasoning part of children's everyday lives? Can you think of a few scenarios in which students use mathematics informally?

_____

_____

The Purpose of Problem-Based Learning

Problem-based learning (PBL) is an essential aspect of a solid mathematics program. It requires complex thinking and challenges students to express their ideas in multiple ways. From solving a problem using the standard algorithm, to creating a mathematical model that represents what they know about a concept, students are challenged to do it all. Moreover, with PBL students are required to think like mathematicians as they look for patterns, try out multiple strategies, apply techniques, and communicate their thinking. Students will not become independent problem-solvers if they are constantly relying on the teacher to tell them how to solve problems. PBL draws on funds of knowledge, or outside school knowledge, brought to the classroom to engage students with authentic tasks in which they must develop their ability to explain their thinking and communicate mathematically.

It is important to recognize the attributes of strong PBL tasks:

- Strongly connects to the underlying mathematical concepts in a way that promotes a rich class discussion.
- Supports students in identifying and utilizing strategies that illustrate both conceptual understanding and procedural fluency.
- Promotes multiple solution paths and provides students with multiple tools to utilize throughout the problem-solving process.
- Allows students to apply the mathematical language and/or notation throughout their work.

© Patricia Dickenson

Putting Research into Practice

You might wonder what the research has to say about PBL and its impact on student learning and achievement. There are many studies that have identified the benefits of PBL. These studies show that PBL can improve students' higher level thinking skills, motivation, and engagement (Wirkila & Kuhn, 2011). Other studies have shown that students engaged in PBL perform academically at or above those who engage in traditional classroom instruction in their ability to flexibly problem-solve, generate hypotheses, and apply knowledge (Dochy, Segers, Van den Bossche, & Gijbels, 2003). Moreover, studies have found increased ability to formulate explanations and generate hypotheses (Hmelo, 1998; Wirkila & Kuhn, 2011). PBL has been shown to benefit students both social and academically.

> Classroom practices in countries with exceptional math scores on international assessments have shown the use of problem-based learning as a part of regular math practice (TIMMS, 2015).

For example, students in Japan spend an entire class period engaged in solving a single problem. When researchers examined math instruction in Japan, they found the typical lesson unfolded with a brief review and then students worked on solving a single, rich problem. After solving the problem, these students shared multiple solutions and the lesson ended with a teacher-led discussion. Unlike math instruction in the United States, in which students are typically shown a demonstration of a procedure followed by practicing many problems, Japanese students worked on only one problem without much demonstration (Stevenson & Stigler, 1992). Instruction of this kind is considered inquiry-based and can also be considered problem-based.

 Across the Curriculum

In English Language Arts engaging with the text requires problem-solving skills. Students can consider multiple solutions to a characters' problem and what steps they must take to overcome a situation. Have your students write an equation to represent a relationship.

Making a Connection with PBL

Let's go back to our example of Timmy and Anna who are second graders learning about place value. Perhaps you are wondering how a standards-based curriculum can connect to the informal strategies these children are using in the game of Minecraft.

In second grade, you find the following standard:

> Cluster B: Use place value understanding and properties of operations to add and subtract. Students need problem contexts in which they must model addition with sums up to 1,000. This includes having students use concrete materials to create addition examples.

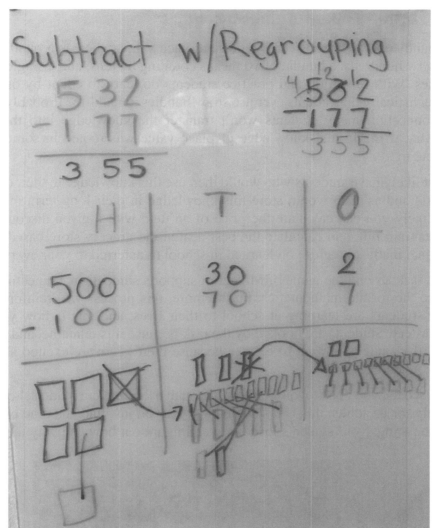

© Patricia Dickenson

As discussed in earlier chapters, teachers should have students begin with the concrete, then move to pictures and last numerals. Also take note of the standard above which focuses on understanding place value and the properties of operations. This means developing students' conceptual understanding of place value and using the properties accordingly to support flexibility with numbers. Nowhere in the standard cluster above are students expected to work with the standard algorithm (carrying, borrowing, etc.); in fact, students do not even encounter this algorithm until they are in fourth grade.

> How might a focus on developing conceptual understanding as illustrated in the subtraction problem above support students' problem-solving skills?

Connecting Formal and Informal Strategies

Traditionally, bundled straws are used to represent place value, whereas a bundle of hundred means counting by hundreds, a bundle of 10 means counting by tens, and a single straw means counting by ones. With repetition and practice students do learn to count by ones, tens, and hundreds, but realistically do students ever use straw bundles in real life? Probably not. Without a purposeful connection many students won't transfer the knowledge into their long-term memory. But what if the formal knowledge of place value was rooted in something second graders can relate to?

You would most likely have students who would then use this knowledge in their everyday lives (outside of class) and as such would store this knowledge in their long-term memory. Think about it, most likely you can calculate the price of an item with a given discount, determine the tip on a restaurant bill, and calculate the best deal at the grocery store based on unit rates because the formal math strategies you learned in school transferred to your everyday life.

Building a PBL task around the game of Minecraft supports students in connecting their informal strategies to the formal mathematics. Furthermore, this process will reinforce the formal math strategies students are learning at school to their lives, and this is how you move students toward mastery. Students are hooked by the task because it is relatable, and even students who don't play the game will want to engage because their peers are excited about the task. Enthusiasm is contagious!

As classroom teachers, you need to know where the math exists in your students' everyday lives, and unfortunately for us adults, this is not something you can just find and read on the Internet. You might try the things your students love to do and figure out how and why they are doing it

© Patricia Dickenson

(e.g., computer games). After investigating the game of Minecraft, a teacher can realize she can build place value concepts into her lesson because students are estimating values and using mental computation strategies in the game when constructing their virtual world. When we tap into these informal strategies, we are accessing students' funds of knowledge, which is their knowledge based on home and life experiences outside of school (Moll, Amanti, Neff, & Gonzalez, 1992).

You've probably heard of these popular games, Pokemon, Fruit Ninja, and Roblox, but did you know these games include mathematical concepts such as fractions, area, addition, and subtraction with base ten? Your students will be so excited when you connect the math to the games they enjoy playing.

 **Try It!**

Discover a few popular games your students enjoy playing at home and then review the games to determine where the math connections are and how you might make formal connections to the math strategies.

_____

_____

Structure of PBL

Designing instruction for PBL requires teachers to make informed decisions about what informal mathematical knowledge, or funds of knowledge, students bring into the classroom. They must then determine how that knowledge can be situated in a problem-solving activity to support students in using their informal knowledge to develop a range of strategies and reach accurate solutions. In our work with teachers, we typically walk them through a process for either creating or modifying an existing PBL task from their curriculum so that it is connected to their instructional context and students. We strongly recommend that you use this process when you create or modify a PBL task from a text or outside resource.

Step 1: Identify the mathematical goals for the lesson.
- What should students know and be able to do by the end of this lesson?

Step 2: Identify how the task will connect to students' informal and formal math knowledge.
- Identify students' prior knowledge they have already acquired that will support them in the task and the concepts and ideas they need to understand in order to engage in the task.
- Determine how the task will connect to the lives of students and what you might do to hook the students and engage them in the problem.
- Determine the language demands for the task and how you will support all learners in your class.

Step 3: Identify the tasks and all the ways the task can be solved.
- Include concrete, pictorial, and numerical representations.
- Share possible misconceptions and errors students might make.

Step 4: Identify student group work, roles, and expectations.
- Determine the time and the process for students to work throughout the task: small group, individual, and partner work.
- Select manipulatives and tools students have access to as they work through the problem.
- Determine how students will record and share their work.

🛍 **Snag It:** Make your own copy of a PBL Planner Template to use in planning PBL tasks PBL Planner template

Let's see this process in action. Dr. Dickenson has mapped out the second-grade Minecraft PBL task we discussed earlier. Each of the four steps listed above are articulated in the planner to support her thinking about how she will create and teach an engaging PBL task.

👁 **View It:** Minecraft Task

Teacher Name	Grade
Dr. Dickenson	2
Content Standards Addressed: (National Math Standard or Common Coro)	
Standard 2.NBT.B.7	
Add and subtract within 1,000, using concrete models or drawings and strategies based on the place value, properties of operations, and or the relationship between addition and subtraction; relate the strategy to a written method. Understand that in adding or subtracting three-digit numbers, one adds or subtracts hundreds and hundreds, tens and tens, ones and ones; and sometimes it is necessary to compose or decompose tens or hundreds.	

Mathematical Goal: Students will be able to . . .	Standard for Mathematical Practice:
Students will be able to compose and decompose tens and hundreds to solve problems using models and strategies.	SMP #1: Make Sense of Problems and Persevere in Solving Them SMP #4: Model with Mathematics
	SMP #5: Use Appropriate Tools Strategically

Informal Math Knowledge: Students can . . .	Formal Math Knowledge: Students need to know . . .
Understand the relationship between items and groups of items. For example, a dozen eggs contains 12 eggs. A package of gum contains 10 pieces.	Relationship between units, tens, and hundreds.

The Task and Hook: State the problem and how you will hook students

Introducing the problem and ask students what they notice and wonder. Post recording in Padlet T-Chart. Review concept of a bundle. We will create a bundle using tree template to compose a group of 10 trees into a bundle and decompose a tree into 10 wooden blocks.

PBL TASK:

In the game, Minecraft, Steve must build a castle to protect himself from the monsters that live in the nearby caves. He will need wooden blocks from trees to make a shelter.

One tree contain 10 wooden blocks. A bundle contains 10 trees
A. On the first day, Steven collected two bundles and four trees how many wooden blocks does Steve have all together?
B. On the second day, Steven collected three more bundles and three trees how many wooden blocks has he collected in total?
C. On the third day, Steve used 540 blocks to make a castle how many blocks does he have left?

In this first part of the planner, the connection between students' formal and informal strategies is identified and connected to the task and what students will actually do to solve the problem. Rather than just having the concept of Minecraft to get students interested, the tools and process of problem-solving is connected to the themes found in the Minecraft game.

Hook:

Students will use create mode in the computer lab to construct a castle in Minecraft. The problem will be presented with a Minecraft background and character for students to illustrate their castle upon problem completion.

Possible Solutions: (include all pictures, models, representations)

Students can build models using counters. Students will illustrate bundles of trees and show with models that one tree is equivalent to 10 blocks and 10 trees is equivalent to 100 wooden blocks.

Students will use the place value chart to compose and decompose tens and hundreds.

Possible Errors and Misconceptions:

Students who are counting with one-to-one correspondence may miscount and not see equivalency.

Students may fail to use estimation strategies to support them in determining if their answer is reasonable.

Students who do not know basic facts may have incorrect answers.

Language Demand	Scaffolding Strategies
Bundle may be a new word that students are not familiar with.	Use 3-Read strategy to read through the problem.
Teachers will need to make familiar associations such as bringing in a box of fruit snacks so students can see the associations between a box and the individual packages that the box contains. Teacher posts language words with picture on math word walls for review.	Create bundles of trees with kids so they can make an association using a representation.
	Have students cut a paper tree into 10 wooden blocks.
	Provide students with place value charts so they can organize their thinking and connect to place value.

Next, the teacher should identify possible solutions that students might consider. This process will support the teacher in providing materials to support as well as determine the kinds of questions to ask while students are engaged in the task. Determining possible errors and misconceptions should also be considered to support students both prior to and throughout the task. Scaffolding strategies can help students avoid possible errors and misconceptions, and the language demands of the task should be addressed at the onset of the task for students to be successful.

Time	Group Roles and Process	Evidence Collected
20	After the first 10 min, students will work collaboratively and share their solutions strategies. They will then create a poster to share with the class.	Group poster

Time	Individual Process	Evidence Collected
10	Students will begin the task individually to think of possible solutions before working in a group to share their responses and create a poster for sharing.	Student individual paper with the problem.

Time	Share Out Roles and Process	Evidence Collected
15	Teacher will circulate the room to determine the order of sharing. Incomplete work will be shared first to see what the students know and how they are thinking. Correct and complete answers will be shared last	Teacher notes on students sharing and questions asked to support thinking.

Notes, Resources, and Materials Needed:

Online tool Padlet is created for teacher to record students thinking about what they notice and wonder about the task.

Trees and bundle templates will be provided for students to make bundles and blocks. Place value charts can assist students to determine values and use mental math strategies for computation. Groups that finish early will be asked to begin constructing a physical model with the paper wooden blocks. Groups that finish their castle construction can use the computers to build a three-dimensional (3D) Minecraft model using an unlimited number of blocks. Comparisons among 3D models will be made and students can ask questions of 3D models during a class gallery walk.

Finally, it is essential to determine how the PBL task will unfold in your class. Depending on your class composition and learner preferences, you might begin by providing students with individual quiet time to map out their thinking process. Then students can work in small groups or with a partner to discuss their ideas and collaborate. Time is always important to consider and as such will influence the instructional choices you make. Regardless of whether students have found a solution, you should always make time for students to share their thinking process with their peers. Peer learning happens when students have an opportunity to share their thinking and listen to classmates discuss their mathematical models and process.

The place value concept is just one example of how you might make the connection to students' informal knowledge and the formal strategies in math. We shared just one way but, believe me, there are countless more.

◉ **View It:** In this video, see additional ideas for connecting math to the game of Minecraft: https://youtu.be/txJFAxg3SQU

Putting Planning into Action

Time is always a factor when implementing PBL tasks in your class. The process of planning has been articulated above but what you also need to consider is how this process will unfold in your class. The below graphic shares a suggested model for you to consider for implementation. The process begins with a teacher-led unpacking of the problem. This will ensure students understand the problem and are capable to work independently. During this time the teacher can have students act out the problem or model a simpler problem to establish understanding and activate prior knowledge. Visual aids are also used to demonstrate the context of the problem and are extremely useful with second-language learners. As noted in the graphic below, this first step should take about 10 min and include the teacher recording students' ideas and questions.

Student work time may include students working independently, in a small group, or with a partner. During this time, the teacher circulates the room to provide support and to identify which strategies will be shared during student-led share out. The teacher can debrief with students and share potential strategies about midpoint through student work time. This process will help struggling students hear what other students are doing and answer any questions students might have.

> An important aspect of getting students to develop strategies and build their confidence in math is providing an opportunity to talk about what they are doing and how they arrived at their solutions.

Pair-share is an opportunity for students to articulate their thinking with feedback and it also holds students accountable for doing the math. Many students are motivated to look competent with their peers and math talk does that.

In the final stage of the PBL task, you select students (no more than 5) to share their solutions and talk about their process. This is when you have a chance to see the Math Practice Standards in action when students have the opportunity to:

- Construct an argument to share their thinking (SMP #3).
- Demonstrate how they make sense of the problem and persevere in solving (SMP #1 & 2).
- Show a mathematical model to explain their thinking (SMP #4 & 5).
- Use mathematical terms and definitions when explaining their thinking (SMP # 6).
- Determine connections across solutions (SMP # 7 & 8).
- Listen attentively to critique others' reasoning (SMP #3 & 8).

By having students engage in the act of teaching their peers, you are truly "teaching outside the box" in which the traditional teacher-directed mode of transmitting information is dismantled and the onus of learning becomes situated where it belongs: on the students.

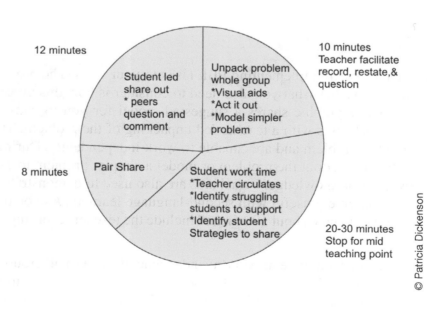

© Patricia Dickenson

Make the Tech Connection: Create

There are oodles of web-based tools and apps that will capture student thinking with digital recordings and images to show what they know. We have found even students in the early grades are excited and able to explain their thinking with these tools. Hand-held devices, such as cell phones and tablets, are the easiest to navigate once the app is downloaded onto the device. Students take a photo of their work and record their thinking as the image is displayed. Apps, such as Adobe Spark, Educreations, and Explain Everything will take a collection of student work samples into a slideshow with student narration. This will be great to share with parents during Open House.

PBL Does it All

PBL is used to engage students in rich problems and enhance their knowledge and problem-solving skills, but there are more reasons than just academic ones for using this approach. Here are five reasons for using PBL (Barrows & Kelson, 1995; Hmelo-Silver, 2004).

Supports the construction of deep and flexible knowledge

- Students gain knowledge and use it in flexible ways.
- Students demonstrate flexibility when they apply strategies and knowledge appropriately when meeting a new problem.
- Flexibility develops stronger understanding of concepts and deepens student knowledge.

Enhances the ability to develop effective problem-solving skills

- Students solve problems effectively by monitoring their own thinking by selecting and applying appropriate strategies, regulating their progress, monitoring their behaviors, and planning progress.
- Students use metacognition and engage in metacognition and critical thinking, which enhances problem-solving.

Develops self-directed learning skills

- Students make decisions about solving problems without being told steps to take.
- Students decide on a plan and reach an end goal.
- Students responsibly select, manage, and apply decisions and actions in problem-solving, and are forced to become self-directed in their learning.
- Students develop life skills for success.

Encourages effective collaboration skills

- Students learn skills of teamwork through collaboration.
- Students explain their ideas, listen actively, and come to consensus about steps to take.
- Builds skills of teamwork and communication shown to enhance learning (Webb & Palinscar, 1996).

Develops intrinsic motivation for learning

- Students feel the power to make decisions and building a sense of autonomy, and feel more motivated to learn.
- Students engage in meaningful tasks.
- Students engage in tasks at their "just right" level which will engage but not frustrate them, according to their zone of proximal development.

PBL packages everything kids crave: choice, autonomy, and meaningful collaborative learning. PBL also embeds the Standards for Mathematical Practice, develops students' 21st century skills, and strengthens students' content knowledge, requiring application of knowledge in flexible ways. Both the purpose for and byproduct of PBL are enhanced motivation and metacognitive skills. Why wouldn't we use this method? Perhaps we would rather see students getting the "right answer" and moving through textbook material or we feel that students are learning most when they solve a series of closed-ended problems.

> We need to examine our choices and reasons for why we are selecting methods of instruction and give opportunities for problem-solving in a variety of ways.

As we have seen across the Big 5 pedagogies, the focus is on 21st century skills, particularly the 4Cs: communication, collaboration, critical thinking, and creativity. Similarly, PBL promotes the development of new skills and knowledge through inquiry as well as critical thinking by using nontraditional methods. Student activities are very open-ended and inquiry-based thus resulting in self-directed learning and greater engagement and motivation.

We have identified some additional characteristics that distinguish PBL below.

Problem-Based Learning is	Problem-Based Learning is NOT
• Collaborative • Student-centered • Focused on complex, ill-structured problems • Set in real-life or fictitious contexts • Student self-initiated problem-solving using prior knowledge	• Independent • Teacher-centered • Focused on an easily solved, predictable, single-answer problems • Textbook driven • Teacher-initiated step-by-step problem-solving

Stop and Reflect

Why would you implement PBL in your classroom? What characteristics of PBL do you value?

_____

_____

PBL Across the Curriculum

Problem-based learning is the sweet spot for making interdisciplinary connections. Creating a context for learning based on what students are reading about in Social Studies or learning in Art can really make math come alive and bring value to a math problem. Students who are not excited about math can shift their perspective when their favorite subject such as Physical Education or Social Studies are taught through a math lens. Likewise, when Social Studies and Physical Education teachers can use math as a lens to examine an issue and problem-solve, students are encouraged to think critically and use the math to highlight a concern about an issue and how math can be used to highlight issues.

👁 **View it:** In this problem-based learning activity, math skills are reinforced through Physical Education and Social Studies content.

https://bit.ly/2SCIqaP

Similarly, math can be integrated in other subjects such as art and dance. When students examine problems in these subject-specific areas, they are also inspired to be change agents and challenge the status quo.

👁 **View it:** Dance Demographics: https://bit.ly/3hjJrN9

👁 **View it:** Fraction Art: https://bit.ly/3qBt6rn

The Role of Thinking in Problem-Solving

Metacognition plays an important role in learning and is responsible for how we think about what we know, such as activating knowledge, applying strategies, and self-regulating thinking. Metacognition is a form of knowledge drawn on regularly while problem-solving. Students have to assess the problem and what is being asked, which requires metacognitive processes to evaluate and sift mentally through ideas. Then, students must select a strategy that best fits the situation. To solve the problem, students must again draw on their metacognitive skills as they continuously regulate their mental activity, staying focused and managing the activation and application of their past and current knowledge. Usually, students have to remember previous procedural and content knowledge in order to respond to a problem (Anderson et al., 2001). PBL stimulates this type of mental activity and is the reason why it is a powerful approach for developing metacognitive and higher level thinking skills.

We want to infuse metacognition across our instruction, so here are some strategies for promoting it in your classroom that work across all grades and ages. You can use these strategies at all points during problem-solving: at the beginning, middle, and the end.

1. **Think-Pair-Share**

   This strategy gives students time to think and discuss a given question about an idea or topic and then share their response in partners. For example, if you want your fifth graders to connect to informal measurement strategies, you can ask students a question about their previous experiences with measurement at home as an introduction. Students may recall baking with measuring cups or building something using a builder's measuring tape. You need to give students at least 1 minute of think time and then share their ideas with their partner. Both partners should share equally about their ideas.

2. **Think Aloud**

   Simply put, to use this strategy you just think out loud whatever thinking process you are trying to get students to use or understand. For example, if you were modeling a think aloud for a problem using money, you might begin with the value of the coins, such as, "I need to remember how many pennies make a dime. Let me think about that. Oh right, it is worth 10 pennies or 10 cents." This type of modeling gives students a clear idea of how they should think. Students can also practice their own thinking aloud for each other in the process of learning a new concept or when solving problems. When students become accustomed to thinking aloud about their processes, they become more comfortable and confident explaining their thinking when sharing problem solutions in front of their peers.

3. **Graphic Organizers**

   Graphic organizers provide ways to analyze, organize, monitor, interpret, and represent thinking. Graphic organizers can be in the form of concept maps that organize content around a single idea, T-charts to compare or record thinking, Notice and Wonder charts, or organizational charts that structure, analyze, or organize ideas, such as the examples we have already provided in this chapter (PBL Planning Template, PBL Student Organizer). Graphic organizers assist the mind in managing and organizing information so that it can be processed and used more effectively and efficiently. Graphic organizers also help us make connections between and across ideas.

4. **Self-Assessment**

   Self-assessments can be used at any point during the learning process and can be focused on behavior or academics. The goal of self-assessment is to prompt awareness of one's self. For example, when solving a problem, you can ask students to simply give a thumb up (agree), down (disagree), or to the side (not sure) to show whether they understand what the problem is asking them to do. You can also provide reflective rubrics for students to answer that prompt specific questions or statements on which to reflect. (See an example of a self-assessment rubric toward the end of this chapter.) Self-assessment can occur while evaluating group process or when writing reflectively about what was learned after solving a problem, whether interpersonally or academically. Self-assessments can be easily captured on tools like Voice Thread or Flipgrid where students can take a picture of their own calculations or representations and record and reflect on the picture or process. Evidence of self-assessment can include just an oral recording instead of a written sentence or paragraph.

5. **Reflection**

   General forms of reflection on learning can happen at any time during the learning process. As the designer of the curriculum, you can purposefully plan reflective opportunities throughout the problem-solving phase during which you can prompt students to discuss in pairs or small groups what they have learned or whatever topic you think is important. You can also just stop at points and ask students to reflect in the midst of learning. By the way, have you noticed that we have the reader stop and reflect at various points throughout this book? We know the power of this strategy and have built it into our content to help you reflect. Take note, whenever you add reflection, you are capitalizing on students' metacognition and its power to engage, transform, and motivate their learning.

 Make the Tech Connection

Waiting for the class to begin in order for learning to occur is a thing of the past. Your class can be asynchronous to provide a place for students to connect and continue learning. Google Classroom allows you to create a virtual class where you can post announcements, share lectures, create assignments, and allow students to stay connected. The question features can promote a peer-supporting-peer platform where students can ask and answer questions. You determine the parameters and let learning be accessible no matter where your students are.

Students' Steps to Problem-Solving

There are essentially five steps students take when they engage in PBL. Each step enhances students' skills across the process of problem-solving.

Student Steps in PBL	Tech Integration
Step 1. Examine and evaluate the problem	Google slides
Students examine the problem and evaluate what is known and what is needed.	Popplet
	Sutori—timeline organizer if problem is story or historically based.

Student Steps in PBL	Tech Integration
Step 2. Make a plan Students develop a plan, including what is needed, where to gather additional information, and strategies to be applied.	Virtual Graph Paper Google docs Google Drawing Seesaw
Step 3. Create a representation to support their problem-solving process Students begin by modeling their ideas through drawing, graphing, or creating a visual to represent their thinking. During the modeling process, students may or may not come to a solution.	Padlet Seesaw Google slides Google Drawing Desmos Equatio Math Learning Center
Step 4. Reflect on and evaluate the results Students assess their thinking process and determine if it is reasonable and meets their planning goals. If it does not, they go back to Step 2 and revise their plan and go through the process once more.	Google Forms Survey Monkey Poll Everywhere Google Docs
Step 5. Share solutions and results Once students have met their goal and solved the problem, they can share their process and their solution with others. Sharing provides opportunities for examining and critiquing each other's process and solution (if reached), learning from others, deconstructing errors, and articulating knowledge using academic language.	Flipgrid to record their solution. Teacher created question with student audio response using Recap Gamify learning and have students respond and share answers using Quizziz or Kahoot

Summary: Putting Ideas into Action

Let's flip the switch and turn on PBL in the classroom. You know your kids and you know their interests, skills, and the community in which you live. If you want to engage students and capitalize on their familiarity and interests, generate problems around those contexts. Let's say your fifth-grade students live in an agricultural area and you want to develop a real-life problem that will support their understanding of converting percentages to decimals. Of course, you can just teach the procedure and explain the step-by-step process, but if you only teach procedures and rules, for many the process just won't make sense. Instead, you decide to use a PBL approach to teach the concept within an agricultural context your students can understand.

Consider the following PBL Task:

> You have 80 acres of land to grow this year's crops. To maximize your earning potential, you decide to grow crops based on last year's sales. According the records, 40% will be strawberries, 15% lettuce, 15% beans, and 30% should be broccoli. How many acres will you need for each crop?

© Christopher Boswell/Shutterstock.com

This problem is based on the standard:

CCSS.MATH.CONTENT.5.NBT.B.7

Add, subtract, multiply, and divide decimals to hundredths, using concrete models or drawings and strategies based on place value, properties of operations, and/or the relationship between addition and subtraction; relate the strategy to a written method and explain the reasoning used.

When students engage in a problem like the crop problem, they need a way to understand and organize the information. Graphic organizers are a great way to scaffold and guide students through the PBL steps as they record and make their thinking explicit. Don't be surprised if you need to explain and guide the students in understanding the problem and incorporating the graphic organizer several times before they are able to work independently. Even adult learners need guidance and step-by-step instruction before they develop competency. Examine the graphic organizer below. There is a place for the problem, and then two sections for students to make sense of the problem.

Sense-making is a critical step in PBL because if students do not truly understand the problem and the variables they know and need to know, they may well be lost in the process.

The graphic organizer has a place for students to record their calculations and thinking as they solve the problem, a representation, and an explanation of their solution at the end.

Students can easily share the graphic organizer on Google docs and collectively record their thinking, or you can require each student to record individual solutions to promote thinking and accountability. This is something you can decide since you know your students best.

As an additional scaffold for this task, we recommend giving students access to graph paper. In Chapter 2, we discussed how students often need support before moving directly to abstract symbolic thinking. Making a representation by using graph paper to show the amount of acres as it is divided helps students to visually keep track of the amount of acres and verify that 100% of the total 80 acres is used.

Make the Tech Connection

Students can use a digital tool such as Geogebra, Google Drawing, or Glencoe Virtual Manipulatives where they can create a virtual drawing to support their thinking and illustrate their solution. Digital tools provide students with the ability to quickly edit, revise, and create an illustration to support their thinking.

Try It!

Use the Glencoe Virtual Manipulatives tool to create a virtual representation of the crop problem below. We recommend clicking on "Backgrounds" and selecting "Workmats" and "Grid" to create your representation. Once you have created a virtual representation select the printer icon at the bottom of the screen.

http://www.glencoe.com/sites/common_assets/mathematics/ebook_assets/vmf/VMF-Interface.html

Student PBL Organizer

The problem

You have 80 acres of land to grow this year's crops. To maximize your earning potential, you decide to grow crops based on last year's sales. According to the records, 40% will be strawberries, 15% lettuce, 15% beans, and 30% should be broccoli. How many acres will you need for each crop?

What is the problem?   **What information do we know?**

What are the next steps?

Notes and Calculations

Representation

Explanation of Solution

🛍 **Snag It:** Make a copy of the Student PBL Organizer.

Here is one of our student's representation of the crop problem. What do you notice about the way this student solved the problem? How was your virtual representation similar and/or different?

PBL Organizer: shorturl.at/ORUY1

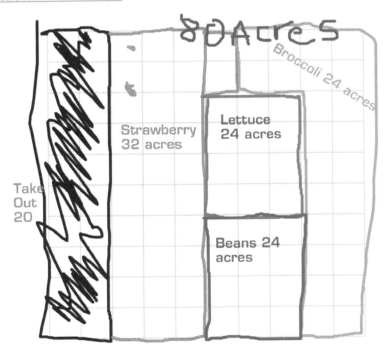

Source: APP Math Learning Center https://apps.mathlearningcenter.org/fractions/.

With PBL, the focus is not on practicing the math but *doing* the math. You might just find that through this process students can do the procedure but they might not understand the math conceptually. What seems reasonable as an approach to this problem? Would it make sense to draw 80 acres and take 40 acres and label it strawberries? Students will quickly realize that there is something more they need to do to make sense of this problem to properly distribute the crop percentages across 80 acres.

Once students have found their solutions, sharing the representations on the document camera and having several groups explain their process can highlight different strategies. Perhaps there is a group who used percent as fractions instead of converting to decimals and this strategy could be shared with the whole class.

> Sharing different strategies or ways of representing the solution can help to expand students' own thinking.

As illustrated in the crop problem, the teacher and students' roles are different than in traditional teacher-centered instruction, where the teacher is in front of the room and students are passive listeners. Below, we highlight some additional role differences in PBL.

Teacher's Role	Student's Role
• Identify math skills that students possess and new knowledge to be acquired • Provide an ill-defined problem set in real-life context that will challenge students that is connected to the students' interests and informal knowledge • Assign students to heterogeneous groups • Set norms for collaborative student work • Assign group roles • Provide scaffolds to support students' reading and solving of the problem • Integrate technology • Provide ways for student thinking to be made visible (e.g., graphic organizers) • Act as tutor when needed • Check groups' understanding • Provide opportunity for groups to share and evaluate solutions • Facilitate reflection on learning	• Work collaboratively with group • Define what is known in the problem • Identify the unknown in the problem • Use prior knowledge • Communicate effectively with group • Fulfill job responsibilities • Use conflict resolution skills as needed • Use mathematical tools and technology to record and demonstrate understanding • Be self-directed and motivated • Seek unknown information • Ask the teacher for knowledge support when needed • Edit and revise work as needed • Record and share solution • Reflect on the learning process

There are many possible types of activities around which to plan a PBL task. Here are some suggestions:

K-2: Driving Question	PBL Task	Technology Integration
Counting and Cardinality	Count the windows in your class. How many windows did you count? Represent the number you counted in as many different ways as you can.	Glenco Base Ten Pieces
Addition and Subtraction With Money	Kelly has $1.75 in her pocket. What combinations of coins could she have?	Money Pieces
Data and Graphing	Whose name in our class has the most letters? Who has the least? Make a graph to find out.	Create a Graph

3–5: Driving Question	PBL Task	Technology Integration
Decimals	Our class is raising money to buy supplies for our class garden by selling ice cream every Friday after school. The ice cream bars cost $.75 each and ice cream sandwiches were $1.25 each. Our class goal of selling $50.00 worth of ice cream was met at the end of the first month: (a) Determine how much and what kind of ice cream was sold during the first month. (b) Draw a representation to show your thinking and write an explanation for your solution.	Virtual Decimal Squares Abcya virtual manipulatives
Adding and Subtracting Fractions	The class is putting on a pancake breakfast for the school. For each pancake, we will serve a ½ cup of blueberries and ⅓ cup of syrup: (a) How many cups of blueberries and cups of syrup will you need for each person in a 28-person class? (b) How many cups of blueberries and cups of syrup you will need if each person brings three guests? (c) Draw a representation to explain each step of your thinking.	National Library of Virtual Manipulatives Seesaw to share illustrations Abcya Virtual Manipulatives Shadow Puppet to record illustrations
Geometry and Graphing	Ball Rolling Problem (STEM) shorturl.at/ahCKT	Desmos Geogebra

(Continued)

6–8	PBL TASK	Technology Integration
Fraction, Decimal, Percent	Given a ten by ten grid design a character for a short story you will be writing about (see image below).	Fraction Pieces
Ratios and Rates	It takes Laila 20 min to burn 40 calories. At this rate, how many calories will she burn in 45 min?	Equatio

6–12	PBL TASK	Technology Integration
Surface Area and Volume	Fish Tank Problem: Students will create and calculate the cost of a fish tank based on specific requirements and a set budget.	Google Sheets to record costs. Internet to identify costs for parts. TinkerCad to make a 3-D Model

Make the Tech Connection: Calculate & Create

In the Fish Tank Project, students used Google Sheets to calculate the cost of constructing a fish tank with a budget. Students created an illustration using graph paper and used the digital tool TinkerCad (https://www.tinkercad.com/) to make a 3-D model. Poster displays allowed students to share their work with a visual representation.

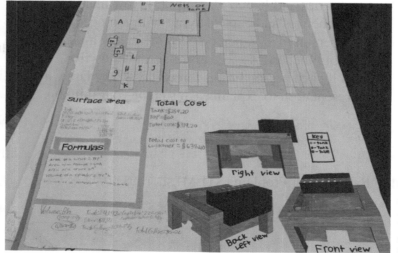

© Patricia Dickenson

Students used the digital tool ThinkerCad to make a 3-D illustration of their fish tank. This tool also includes a 3-D printer feature.

In the photo below, fourth-grade students were given the task of using a ten by ten grid to create a character for a short story they will write about.

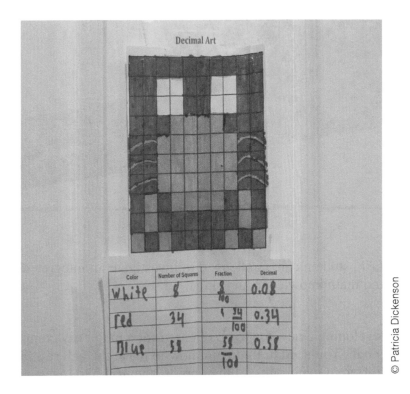

Color	Number of Squares	Fraction	Decimal
White	8	$\frac{8}{100}$	0.08
red	34	$\frac{34}{100}$	0.34
Blue	58	$\frac{58}{100}$	0.58

Make the STEM Connection

PBL is also a natural place to integrate STEM-related problems. STEM stands for Science, Technology, Engineering, and Math. Both scientists and engineers focus on questions and problems in the real world. While scientists seek knowledge to questions, engineers find solutions to problems that can be applied and tested. When it comes to STEM the data must be collected and analyzed in order to reach a conclusion. Conclusions are made possible with mathematics. STEM-related problems are also inquiry based so that students learn the mathematics through investigations, which includes mathematical modeling, justifying, critiquing, and thinking.

Think about the features of PBL we have already described, such as connections to informal and formal strategies, multiple solutions, basing problems in real-life contexts, engaging in classroom discourse, and metacognition. These features of problems also extend to scientific problems in which students grapple with scientific concepts, collect data, and examine patterns.

PBL Task: Ball Rolling Problem

© Deanora/Shutterstock.com

In the Ball Rolling task, students are challenged to investigate an integrated problem in which they apply science and math knowledge and skills.

PBL Task:

You are a scientist developing a new toy to be released for a major toy company. A critical part of the toy is a rolling ball. You need to figure out how to make the ball roll faster and slower by experimenting with different materials on the ramp. It is your job to investigate these materials and identify which ones increase and decrease your ball's speed. Your findings are key to making this toy a success.

1. Roll your ball three times and take an average measurement of the distance from the end of the ramp to where the ball stops. Record your results on the graphic organizer.
2. Select a new material to put on your ramp and write a prediction whether you think it will increase or decrease the ball's speed in your science journal.
3. Try several different materials on your ramp. For each material, record your ball's distance from the end of the ramp, rolling the ball three times and then calculating the average for each different type of material.
4. When all the data has been gathered, graph the results for each type of material. Each group member must create his or her own graph.
5. Discuss your findings as a group.

Write an explanation of your findings in your science journal. What materials increased the ball's speed? What materials decreased the ball's speed? Why do you think these materials made this change? Were you surprised by any of the results?

🔖 Snag It: shorturl.at/ahCKT

Make a copy of this lesson below for your use. Although this lesson was geared for third grade math standards, the domain Measurement and Data extends across the K-5th grade span and this lesson could easily be modified to reach these grade spans. In this lesson, Dr. Coddington makes interdisciplinary connections with math, science, and English Language Arts.

Teacher Name	Grade
Dr. Coddington	3rd

Content Standards Addressed:(National Math Standard or Common Core)

CCSS.MATH.CONTENT.3.MD.B.4
Generate measurement data by measuring lengths using rulers marked with halves and fourths of an inch. Show the data by making a line plot, where the horizontal scale is marked off in appropriate units—whole numbers, halves, or quarters.

CCSS.MATH.CONTENT.3.MD.B.3
Draw a scaled picture graph and a scaled bar graph to represent a data set with several categories.

CCSS.MATH.CONTENT.3.OA.A.3
Use multiplication and division within 100 to solve word problems in situations involving equal groups, arrays, and measurement quantities, e.g., by using drawings and equations with a symbol for the unknown number to represent the problem.

NGSS
3-PS2-2
Make observations and/or measurements of an object's motion to provide evidence that a pattern can be used to predict future motion.

PS2.A: Forces and Motion

Each force acts on one particular object and has both strength and a direction. An object at rest typically has multiple forces acting on it, but they add to give zero net force on the object. Forces that do not sum to zero can cause changes in the object's speed or direction of motion. (Boundary: Qualitative and conceptual, but not quantitative addition of forces is used at this level.) (3-PS2-1)

CCSS ELA/Literacy
W.3.8 Recall information from experiences or gather information from print and digital sources; take brief notes on sources and sort evidence into provided categories. (3-PS2-1),(3-PS2-2)

A benefit of STEM-integrated problems is maximizing many standards at one time. When planning this type of instruction look for ways ideas intersect across content areas. Writing and reading in the content areas is also an important skill you can integrate naturally. Students need to see that language, math, and science are interconnected. Notice in the Ball Rolling task how standards from math, science, and writing are included.

> In real life, most learning does not come separated neatly into content areas. Integrated problems help students see that life is full of math, science, engineering, and technological concepts that are naturally interconnected.

Possible Solutions: (include all pictures, models, representations)

Students will graph results.

Will find that the terry cloth will slow down the ball and smooth materials and tinfoil will make the ball increase its speed.

Possible Errors and Misconceptions:

Students will try and push the ball down the ramp rather than allowing the velocity of the ball to carry it naturally down the ramp.

Students may not calculate average correctly from the three attempts.

Students may not measure correctly.

Not recognize friction or reduced friction is responsible for the slowing of the ball.

Students may not realize how to represent the data on the graph and then infer a reasonable answer.

Language Demand	Scaffolding Strategies
Ramp	Graphic organizer to record information video to be reviewed
Increase	
Decrease	
Average	
Measurement	

(Continued)

Time	Group Roles and Process	Evidence Collected
40 min	Students will be assigned roles: Recorder, Facilitator, Team Leader, Resource Manager	**Graphic organizer** **Video Observation**
	- 3-Read strategy to review problem	
	- Groups will begin to plan what materials they need to use	
	- Groups predict what they think may result	
	- Groups begin experimenting and will record video and written work on graphic organizer	
	- Together they will calculate and make graph	

Time	Individual Process	Evidence Collected
10	- Students will reflect in their science journals after completing the experiment	**Science Journal**

Anticipating students' misconceptions is not always easy. Examining strategies and solutions will help hone your skills in identifying error. Asking students to provide verbal explanations as you roam the room can also be helpful to monitor student progress and make thinking visible. When you see emerging solutions that show misconceptions, ask students what they mean by their representation or calculations. Listen closely because student explanations will give you a window into your students' thinking and help you identify errors and misconceptions as they occur.

Time	Share Out Roles and Process	Evidence Collected
15	- Each group share their findings along with graph	**Graphs Graphic Organizers**

Notes, Resources and Materials Needed:

Ramps

Balls

Various material (terry cloth, cotton smooth cloth, tin foil, wax paper)

iPad—video

Rulers and yardsticks

Providing opportunities to share solutions is a critical part of wrapping up student learning. Students hearing peer explanations and seeing multiple ways of thinking and solving a problem is not just lesson closure but allows for some final instruction via student explanation.

Scaffolding for Success

The research on PBL as a teaching method shows both benefits and challenges for students. PBL promotes better retention and application of students' knowledge as well as enhances students' ability to argue based on evidence (Pedersen & Liu, 2003; Wirkila & Kuhn, 2011). Research has also demonstrated that PBL can increase student motivation and engagement (Pedersen & Liu, 2003). On the other hand, PBL can also present challenges to consider. Some studies have shown students need scaffolding in both content and organization to be successful (Simons & Klein, 2007). Scaffolding needs to be planned and organized by the teacher, and can include supports such as generating ideas, note-taking, journals, graphic organizers, and supporting students' language and discourse, among others (Simons & Klein, 2007; Wirkila & Kuhn, 2011).

© Patricia Dickenson

Let's talk about why you would use scaffolding when using PBL. Since PBL requires higher levels of thinking, self-regulation, and independence, you might find your students inexperienced in managing their own problem-solving. This may be evident in students who already exhibit challenges in the academic setting, such as students with special needs or English-language learners; however, even the average or strong student may need support, since this style of learning may be new and present a new kind of challenge. That is why we recommend building scaffolding into the problem-solving experience. With intentional scaffolding, students will more likely experience success.

We like to think about scaffolds as the structural support you would find on the side of a building under construction. Scaffolds are temporary and there to provide extra support while students are constructing the knowledge necessary to move to proficiency. Proficiency occurs when students have mastered a cognitive process. When this happens, the scaffolding needs to be removed; however, as students begin to work with new challenging concepts beyond their level of mastery, the scaffolds may be needed again. This cycle continues as scaffolds are given and then removed as needed.

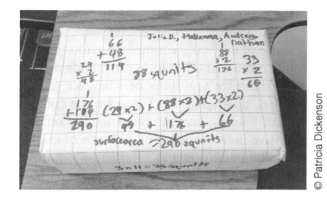

© Patricia Dickenson

© Patricia Dickenson

In the above images, students determined the surface area of a rectangular prism by calculating the area of each face of the box. The scaffold of square unit paper and a physical box allows the students to see that a rectangular prism has six sides in which the opposite sides have equal area. Having a physical scaffold promotes meaning making and allows the students to make sense of the formula for surface area. A= 2 (wl + hl + hw)

Scaffolds should be individualized based on student need. Some students with learning disabilities may need more scaffolds or scaffolds for longer time than other students. English-language learners may need scaffolds around language. It all depends on where students are in their learning and what their individual needs may be.

Since scaffolding is a common need for students in PBL, we want to highlight three methods of scaffolding that will benefit your students:

1. Scaffolding tools
2. Scaffolding organization
3. Scaffolding language

Scaffolding Tools

Students often need scaffolds to support mathematical thinking by using tools such as calculators, hundreds charts, concrete manipulatives, or graphing paper. In the fifth-grade crop problem, graphing paper was a scaffold for students' mathematical thinking for creating a visual representation. As discussed in Chapter 2, concrete materials and representations scaffold students' thinking as they move toward the abstract/symbolic stage. It is valuable to provide these materials to give students the extra support they need.

Scaffolds may include the following:

- Manipulatives (physical or virtual)—blocks, counters, Rekenrek, tangram blocks, ones-tens-hundreds blocks
- Calculator
- Hundreds charts, multiplication charts
- Graph paper of different size squares
- Drawing paper or individual whiteboards, virtual whiteboards

Scaffolding Organization

When students are learning new content, they make sense of it by connecting to previous knowledge because our brains thrive on structure. We refer to the mental map in our minds of how ideas are connected as *schema*. For example, if we asked what you think of when we say the word "dog," you likely say a pet with two ears, two eyes, a tail, and fur. These are the connections you have in your mind because of what you already know, and can be called the schema that you have about dogs. Our experiences build cognitive understanding of all kinds of knowledge and ideas in math, such as basic operations including addition and subtraction, multiplication, fractions, area, volume—the list goes on and on. When we expand our mental map, we are learning new information (Ausebel, 1968). We always want to connect new knowledge to previous knowledge when teaching new concepts and ideas. Graphic organizers help us to make connections for students and organizes and structures new information so that it can be used and remembered more easily.

> Graphic organizers naturally build on our brain's tendency for cognitive structure and are a useful scaffold for students when learning and working with new information.

The organization received through graphic organizers helps the learner make connections between ideas, chunk information, and make visual connections. In many ways, graphic organizers simplify thinking and provide ways of organizing information and making connections to prior knowledge. This is the reason we included a graphic organizer in our crop problem above. Graphic organizers come in all shapes and sizes and can be custom designed based on the specific task your students are completing. The sky's the limit!

Virtual Tools for organizing information: Popplet, kidspiration, Seesaw.

◉ **View It:** The below graphic organizer is used to help students approach problem solving. Here is a link to some additional graphic organizers you might find useful. shorturl.at/bdoL1

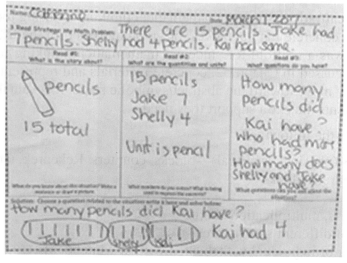

© Patricia Dickenson

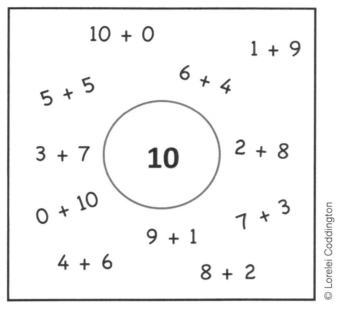

© Lorelei Coddington

Scaffolding Language

In Chapter 4, we discussed the value of sentence stems as a scaffold for language production. Sentence stems give students the words they lack or the confidence they need to formulate and articulate their thoughts. You might find that even your non–English language learners benefit from this type of support, since language in math can be intimidating for some students. Sentence stems can be provided either visually on the board, chart paper, or on a wall poster, as long as they are visually accessible. Some additional sentence stems can be found in the 3-Reads chart below. Sentence stems can support both oral and written language production.

The language of math, especially in math problems, can be difficult for students to understand, since problem situations are language-rich and often very complex. The text of the problem may require students to figure out relationships between words, numbers, tables, graphs, diagrams, and symbols which is very challenging. Students must become familiar with the ways that mathematicians talk and use the language of the discipline in order to participate in the discussions and thoughts presented. If the meaning of the problem and what students are to do is not understood, students will not be successful in problem-solving nor will they be able to participate or contribute to the construction of knowledge. Our goal is to ensure that students are successful; a goal in which scaffolding is a must.

3-Read Strategy

To scaffold the language of a problem and provide access for students, we recommend using the 3-Reads strategy since it breaks the reading of the problem into three steps and scaffolds students' understanding (Kelemanik, Lucenta, & Creighton, 2016). The purpose of the 3-Reads strategy is to make the content of the problem explicit through three specific readings in a row so students understand the meaning of the problem at a much deeper level before trying to solve it. This strategy assists students in identifying the meaning by examining the context and quantities and then interpreting the problem.

Below is a chart to use with your students which takes them through the stages of the three readings of the problem. By adding sentence stems to each step, you support English-language learners and other students who need more tools to feel confident using their academic language.

3-Reads Chart

Read #1: Choral Read and draw an illustration or write a sentence about what the problem is about.

Sentence Stems:

This problem is about . . .

In this problem there are . . .

Read #2: Choral Read and identify the quantity (the numbers) and identify the units (what is being counted).

Sentence Stems:

In this problem there are . . .

The problem tells me that . . .

Read #3: Choral Read or Partner Read and record any mathematical questions or statements you have about the situation.

Sentence Stem:

I wonder if . . .

How does . . .

I think that . . .

🛍 **Snag It:** Use this chart to guide your 3-Reads activity with your students.

3-Reads Chart: shorturl.at/fjLNW

Developing Group Norms and Roles

Have you ever worked in a group where members didn't get along, where one person dominated and did all the work, or group members valued other people's ideas but not yours? Disagreements, domination, and exclusion are classic examples of dysfunctional groups. In contrast, our goal is to develop high-functioning groups, and to do this we must first establish group norms. Before engaging students in group work, we must lay the ground rules and make sure everyone knows what is expected and how groups are to work together successfully.

Step 1. Identify a list of group norms.

To begin the process of establishing group norms, we suggest having students generate a list of characteristics of effective groups. Children are usually perceptive and can draw on their prior experiences to create a comprehensive list. From this list, we suggest grouping the students' ideas into categories that represent the following expectations:

1. Everyone participates in the math.
2. Everyone contributes by sharing ideas and strategies.
3. Everyone listens actively by asking questions and clarifying.
4. Everyone genuinely values each other's mathematical ideas.
5. Everyone willingly takes risks.
6. Everyone supports the group members to meet goals and responsibilities.

It is valuable to state your expectations in positive terms to emphasize the desirable behaviors rather than emphasizing undesirable behaviors.

Step 2. Communicate the norms in writing.

Post the expectations on a chart to be visually prominent in your classroom and review the expectations daily at first and then periodically as you move through the following weeks and months. You can even have students sign the poster as a sign of commitment to your agreed upon norms. When you hit periods of disrespectful, bossy, or disagreeable behavior, go back and revisit your group norms to reinforce your expectations.

Step 3. Practice and reinforce group norms through role-play.

With all ages, you can role-play exactly what is meant by each one of the expectations. Assign students a scenario of a challenging group situation and ask them to act out an appropriate group response as an example along with a non-example showing the opposite so that students clearly envision the expected norms. Providing both examples and non-examples makes it very clear what is expected and what is not. You can even take pictures of students role-playing and post on a virtual board like Padlet and have students reflect on the characteristics.

Creating an Emotionally Safe Classroom

If one of your group norms is to take risks, it is fair to say that you must create a space in which students are willing to take risks. Though it takes work and effort to create and maintain an emotionally safe classroom, it is extremely important and provides enormous rewards. So, how does a teacher make a safe classroom for risk-taking? Consider the following ideas.

- **Value contributions**
  This means everyone gets a chance to share and ways are found to applaud each student's effort, process, and risk-taking. We certainly want to value precision and accuracy but, if you only call on the "smart" kids and give positive feedback for the correct answer, you create an environment in which students feel they must have an accurate answer to present or even to volunteer. This puts great pressure on students and they quickly realize it is easier and safer to let someone else share. Of course, it is also critical that you as

a teacher not humiliate or call out students in negative ways, as this also reinforces fear and anxiety. Remember, even your tone matters.

- **Normalize error**

  We have mentioned this in several places in this book so far. Normalizing error means that students see error as a natural and beneficial part of learning. If student error is used regularly as a valued part of the learning process, students become less anxious and more accepting of the benefits of deconstructing error as a valuable tool from which to learn. This realization decreases fear and allows students to have a positive association with error in relationship to learning. You might be interested to know that research shows benefits to achievement when using student error in this way (Wells & Coffey, 2005). Normalizing error is a common practice in other countries with high achievement, such as Japan, where problem-solving is used as an exclusive model of instruction (Stevenson & Stigler, 1992).

- **Model a positive attitude**

  Students pick up on teachers' attitudes toward subject matter, especially in math. Having a positive attitude is critical since how you approach the subject can impact students' attitudes. Regardless of how confident you feel about math, be positive and approach the content with energy and excitement. Your attitude will be contagious, and you will actually enjoy yourself!

Establishing Group Roles

Once your class has a strong understanding of group norms, it is also beneficial to include group roles to delegate responsibility within the groups. Similar to establishing norms, role-playing the responsibilities of each role provides a clear set of expectations. We suggest rotating roles regularly so that all students get the opportunity to lead and grow in their group responsibilities. Here are a few possible group roles:

1. **Team Leader**—Responsible for ensuring that the group stays focused and on task. Regularly checks with group members to make sure everyone is on task and acting responsibly.
2. **Facilitator**—Responsible for reading the problem and ensuring all members understand the problem. Makes sure all group members are contributing and communicating about the solution.
3. **Technology Manager**—Responsible for gathering tools and supplies.
4. **Recorder**—Responsible for recording ideas and solutions.

 Make the Tech Connection

You must also consider group roles and expectations when it comes to technology use. Be sure you set clear expectations for digital use including time frames and what sites students are to use. If expectations are not being met, determine a fair consequence and follow through.

👁 **View It:** Tips and Tricks for managing technology in the classroom https://www.edutopia.org/discussion/classroom-management-tips-technology-rich-classroom

Assessment

With group responsibility comes group accountability. Using a rubric to self-assess participation in the group as well as an assessment to evaluate the function of the group can be beneficial, not just for you, but to develop self-awareness and prompt metacognitive thought in your students. We have provided both a self-reflection rubric and a group evaluation assessment below.

Self-Assessment Rubric—Group Work

	3 ☺	2 ☺	1 ☹
Math contribution	I contributed to the math ideas.	I sometimes contributed to the math ideas.	I did not contribute to the math ideas.
Responsibility	I was responsible and did my job very well.	I was sometimes responsible and did my job most of the time.	I was not responsible and did not do my job.
Effort	I tried my best and was on task all the time.	I tried at times and was on task some of the time.	I did not try at all and was off task most of the time.
Cooperation	I had a good attitude and was a cooperative group member.	I had a good attitude some of the time and cooperated with my group some of the time.	I did not have a good attitude and I had difficulty cooperating with my group.

🔖 **Snag It:** Get a copy of the self-assessment. Self-Assessment — Group Work Rubric

Group Assessment

Write in your group members' names. Rate yourself and your peers based on the following scale: 4 — Excellent 3 — Average 2 — Below Average 1 — Weak				
Description	Myself	1.	2.	3.
Contributed ideas for solving the problem				
Participated as an active group member				
Kept the group on task				
Responsibly fulfilled assigned job				

Worked cooperatively with the group				
Comments:				

🔖 **Snag It:** Go Digital and get a copy of the Group Assessment. <u>Group Assessment</u>

Distinctions of PBL

Though PBL and project-based learning (PjBL) are both inquiry methods that allow for much autonomy and student direction, there are some key differences you should note. One difference is that PBL is centered on solving problems while PjBL is focused on creating projects. Another difference is who initiates the problem; PBL has a teacher-initiated problem, while PjBL has a student or teacher-initiated driving question. Both PBL and PjBL can include content-area integration though in PBL the problem can be fully centered in the content-area. A final difference is the type of outcome of the student work: in PBL students produce a solution and PjBL they produce a product or presentation. Both methods do require communication of the final outcome but PBL is solution-based while PjBL is product-based.

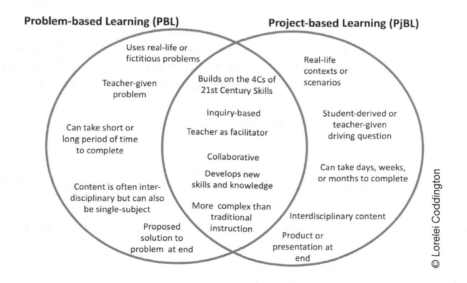

© Lorelei Coddington

Resources for PBL Problems

There are many resources available to support you in PBL. Here is a brief collection of websites and books with problems to be used or adapted as you plan PBL tasks.

Websites

http://www.cemc.uwaterloo.ca/resources/potw.php—This website from the University of Waterloo has hundreds of problems from 3rd to 12th grade that can be adapted or used as PBL tasks.

https://robertkaplinsky.com/prbl-search-engine/—This website has a search engine that can search for problems at a particular grade or content. Additional links to many other websites with other math resources and problems are available at this site.

https://illuminations.nctm.org—This website contains problems K-12 that are connected to the Common Core State Standards Mathematics (CCSS-M).

http://www.insidemathematics.org/performance-assessment-tasks—This site contains many different problem tasks connected to the CCSS-M that could be adapted for PBL.

https://www.illustrativemathematics.org/ Tasks are aligned to CCSS-M and learning progressions.

Books

Blanton, M. (2008). *Algebra and the elementary classroom: Transforming thinking, transforming practice* (4th Ed.). Portsmouth, NH: Heinemann.
    There are problems used throughout the text and also provided at the end of the book which can be used or adapted.
Burns, M. (1992). *About teaching mathematics: A K-8 resource*. White Plains, NY: Math Solutions Publications.
    This resource provides many problems throughout the text. There are many problems that can be used or adapted.
Carpenter, T., Fennema, E., Franke, M. L., Levi, L., & Empson, S. B. (1999). *Children's mathematics: Cognitively guided instruction*. Portsmouth, NH: Heinemann.
    This text explains student strategies across content areas and how to learn from students' thinking. Problems are discussed with student work samples throughout the text.

Summary

In this chapter, we examined PBL as a valuable approach to instruction that not only motivates and engages students but also connects them to challenging real-world problems in active problem-solving. In this approach, teachers capitalize on students' informal knowledge that connect to students' home lives and personal experiences, otherwise known as funds of knowledge. Our problem at the start of this chapter showed how a popular video game like Minecraft can be harnessed to hook students' interests and engage them in problem-solving, while connecting their informal knowledge to the formal knowledge of school. We discussed the importance of building on students' experiences in mathematics so they can see the relevance of math to the world and thereby transfer formal strategies into real life.

When planning PBL tasks, it is important to structure the learning experience and anticipate students' scaffolding needs. Teachers should plan around standards and develop a hook to engage students and make connections to real-world contexts. PBL tasks may integrate other content areas such as STEM content. Teachers must also think about grouping, language demands, tools, and structuring the learning experience in manageable ways. Scaffolds are purposeful supports that we can provide for students to assist them in the learning process.

PBL requires students to work cooperatively in problem-solving which can be challenging socially. Students must develop skills to be successful and we must create environments that are safe and conducive to taking risks. Developing classroom norms and role-playing expectations is an important place to start before beginning PBL. Students can also take on roles within their groups adding to their responsibilities. You know your students best, so use what you know to make connections and support students throughout the PBL learning process.

Additional Activities/Discussion Questions

1. In what ways do PBL tasks challenge students' thinking according to the revised Bloom's taxonomy from Chapter 2? Consider the tasks presented in this chapter as well as some from the websites provided above.
2. Make a list of ways that math intersects with daily life. Which of these intersections could be a starting place for developing a PBL task?
3. Go to one of the PBL websites listed above and select a problem. Adapt the problem into a PBL task using the PBL Planner Template. Identify standards, hook, and subsequent steps of instruction.

Instructor Activities

1. Engage your students in a PBL task, requiring them to use the Student PBL Organizer to plan their steps. Discuss how the graphic organizer influenced their metacognitive thinking. Brainstorm additional scaffolds to support students' language and cognition.
2. Generate a list of STEM topics that could be developed into PBL tasks. During this process, explore the Next Generation Science Standards and identify mathematics connections to science and engineering.
3. Use the PBL websites or book resources to evaluate problems that could be adapted as PBL tasks.
   a. Examine the different tasks for levels of cognitive demand. What makes one task stronger and more robust than another? How to increase critical thinking across the task?
   b. Together discuss whether the problem can be adapted for PBL or not.
   c. If adaptation is necessary, discuss what would make the problem stronger.
4. Discuss the characteristics of linguistically challenging tasks and examine various PBL tasks for language demands. Generate appropriate scaffolds for English-language learners and students with varying special needs.

Chapter 8

Math Centers

Self-Reflection

What inspires you to get things done and achieve your dreams?

"Leadership is the art of getting someone else to do something you want done because he wants to do it."

—Dwight D. Eisenhower

One of the most common challenges of being a teacher is finding the time to do it all: support students where they are and not just where the curriculum says they should be, create challenging learning tasks that encourage students to work cooperatively, provide opportunities for unstructured activities that are student-directed, and make time for students to engage in gameplay that will build their confidence and fluency of facts. The students in your class might be the same age, live in the same neighborhood, and have similar childhood experiences, but they learn differently, achieve milestones at various points in time, have unique preferences to express what they know, and most certainly vary in confidence and beliefs about themselves as learners. All of these factors matter not just when it comes to learning math, but in the instructional decisions you make as a teacher.

© Patricia Dickenson

With reading instruction, students' reading assessment indicates their grade level fluency and, as such, you provide reading materials that are within their zone of proximal development to promote challenge and not frustration. Unfortunately, the same is not true when it comes to traditional math instruction. If you are teaching fifth grade and a student is working at a third grade level, chances are you are still teaching them fifth grade standards. Creating time and opportunity for all students (even those working above grade level) to work in their zone of proximal development is critical, and math centers do just that. Math centers provide students a chance to work within their zone of proximal development through structured and unstructured activities, blended learning programs that adapt to students' level of proficiency, and small group and individualized instruction provided by the teacher.

So how do teachers manage it all when it comes to instruction? They don't; they teach kids how to manage themselves, identify areas for growth, and create structured and unstructured tasks to promote independent learners who strive towards mastery and self-improvement.

This approach to instruction can be achieved even in the early elementary grades with established routines, purposeful planning, and the ability to "let go." By letting go you are giving your students the power to control their learning. Teachers who trust in their students' ability to struggle and persevere when engaging in tasks, are creating a foundation for young learners to develop the overarching habits of mind that are essential to becoming productive mathematical thinkers.

For many students, the satisfaction of knowing they accomplished a task is more important than the grade they received. Math centers create a consistent space for students to work independently as well as cooperatively with other classmates to construct ideas and negotiate meaning. With self-directed activities at each center, students must take the responsibility for learning. This means students can **choose** the activities they will work on, **manage** their work products independently, **reflect** on their accomplishments, and **self-assess** their learning. This four-stage process (choose, manage, reflect, and self-assess) is important for students to experience in order to become independent learners (see figure 8.1 below). As the classroom teacher, you participate in this process by **designing opportunities** for student to choose what they want to do during math centers, **direct** the goals and management of their learning, create **access and experience with digital tools,** and most importantly, provide **feedback to direct the learning process** (see figure 8.2 below).

Teachers also provide support through scaffolds such as graphic organizers, criteria charts, interactive documents, and self-reflection logs that support students in meaningful ways. Throughout this process you are collecting data both formal and informal that you will use to design center activities and provide differentiated instruction to support students where they are at and not just where the textbook says they should be, by doing this you are truly "teaching math outside the box."

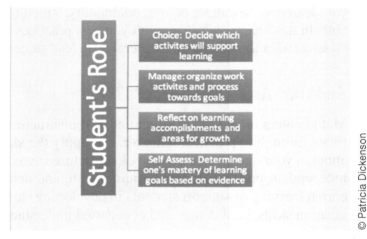

Figure 8.1 Student's Role: Student-centered approach to instruction that provides choice and the ability to manage learning with an opportunity to reflect and self-assess.

In this chapter we will provide you with tools and resources to support you in each of these four areas: choice, manage, reflect, and self-assess.

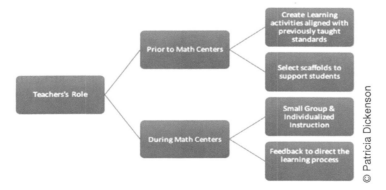

Figure 8.2 Teacher's Role: the teacher plays an active role behind the scenes in designing and creating center activities. During math centers, the teacher can provide individualized and small group support with feedback to students that will help direct their learning process.

The Purpose of Math Centers

Math centers in many ways become the glue that binds together all of the pedagogical practices you have been learning about in this book. With math centers, you are not doing anything new except providing an opportunity for students to develop their skills, fluency, and confidence in math. As such, we have positioned math centers as our last pedagogical practice.

> With math centers you can do it all: differentiate instruction, provide personalized and small group instruction, foster independence, reinforce skills, support student reflection, and challenge gifted learners.

We love math centers, but we also recognize there is no perfect script or way of organizing and structuring this practice. Like many things we do as teachers, math centers need to fit the needs of your learners, the culture of your community, structure of the school, and resources that are available. In this chapter we share with you best practices for facilitating math centers and what great classroom leaders (we mean teachers) do to lead students towards becoming independent learners.

So What Are Math Centers?

Math centers include both structured and unstructured activities that small groups of students rotate through to practice, rehearse, and apply the skills and strategies they have been learning about in your math instruction block. Structured activities in math centers includes games, drills, independent practice, adaptive online math, and activities with the teacher that can reinforce, enrich learning or support students in developing skills such as computational fluency, communication skills, confidence, and conceptual understanding.

Unstructured activities include exploration and creative activities that support reasoning, logic, problem solving, real-life application, and most importantly a love of mathematics. Depending on the age and grade level of your students, unstructured activities might include

Source: Patricia Dickenson

blocks, Legos, counters, building toys, online and board games, and puzzles that support logic and reasoning. There should be a good balance between structured and unstructured activities at your math centers. While structured activities can reinforce concepts learned, unstructured activities develop students' efficacy and promote a positive attitude toward math.

Think About It!

How might an unstructured activity of playing with magnetic tiles support a Kindergarten student with content standards such as Counting and Cardinality (in which the child counts to tell the number of objects) and Geometry (analyze, compare, create and compose shapes). What is the value of participating in unstructured activities in the classroom? How might this process support and/or challenge students' attitudes and beliefs about learning math?

_____

_____

Putting Research into Practice

The concept of math centers has its roots in the 1970s with a program called *Mathematics Their Way* by Mary Barrata Lorton (1976) which explored math concepts with concrete objects as a way to build conceptual understanding. The focus of math centers was to deepen students' understanding and promote independent work time.

> The idea of choice is a strong component of math workshop which has been found to foster ownership and self-direction of student learning.

Math centers provide a student-centered learning environment based on choice. Choice has been found to be significant in motivating students and engaging them in the learning process. This is critical since national assessment data shows that students struggle with boredom in math (Mullis, Martin, Foy, P., & Arrora, 2012). In authentic learning experience, like math centers, choice increases students' motivation and interest in learning. When students experience choice, they find the learning more engaging than traditional forms of instruction (Cordova & Lepper, 1996).

Collaboration is also a component of math centers as students work in groups to problem solve, share ideas, discuss a solution or play a game. According to the Partnership for 21st Century skills (2012), collaboration is "essential in our classrooms because it is inherent in the nature of how work is accomplished in our civic and workforce lives" (p.20). These 21st Century skills prepare students to be college and career ready, and bolster students' cognitive development and social and emotional growth as well. Peer-to-peer interaction promotes higher-level reasoning and enhances retention of learning. Motivation, positive attitudes, and increased self-esteem are also benefits of collaborative group work. After working in groups, students are excited to participate in whole-class discussion and present their ideas to the class. The benefits from cooperative learning are found to be universal, enhancing students' schooling experiences while also developing their life skills (Nastasi & Clements, 1991). These skills will be drawn on throughout students' entire lives and can begin to be developed at a very young age.

Within math centers, collaborative group work must be explicitly taught and modeled. The routines you establish during math centers must be intentional to support collaboration, active listening, and peer discussion. Don't assume your students know how to share their thinking, listen to their peers, and work cooperatively. The instructional decisions you make as a teacher must reflect your students' areas for growth and development. That is why during math centers you must make time to observe your students in action.

During centers, if a teacher is isolated to a classroom corner with a small group of students a huge opportunity is missed to determine what skills are needed to make math centers a success.

Math Workshop

Looks Like	Sounds Like
• Everyone working	• Math talk
• At stations (chairs or floor)	• Level 1 voices
• No bathroom (unless emergency)	• Asking questions about math
• Supplies being used correctly	• Thinking out loud
• Teamwork	• Talking through problems
• Problem solving	
• Helping friends	
• Having fun	

Teacher's Job	Student's Job
• Work with a group at the kidney table	• Stay focused and on task
• Answer questions	• Work on your assigned station
• Teach about math	• Solve problems
• Listening and learning from you!	• Work together
	• Practice math skills
	• Listening and learning from your teacher and your classmates.

© Kendall Hunt Publishing Company

We're sure you are curious right now about what math centers look like in action. The following videos show the implementation of centers in both a kindergarten class and fourth grade.

◉ **View It:** In this video Mr. Warren demonstrates how to introduce centers in his kindergarten class: https://www.youtube.com/watch?v=ZdEK2RMGSs0

◉ **View It:** Watch this fourth grade teacher and her students explore the different kinds of math centers in her math workshop block: https://www.youtube.com/watch?v=Z_vDV_UkP_0

Characteristics of Effective Math Centers

❑ Furniture is arranged so that noisy and quiet areas are separated and the teacher has a view of the entire room.

❑ Designated places for students to store their finished products and any incomplete work.

❑ Centers are organized with clear expectations and managed so that students can work independently.

❑ Materials and manipulatives are clearly labeled and within easy view and reach of the children.

❑ Variety of structured and unstructured activities support both conceptual understanding, procedural fluency, and problem solving skills.

❑ Tasks are open-ended and provide students with a low-floor and high-ceiling that can challenge and support all learners.

❑ Students can work together and engage in meaningful productive struggle.

❑ Center activities are aligned with curriculum and based on ongoing assessment.

❑ Students are accountable for their work and exemplars are provided to model expectations.

Source: Patricia Dickenson

Getting Started with Math Centers

Just like the first few days of school when establishing routines and procedures for activities and transitions are essential for classroom management, the same is true when it comes to math centers. You begin math centers just like you begin training your students for other classroom routines such as putting their materials away or lining up at the door.

1. Start by introducing students to one center and practice the procedures and skills students need to learn.

2. Review how to take out, use, and put away materials.
3. Clearly model and communicate expectations for independent work or when working with a partner.
4. Demonstrate how students should record their work and seek assistance if they need help.
5. Debrief with your students at the end of math center time and share what you observed. Ask students what went well and where they need to improve. Feedback is crucial!

For example, let's say you are introducing the Game Center with your students. You have two games that your students can choose from which they have learned how to play during whole group instruction. At your math center the games are stored in reclosable bags or bins with lids and includes directions, game board and pieces. Students should model how they take out materials, communicate, record their responses, and put away belongings. You can make a poster for each center or use table tents to serve as a reminder of the rules and expectations at each center or take a picture of students modeling actions and post as a reminder. Be sure you set expectations for noise level and how you expect students to communicate during math centers. At the closing of the math centers, spend a few minutes sharing what you observed, what went well, kudos to students who were on task, and what you hope for next time.

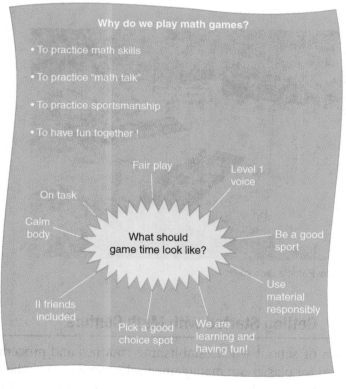

© Kendall Hunt Publishing Company

Now that you have set up one center, put the process into action and practice for a few days or longer until students have demonstrated mastery for each center. Once students can work independently it's time to introduce another center. Repeat this process until all math centers are introduced, rehearsed, and running seamlessly.

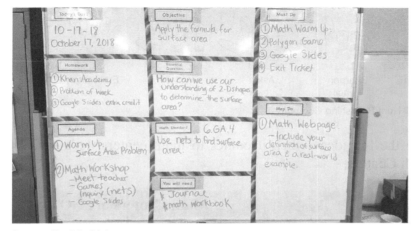

Source: Patricia Dickenson

If you have five centers through which students will rotate, it might take up to five weeks before you have your Math Workshop fully established. While students are learning what to do at each center, we create a "Must Do" and "May Do" board. The "Must Do" board can highlight tasks students must complete before moving on to a choice activity. For example, students must complete page five of their workbook before they can choose to work in a center. The "May Do" list can include centers students can choose from in which they work independently. For example, if you practiced several games and students know how to work on a blended learning activity independently your "May Do" list might include a game center and tech center as a choice if all items in the "Must Do" list have been completed.

 Make the Tech Connection: Present it!

Prepare your introduction and rotations of math centers with a presentation to facilitate this process. If you have access to a whiteboard or projector display the rules, procedures and rotations to review and keep students on task. Use an online digital timer such as your phone, tablet or a webtool such as online stopwatch (https://www.online-stopwatch.com/) to keep students on task and manage your time as well.

🛍 Snag It: Introducing Math Centers with Google Slides

Use the Google Slides "Introducing Math Centers" to review expectations and procedures. We recommend you review each of the big ideas for setting up rules and procedures for math centers with your class. Effective communication is key when it comes to establishing effective math centers. As you can imagine, it is difficult to teach a small group of students when there is much noise and distraction around so be sure you emphasize the rules and expectations for classroom volume while students are at one of the centers. Another key aspect that is discussed in this presentation is hand signals that students should learn and use to get the teacher's attention.

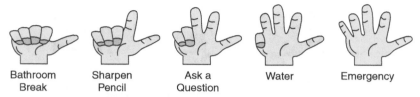

Bathroom   Sharpen   Ask a   Water   Emergency
Break   Pencil   Question

© Kendall Hunt Publishing Company

Now that you have the big ideas when it comes to math centers, let's review the essential components of Math Centers:

Math Centers are	Math Centers are NOT
• Student-centered • Foster creativity for the students and the teacher • Comprised of open-ended tasks • Structured and unstructured activities • Aligned with curriculum • Planned and organized by the teacher in advance • Organized with all materials available for students' independent use • Modeled and practiced in advance as a whole class • Provides opportunities for student choice, independence, and self-assessment • Promotes challenge and productive struggle, yet is supportive • Opportunities to work with a teacher-led small group	• Teacher-centered • Dependent on teacher-directed instruction • Comprised of closed-ended, predictable tasks (worksheets) • Haphazard learning experiences independent of the curriculum • Planned last minute or instituted without modeling or practice • Low-level busy work to keep students occupied while the teacher is working with a small group

Remember math centers foster collaboration, inquiry, and student-directed learning. So don't be alarmed if you hear laughter, chatter, and excitement around the room - harness it. This is the goal of math centers and you are an essential part of the process from planning student activities to feedback and support. Don't be surprised if math centers become the most vibrant time of your classroom practice and you'll learn so much about your students when you observe, support, and ask open-ended questions.

Conceptions of Math Centers

Math centers can be conceptualized in many different ways and used for a variety of purposes. For example, one teacher might have math centers every day of the week with students rotating one center each day until students move through each of the five centers in a week. While another teacher might have "Fun Fridays" during which students rotate through a set of three centers on one day, once a week. In another classroom, math centers might be independent choice in which students select from a variety of activities (e.g., games, independent work, Marcy Cook tiling activities, tangram activities) once they have completed required "Must Do" class work. In another classroom, math centers can be highly structured and include a teaching center and several independent activities around a single standard. That said, there is not one single way that math centers occur; they vary in organization and purpose depending on the teacher and the classroom. As you will note, we are presenting the last model in more detail in the remaining part of this chapter, but realize that you have discretion to make math centers fit your math program and students' needs.

Getting Structured with Math Centers:

One key aspect of having a successful math center block is providing a structure that will cue and prompt student behavior. Going digital will help facilitate this process by setting a timer or your phone that cues students to move and rotate to the next station. We recommend no more than six stations with a maximum of four students in a group. If you have more than 24 students in your class then add additional students to each group, but try to have an even number of students in each group since math games and routines typically require partner work. We've created a digital math rotation board to use and display during math centers. This is an editable presentation so you can change student and center names to best meet the needs of your classroom. In the first slide, all center names and rotations are shown, however after your students finish the first rotation, switch to the second slide and your first rotation is blanked out. This will allow you to visually cue your students to which rotation is occuring.

Math Workshop

Group	Group Members	Rotation #1	Rotation #2	Rotation #3	Rotation #4	Rotation #5
1	Cathy Michael June Cory	Math & Teacher	Math & Tech	Math Games	Math Inquiry	Math Journal
2	Hal David Mary Dillon	Math & Tech	Math Games	Math Inquiry	Math Journal	Math & Teacher
3	Branden Cullen Catherine Jake	Math Games	Math Inquiry	Math Journal	Math & Teacher	Math & Tech
4	Lorelei Patricia John Sara	Math Inquiry	Math Journal	Math & Teacher	Math & Tech	Math Games
5	Lane Jo Miguel Paula	Math Journal	Math & Teacher	Math & Tech	Math Games	Math Inquiry

Snag It: https://goo.gl/pC9uAa

Make the Tech Connection: Productivity Tools

During math centers, display the above presentation so your students know where to go and what to do. You can also display a digital timer that will help students stay on track and manage their time wisely. Online Timer: https://www.online-stopwatch.com/countdown-timer/

Tips for Managing Groups of Students

- Start with a highly structured activity at each center to provide students with an opportunity to work effectively with purposeful goals. Once students have demonstrated the skills and behaviors to work effectively, build in unstructured activities which require a greater capacity to self-manage their behavior and effort.
- Include a system to support students in self-managing their behavior and work. This might include a basket to turn in work, journals to record their ideas, a checklist to report which centers they visited, and self-assessment rubrics for reflecting on their effort.
- Be sure students are engaged in ongoing activities and, as they complete their work, they know what to do next.
- Effective centers have a built-in accountability system. This means at every center students are recording their ideas and producing evidence of work. Examples of the forms of evidence you might collect are included in each station idea below. We also share ideas for integrating technology at each station.

Station	Evidence	Technology Integration
Fluency/Math Facts	Student running records which include skills worked on, number of problems completed, and percent correct.	Use the webtool Symbaloo to create a collection of approved online math games for students to play. https://www.symbaloo.com/mix/elementarymath1
Journals/Problem Solving	Student can watch a video from Math Antics or Khan Academy and record what they learned, what they want to know more about and a question they have in their math journal.	Use a digital journal such as a blog or a website to record student ideas. Use the internet to research statistics and facts about a concept and record in their journal. Use online math dictionaries to define key terms and record in their math journal.

Station	Evidence	Technology Integration
Technology	Have students work through a Google Slideshow that includes interactive tasks. Provide an opportunity to practice math skills with a blended learning program such as Prodigy. Students can record time with a log and include a reflection to share what they learned.	Use Google Slides to have students work through activities to practice math skills. Include links to webtools for students to use virtual manipulatives. Use Edpuzzle to make videos interactive and include questions for students to reflect and respond as they watch.
Inquiry	Students can respond to open-ended tasks that explores what they know about a concept.	Use digital tools such as Educreations or FlipGrid for student responses to a prompt.
Small Group/ Teacher Center	Student oral responses are critical during small group work to evaluate understanding. This is a great opportunity to ask probing questions.	Use digital webtools such as Desmos or Math Learning Center tools to show what they know and express their ideas.

Fluency Station: Determine what particular computational skills students need to develop fluency and provide opportunities to practice, practice, and practice. This might include computational skills such as multiplication, addition, subtraction, or division facts where students complete a worksheet and record their percent of accuracy in a minute. You can use sand timers for students to keep track of their time. You should also provide a template for students to record their time and graph their results. Carefully scaffold goal setting and monitoring to help students develop a mindset of skill development with practice and effort. Fluency can also include games that focus on developing accuracy of computational facts. Students should record their scores to self-monitor progress. Tablets also have free games that can support students in developing these skills. We created a Symbaloo which contains a variety of math games for students to choose from and posted this on our class website.

👁 **View It:** https://goo.gl/2eAKps

Fluency Expectations with Common Core Math Standards

Grade	Expected Fluency	Example
K	Add & Subtract up to 5	$3 - 2 = 1$
1	Add & Subtract up to 10	$6 + 4 = 10$
2	Add & Subtract up to 20	$12 + 5 = 17$
	Add & Subtract up to 100 (using paper and pencil)	$42 + 31 = 73$

Grade	Expected Fluency	Example
3	Add & Subtract up to 100	$512 + 310 = 822$
	Multiply/Divide up to 100	$22 \times 3 = 66$
4	Add & Subtract up to 1,000,000	$68,983 - 12,008 = 56,975$
5	Multi-digit multiplication	$456 \times 212 = 96,673$
6	Multi-digit division	$465 \div 25 = 18.6$
	Multi-digit decimal operations	$62.8 \div 4 = 15.7$
7	Solve algebra equations	$4x + 7 = 19$
8	Solve simple systems of equations	$X + y = 17$
		$X - y = 22$

Small Group/Teacher Center: One of the best advantages of having a well run math center block is the ability to work with a small group of students. Typically, small groups of students are arranged homogeneously so you can provide remediation or challenge to meet students' needs and abilities. It is important to determine student groupings based on their strengths and needs. The teacher can create a place for students to share their thinking privately and provide timely support to address students' misconceptions and areas of challenge. Explicit instruction can be provided by the teacher to model strategies, frontload vocabulary, and reinforce concepts. Teachers have an opportunity to ask questions that promote student thinking and deepen student understanding. The teacher can also monitor students more closely to understand what the student can and cannot do with assistance. Small group instruction does require additional planning that is intensive and specifically targeted to meet learners' needs. A typical block of small group instructional time is about twenty minutes.

Small group instruction is a good way to build in assessment for learning. It is ongoing and allows you to respond to the learners' needs and provide feedback to let students know what they need to do to move towards their learning goals. We believe that groups should be flexible and, as such, groups may vary from one math standard to the next. You should also use initial assessments to determine your students' needs and how they should be grouped. A pre-test at the beginning of the unit can help you determine student groupings based on needs. An exit ticket at the end of a lesson can tell you who might need reteaching. Students who perform poorly in certain areas can be grouped together for remediation, whereas students who have strong performance can receive additional challenge.

Source: Patricia Dickenson

Here are some frequently used materials for small group instruction:

Paper and Pencils

Manipulatives and Measuring Tools

Crayons and markers

Work mats and whiteboards

Curriculum material for review/reteach

Tech Station: This is where blended learning happens. Students rotate to computers to work on standards-based adaptive curriculum which provides detailed report and summaries of students' progress. With adaptive learning programs, students can move at their own pace and learn concepts for mastery rather than being constrained by pacing guides. Teachers can assign tasks based on students' level of proficiency from summative assessment and pre-assessment data prior to beginning a new unit.

We've curated a list of blended learning programs for mathematics. We recommend you work with your administrator to determine a program that best meets your students' needs and available resources. Some blended learning programs like Khan Academy and Prodigy are free whereas other programs such as IXL and Ten Marks have a cost.

👁 View It: Look for the category "Blended: to see our recommendations for adaptive learning programs that are Common Core aligned. https://goo.gl/1oZvjR

Blended learning can take place in the class or at home. When bandwidth is slow and access to computers is limited, homework might be the best option for using an adaptive math curriculum with your students. Our parents have shared with us they enjoy watching instructional math videos with their child, especially as the Common Core focuses on conceptual understanding which is different than how they were taught.

If access to computers and Internet is not an option, we recommend that students have the opportunity to experience blended learning in your class. As high stakes standardized assessment takes place through computers starting at third grade, it is important for students to develop the digital skills to work and complete math tasks online.

Source: Patricia Dickenson

We developed a Blended Learning Log for students to record time spent working digitally online. Although most programs will record students time we believe students should also have an opportunity to reflect on their learning, monitor their progress, and ask questions. This template does more than just track student time, it also helps them set goals for improvement.

🔖 Snag It: https://goo.gl/EG1qXp

Weekly Blended Learning Log

(This form is due each Monday; 100 minutes a week required)

Name _____

Date _____

> Please name two or three activities/
> topics that you worked on this week:

Complete the **line graph** below to record your activity for the week. Place a dot to show the number of minutes each day. You may round to the nearest five minutes. When you're done for the week, connect each dot to the next with a straight line.

90							
80							
70							
60							
50							
40							
30							
20							
10							
0							
	Mon.	Tues.	Wed.	Thurs.	Fri.	Sat.	Sun.

You completed_____ minutes at home this week.

Reflection:

What did you learn this week? What questions do you still have? What do you want to learn more about?

_____

_____

_____

Goal Setting: What is a goal you have to improve and how will you meet this goal? _____

Parent signature _____

Going Digital

Our students enjoy the opportunity to work digitally on tasks that we have been exploring in math. We often design Google Slides that include additional practice problems and activities to support students in deepening their understanding about a particular math concept. Using Bloom's Taxonomy as a framework, our Google Slides move students from the knowledge domain to application of a concept. For example we might include a video in our Google Slides to represent the domain of understanding. After students watch the video, they can record in the notes section of the Google Slide: three things you learned, two things you want to know more about, and one question you still have. When students get to the application slide, we might

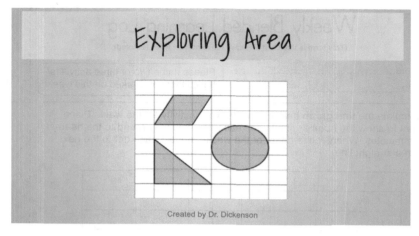

Exploring Area

Created by Dr. Dickenson

🛍 **Snag It:** https://goo.gl/sbNnQ6

ask them to create a video using the tool Flip Grid or Educreations that demonstrates how they apply the concept we are learning about in the real world. This approach to developing increasingly challenging tasks on a Google Slide provides much needed differentiation for students who work at different paces and come into our classroom with different levels of math proficiency.

Journals: In Chapter 4 Daily Routines, we discussed a variety of approaches for using a journal in your math block. Math Centers are a great way to utilize the journal in a variety of ways. First, students can use their notes to support their problem solving skills in their center activities. For example, when students are at the Inquiry Center they can refer to their notes to remind them of the strategies they have learned to solve a problem or complete a task. Students can also use their journals to work independently on a task such as defining key terms which can be recorded in the glossary of their journal. You can also have students use their journal to reflect on their learning while at each center. For example when playing a math game, students are asked to record or illustrate what they learned from playing the math game Blast Off in their journal.

© Patricia Dickenson

As a way to organize the math journal, we have our students paste a Table of Contents into the first page. We often create printed notes for students that they cut and paste into their journal and further highlight key ideas or ask questions for us to respond. This approach to note-taking provides accommodations for many students in our class with Individualized Education Plans (IEP) or for those who need additional support.

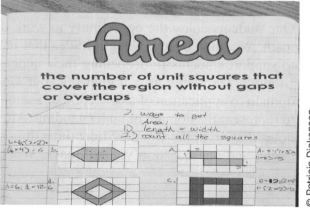

© Patricia Dickenson

We often use journals as a summative assessment with older students which also supports students in learning the skills of how to take notes and organize their thinking. These skills are essential for secondary school and must be explicitly taught by teachers. If these skills are not taught, they will not develop on their own.

🛍 **Snag It:** See the Appendix for a copy of the Math Journal Table of Contents we have created.

Inquiry Center: The inquiry center is a place where the teacher and the students can get creative and explore concepts in greater depth. Here you can create a task for students to develop and demonstrate mastery of a standard. We love the idea of just having a large sheet of butcher paper for students to illustrate ideas, ask questions, create representations and see their peers' thinking visually. In Chapter 5 Open-ended Tasks, you can post a task for students to solve with a peer or independently. In the image on the previous page, students were asked to make an irregular shape of an object they are familiar with and record a math expression to determine the area. The large butcher paper with square units was a great scaffold for students to either compute the area using the formula (length times width) or count square units. Inquiry works best when it is rooted in the lives of the students you teach!

Digital tools can also be used at the inquiry center to respond to tasks and record their thinking. Taking photos of student work as they construct and build representations is a great way to share what you are doing in math with parents and peers. We also create a prompt using the webtool FlipGrid. This tool allows students to create a video response to a question and provide comments on their peers' videos. We think our students especially like the ability to get creative with icons and emoji's in their response. A little bit of silliness is all you need to keep students on task and motivated to complete their FlipGrid which we typically place at the end of our Google Slide tasks.

© Patricia Dickenson

In the photo above students are constructing a model using square units to represent area. Then they will use their tablet to access the FlipGrid where they will create a video to explain their model and how they determined the area.

Math Games

Math Games are necessary for students to develop automaticity in a way that is fun and engaging. With math games, students engage in game play and don't even realize they are "doing the math." We typically select a math game for a center that provides students with an opportunity to either reinforce the skills explicitly being taught or rehearse the concepts and strategies they should have already mastered.

Here's What You Will Need:

- Game boards can be inserted in a clear sheet protector for students to write with a Dry Eraser or you can use laminated copies of a game board
- Erasable markers and cloths for recording and cleaning boards
- Dice and number spinners for games
- Poker chips or transparent counters in various colors
- Plastic storage bags or clear shoebox bins for game storage
- Cubes for counting
- Calculators to check answers

Here's What You Will Do:

1. Prepare enough game boards for all students in your class to work with a partner during whole group instruction.
2. Project your game board to explain and review the game rules and model how to play.
3. Send home a print copy of the game boards for students to play with their parents or siblings to practice.
4. Once students have demonstrated how to play independently without your support th the game can then become a part of your math center "Game Station."

Games can also be used for students who are "fast finishers" or for students who receive intervention as an activity for support or remediation. If you have students who receive resource and support outside your classroom, have them practice the games in these settings to build their confidence. Once students have developed mastery of the game skill, you can also have them work with another grade or class to teach students how to play.

🔖 Snag It: Dr. Dickenson has posted games for printable use and sharing in a variety of math skills. https://teacherprep.wordpress.com/

 Make the Tech Connection:

Students can create videos of how to play a math game. The video can be shared with parents before a math game goes home for practice. Having students explain and share their thinking promotes mastery of understanding as well as provides second language learners an opportunity to develop academic language in mathematics.

Grade	Game
K	Go Fish
1	Making 10
2	Subtraction War
3	Math Facts Baseball

Grade	Game
4	Stand Up, Sit Down
5	PIG
6-8	Pico Fermi Bagel
	Krypto

👁 **View It:** Game Presentation

https://bit.ly/3iMDmLu

Make the Tech Connection:

Students can use any of these free math apps for support while playing a game. We think technology is a great tool to support students who might struggle but games should be played with a partner to support math discourse.

https://goo.gl/qDJ4w3

Math Planning Sheet

When it comes to putting it all together, get started with this math planning sheet.

The top half of the planning sheet provides a space for you to designate groups that will meet with you and what the math focus will be. You can then brainstorm ideas for each center activity and resources needed such as the student workbook and journal. This sheet is editable just "make a copy" and save it to your computer or drive. Once you have your own copy, you can add additional groups or change the centers.

🛍 **Snag It:** https://goo.gl/4hh5iD

The notes section of this template is a good place to reflect on highlights and successes. You might also include anecdotal notes on student performance. We typically end our math block with a wrap-up and share. Have students share something they noticed or learned during centers.

Math Centers Planning Sheet

Teacher Center: Small Group Work

Group 1:		Group 2:	
1.		1.	
2.		2.	
3.		3.	
4.		4.	
Focus:		Focus:	

Group 3:		Group 4:	
1.		1.	
2.		2.	
3.		3.	
4.		4.	
Focus:		Focus:	

Journal	Computers	Independent Work

Games	Problem Solving	Inquiry/Projects

Notes:

Assessment & Math Centers

There are a variety of ways to assess students' progress at math centers. You may want to establish record-keeping procedures to record the activities in which students engage. Here are a few ideas that can be implemented to enhance your assessment.

1. Have students take a picture of themselves during the center activity and then reflect on their learning or skill practice in Seesaw. Use this app to collect students' work and reflections which can later be viewed and evaluated.
2. Promote self-reflection at the end of the math block using Google Forms which allows you to collect students' reflections as assessment.
3. Provide a record-keeping sheet that requires students to record activities in which they engage as they move to centers, their partners, and how many times they repeat an activity or center. This sheet travels with students throughout center rotations and is kept in the students' math center folder. You can collect the folder weekly for evaluation.
4. Use a self-reflection rubric that encourages students to reflect on their cooperative skills while working at the centers. These skills may be: contributing ideas, taking turns, giving "put-ups" or encouragement, listening, being responsible, or helping.
5. Use math journals to record activities and productivity at the end of math centers.
6. Use a planning/reflection form before starting math centers where students identify what they plan to do during the math center. Have students reflect on the same form at the end of math centers on what they learned or the skill they practiced. Keep these assessments to reflect on students' self-assessment and perceived growth. These could be added to student portfolios to reflect students' progress and self-assessment and could be shared with parents at conferences.
7. Keep anecdotal notes to record your observations of students' behaviors and actions at centers. Use these to inform instruction and as reference when conferencing with parents.

Summary

This chapter has explored math centers as a Big 5 pedagogical strategy. Math centers include both structured and unstructured activities in which students rotate to practice, rehearse, and apply skills and strategies learned in math instruction. These activities may include games, drills, independent practice, collaborative work, and adaptive online math activities. Math centers promote students' development in computational fluency, communication, confidence, and conceptual understanding. There is no one way to implement math centers and teachers must determine the best approach by knowing their students' instructional needs and the needs of the learning environment. Typically, math centers involve rotations through centers, but math centers can also be conceived as activities occuring at the end of instruction. Math centers may occur daily, weekly, or as desired by the teacher and offer opportunities for self-directed learning and choice. Students learn to be autonomous and engage in math activities that promote collaboration as well as enhanced skill. Teachers can use math centers as a time to work with small groups of students while the class is engaged in independent learning. Math centers might include blended learning in which technology is integrated as an essential part of center activities. Regardless of how math centers are organized or implemented, teachers can use centers to differentiate for students' learning needs and provide reinforcement of core skills and concepts in a highly engaging learning environment.

Additional Activities/Discussion Questions

1. Develop a plan for implementing standards. Determine how you envision math centers working in your math block. Consider the following:
   a. How often will you use math centers? (e.g., Daily or weekly)
   b. Will you group students or will students self-select the center?
   c. What materials do you have or need for your centers?
   d. How will you have students record their progress?
   e. Will you use a teacher center?

2. Before implementing math centers. Determine the goals you have for student learning based on their current math needs. Make a list of math skills or knowledge needed by your students according to current assessments. In particular, identify areas in which students may be struggling or need more practice. Once you have determined general needs and target areas, match games, technology, and other engaging math activities to reinforce the needed learning. Contemplate the games and skills provided in this chapter to jumpstart your ideas for developing centers to match your students' learning needs.

3. Now that you have a plan in place, anticipate the order in which you will implement the centers. Remember that teaching the behaviors and expectations explicitly for each center is necessary as a whole class at the onset of the center to ensure success. Develop a lesson plan for how you will implement the first center and those that follow. Include in your plan how you will model each one and reinforce your social and academic expectations. Introduce one center at a time during whole class instruction by teaching, reinforcing, and repeating the expected behaviors and academic learning expectations. Take pictures of your students while their are exhibiting desired behaviors and post the pictures and directions for each center to remind students of your expectations.

Instructor Activities

1. During class, have students develop a math center plan including an explanation for five different centers with details for each center including:
   a. The standards and skills/concepts to be reinforced.
   b. A list of the materials needed.
   c. A plan for how and in what order each center will be introduced.
   d. Student-friendly descriptions of behaviors and expectations.
   e. A lesson plan with details for the initial teaching of each center in a whole-class lesson.
   f. Students should present in detail one of their five centers to the class explaining their rationale for their overall center plan and the learning goals.

2. Students can develop a file of math games and activities for their choice of grade level that could be used in centers. They can choose from games listed in this chapter and find others online related to standards or content. Assign students to write rules for 3-5 games that could be used by children in math centers. For one of the games, assign students to work in groups to create a video with playing directions using Flipgrid. Have students share their video rules and play the game in class. Create a bank of videos so that students can have access to each other's game videos to use in future classrooms.

Chapter 9

Putting It All Together

Self-Reflection

How do you approach change? How do you gain inspiration? What is one goal you have for renewing or revitalizing your math instruction?

© Poznyakov/Shutterstock.com

We remember the start of our first year of teaching. School wasn't in session yet, but we were anxious to see our classroom. The key was handed to us and we went to our room, venturing down the hallway. We opened the door and we were surprised at how bare the space was: the walls were empty, void of color, and the desks were stacked in a corner. What we imagined as a warm, welcoming, and organized environment was now completely left up to us—a daunting task, it seemed!

This is sometimes how it feels when we approach planning a year of instruction or thinking about how to implement new ideas related to curriculum. It feels like we are looking at bare walls, not sure where to start or what to hang up. We look around at all that needs to be organized and wonder how it will take place. There are usually lots of questions. You might be asking, *How do I put all of this together and make it work in my math block? Where do I start? How do I organize and prepare myself and my students for implementing these ideas in the classroom?* In this chapter, we answer these questions and help you think through the process of implementing what you have learned. We discuss how to put it all together, and make your classroom work effectively and efficiently while centered on the technology-infused Big 5 pedagogies.

Let's take a moment to review what we have highlighted so far. In the early part of this book, we spent time exploring good teaching, planning with students in mind, and encouraging critical thinking and engagement. We also discussed the importance of structured learning for all students and knowing how to meet students where they are at and not just where the textbook says they should be. Most recently, we unpacked the Big 5 pedagogies which included:

1. Daily Routines
2. Open-ended Tasks
3. Project-based Learning
4. Problem-based Learning
5. Math Centers

We explored how the pedagogies align with the Common Core Mathematics Standards and how to incorporate technology for assessment, instruction, engagement, and creating products of learning. As you may recall, these student-centered pedagogies develop 21st-century skills: communication, collaboration, creativity, critical thinking, problem solving, and digital literacy.

As you wrap up your thinking and make steps toward putting these ideas into practice, we cover five aspects to keep in mind during your preparation for implementation.

1. Organizing your math block
2. Setting goals in your math practice
3. Fostering a mathematical mindset
4. Supporting inclusive practice
5. Developing digital literacy

Before diving into classroom and instructional organization, let's first take a moment to ground ourselves once again in research.

Putting Research into Practice

Our approach to implementing the Big 5 pedagogies depends a lot on who we are as people, our beliefs about ourselves, and how we approach problem solving, which is similar to how students respond when faced with a challenge. Developing curriculum and organizing learning is a form of problem solving and how you approach this challenge reveals a lot about you. So, do you believe you can grow and change in your knowledge and abilities, or do you believe your knowledge and abilities are fixed? These beliefs reflect research on mindset theory (Dweck, 2006). Examining your own growth mindset will help you take what you learn from this book and challenge yourself to apply it to your classroom. As in anything that is new, there are inherent challenges.

Mindset theory is based on two opposing beliefs about self. If someone believes his intelligence is fixed and cannot grow, this person is said to have a "fixed mindset." If someone believes attributes of intelligence can continue to grow, change, and improve then this person has a "growth mindset" (Dweck, 2006).

So, back to you—how do you approach problem solving? What do you believe about yourself and your abilities? Do you believe you can take on the challenge and implement the Big 5 pedagogies we have introduced in this book? Evaluate your mindset by taking the Mindset Interactive Quiz.

 **Try It!**

What mindset are you? Take the quiz and read more about growth mindset here.

Growth Mindset Interactive Quiz: https://www.idrlabs.com/growth-mindset-fixed-mindset/test.php

Stop and Reflect

What did you learn about the way you approach problems? How might your mindset impact your ability to implement the Big 5 pedagogies? How can you support your growth mindset?

_____

_____

Mindset in Mathematics Instruction

There is a growing body of research to suggest that your beliefs in mathematics also predicts your performance (Boaler, 2013). Students' beliefs are largely shaped by their prior experiences with math and the type of classroom environment espoused by the teacher. Teachers who view mistakes as an opportunity to grow and improve are likely to promote a growth mindset, whereas teachers who attribute students' performance based solely on their achievement promote a fixed mindset. An important aspect of changing students' mindset about math, is evaluating your actions as a teacher, from the tasks you provide to the way you celebrate student success. When you allow students to improve their work, retake an exam, and celebrate their effort you are setting the stage for a growth mindset. The kinds of tasks you select for students also contribute to the mindset they adopt. Many of the pedagogies we have discussed throughout this book support a growth mindset as they are open-ended, tiered, have multiple solution paths, and provide an opportunity to improve with effort. Supporting students in changing the messages they tell themselves when it comes to learning math is also an important consideration. Boaler (2010) found that mathematics sends the strongest messages of fixed ability and thinking. What that means is students are likely to believe their effort cannot change their ability in math. We know this message is likely to cause students to disengage and give up when faced with a challenging task. The beginning of the school year is a perfect opportunity to reframe these messages while getting to know your students.

👁 **View It:** In this blog post Dr. Dickenson shares strategies to support a growth mindset the first week of school. http://www. teacherpreptech.com/2018/08/first-day-of-math.html

🛍 **Snag It:** Create a bulletin board around growth mindset. Use these posters to reinforce the idea that students' messages about themselves can change and promote a growth mindset. http://bit. ly/2MFinXz

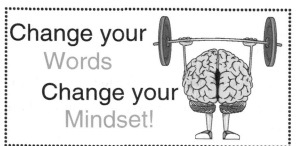

◉ **View It:** Dr. Jo Boaler shares math tasks and videos to support students in adopting a growth mindset in math

https://www.youcubed.org/

Organizing Your Math Block

Planning and organizing your math classroom is like putting together a puzzle. Each part plays an important role in efficiency and organization since there are a variety of pieces to put together. How you organize all the parts will aid in making your room run efficiently and smoothly while supporting your students' success.

Here are some aspects to consider while organizing your effective and efficient math classroom:

    A. Timing and organization of daily tasks
    B. Developing systems for organizing, collecting, and documenting student work
    C. Tracking student progress
    D. Communicating with students and parents
    E. Arranging your classroom

We will focus on each of these areas and give you tips for best practice in organizing and staying on track to make your classroom effective, efficient, and organized.

    A. **Timing and organization of daily tasks**

Timing and organization are critical components of quality math instruction and are not only important for you as the teacher but also essential for your students. Children thrive in environments with organization and structure since this type of environment communicates safety and security. To provide structure, you need to have a schedule for instruction that is followed on a daily basis. Using agendas, posted schedules, and timers can be extremely beneficial to communicating the classroom organization to your students as well as for keeping yourself and students on task and on time.

Agenda—Agendas can be written on your whiteboard, but they can also be interactive and placed in a Google Slide or posted on Google Classroom. On the slide, provide any hyperlinks to a particular video you might like students to watch, math warm-up task that you have made on a Google doc, or give students information about Math Center rotations. Whatever you want to put on your agenda, it can be transformed into a digital agenda. Agendas can be easily stored and revised for another lesson, for another year, or updated for daily use.

Digital agendas work best when your students have one-to-one access to technology. Agendas as self-starters or independent work at the start of math instruction allows time to monitor and check-in individually with students, collect homework, or pull a small group to the back table for a preview of the upcoming material. The activities within an interactive agenda can be informative, directive, or more. Using agendas in this way helps students to know what to expect, what to do, and how to begin. Requiring the students to be independent encourages self-monitoring.

We have included an example of a Google slide agenda for you to view or modify.

> ### Agenda for October 10, 2020
> 1. Number Talk Warm-up
>   a. Solve the math puzzle of the day (mental math only!)
>   b. Be prepared to share your solution with your partner.
>
> 2. What did we learn yesterday? - Review arrays (Khan Academy) complete the Give me 5 slide
>
> 3. Exploring and Recording Arrays - Cooperative groups
>
>   a. Create as many arrays as you can and take a photo to share with the class
>
> 4. Exit Ticket (Google Form)

🛍 **Snag It:** Agenda link https://docs.google.com/presentation/d/1Vv31ZvfTfvLaVTG3wbxds WbulR8fbk-Jm3hEtHOB4VY/edit?usp=sharing

Timer—A simple timer can keep both you and your students on track during a lesson, since time management is a common struggle. Using an online timer or a phone timer are easy ways to be aware of passing time, but you can also buy a simple kitchen timer to do the exact same thing. We have included a link to free online technology timers that we have used. Regardless, timers can be used to keep rotations between math centers moving at just the right time, ensure group work does not go beyond what you had planned, and help you to know when to bring closure to independent work time. An extra benefit of a timer is that it provides a psychological end time for students. If you place the timer under a document camera, students can use the visual countdown to self-regulate and manage their own time. It also can be used as differentiation for students who need time in advance to mentally prepare for transitions or for those who need extended time to do their work. Teaching students to use a timer to their own benefit is another life skill that you can practice as a whole class.

Make the Tech Connection: Productivity

Review the digital timers we have included in our Tech Tool List (under the term productivity). Many of these tools include additional features such as random calling on students, textbox to include agenda, and voice monitoring. As this list is on an editable Google Sheet feel free to include useful tech tools that you come across.

Tech tool list: http://www.teacherpreptech.com/p/tech-tools.html

Source: Screenshot from Classroom Screener: https://classroomscreen.com

Weekly Schedule—Having a weekly schedule is important for you to steer the course of your instruction and to let your students know what to expect. Of course, you should also have a record of your daily plan in a teacher planner, whether on paper or on a digital document. Ideally, you should have a year-long plan, as well as a semester and weekly plan. At the daily level, we like to plan one week in advance in a weekly planner. If you choose a paper document, you can buy a teacher planner at any stationery/teacher supply store or online store. You can also find pages online to print that are free. Regardless of how you organize your plan, you should make it easily accessible so that you can refer to it throughout the teaching day. In our experience, planning and classroom management go hand-in-hand. Teachers who have spent the time to pre-plan their day know what they are doing, what they need, and are more able to seamlessly connect one lesson to the next. Planning also influences student engagement, and when a teacher is well planned, there is usually less "down time" during which students can be off task and get into trouble.

Below is an example of a weekly planner that can be either digital or paper. We like Monday through Friday pages with a lot of space to record daily information across all subjects, including math. You can customize your own planner on an Excel spreadsheet or purchase a planning calendar. Record your day according to your hourly schedule. If you have daily routines, place them on your schedule as well, such as calendar or number talk. Then organize the content area instruction by time blocks. Include your recess and lunch break on your schedule. In mathematics we include the objective, an essential question, the math standard, and a brief description of the evidence of learning to be collected or assessed. Doing this for each day across your entire week will ensure that you are thinking about the progression of teaching and learning and what students need from day to day to be successful. We also recommend sharing this information on your bulletin board so students can conceptualize what they are learning about. Creating this visually establishes a mental frame for students.

🔒 **Snag It:** shorturl.at/bGJRT

Daily Schedule—Once you have the general weekly planning taken care of, you need to organize the timing of activities within your math block. Research has shown that teachers often do not teach math as long as they should and instead shorten the period, so it is always better to spend more time than less in teaching math content (Stevenson, Chen, & Lee, 1993). Depending on the grade level, your math block may be 30 to 90 minutes or longer. Younger children tend to have shorter instructional blocks due to shorter attention spans when using traditional instruction; however, activities and methods of instruction as we have described in this book are highly engaging and will occupy younger students for longer periods of time; so again, you must know your students as well as their engagement level and plan accordingly. If you are engaging students in Problem- or Project-based Learning, expect to have longer periods of instruction. Starting students in a significant task and then cutting them off after they have just begun is not recommended. Not having enough time to authentically engage in an investigation can be very frustrating for students. Thus, carefully planning your schedule to match the needs of the task and your students is essential.

We have included a sample math block schedule around an open-ended task. As we noted earlier, this structure may depend on your school site and district expectations, teammates at your grade level, personal goals, learning rhythm of your students, or the task at hand. If you are engaging students in a Project-based Learning task, you will want to provide students enough time to engage in the investigation. Also remember to include enough time for closure and wrap-up as it is an essential part of the learning. A schedule for a project-based task will be different than the one below, since this schedule is for an open-ended task. We also provide a short explanation of the activities in the schedule.

60–90 Minute Math Block

Daily Plan Sample:

1. Daily Routine	10 minutes
2. Open-Ended Task (Group Work)	15 minutes
3. Learning Target Discussion	5–10 minutes

4. Practice and Quick Check	15–20 minute
5. Math Centers	25 minutes
6. Exit Ticket and Wrap Up	10 minutes

1. *Daily Routine* In this example, you will see that the math block starts with a daily routine. We covered many examples of daily routines in Chapter 4. This could be a Number Talk, calendar, or a math warm-up problem.
2. *Open-Ended Task* The open-ended task is independent and group work around a rigorous open-ended task that challenges students' understanding of a concept. Recall, open-ended tasks are characterized by the following attributes:
   - Open-ended with multiple solutions
   - Multiple entry points at differing levels
   - Various student learning levels possible
   - Engage and interest students
   - Conceptually-based
   - Increased levels of cognitive demand
3. *Learning Target Discussion* After students have engaged in the open-ended task, the teacher orchestrates a class discussion around the findings, sharing their solutions while the teacher purposefully probes and questions students' thinking about the concepts, highlighting ideas that connect to the learning target.
4. *Practice and Quick Check* Students next engage in individual practice (perhaps whiteboards or math journal) and the teacher assesses their progress informally.
5. *Math Centers* As students finish their independent practice, they can move to a pre-designated math center where they explore the same concept in more depth or practice other ongoing skills or concepts. During the math centers, the teacher can differentiate instruction by pulling students who might be struggling with the new learning to a small group in order to provide additional support and re-teaching. Math centers at this point in the lesson may be optional. Some teachers may want to use math centers as the instruction focus for the whole block, but centers can also be integrated into regular daily instruction. As discussed in Chapter 8, there are many ways to implement math centers.
6. *Exit Ticket and Wrap Up* Near the end of the block, briefly discuss the learning that has taken place and follow up with a final problem that can be analyzed as an assessment of individual learning. This exit ticket can be conducted on tablets using a tool such as Go Formative or with a prepared final exit ticket question on Google forms. Assessment results is a record of student progress and should be used to determine next steps in teaching.

Posting your daily math block schedule for students to see is another way to communicate daily math activities. Using a poster or pocket chart, provides a visual to show rotations for math centers or student names for groups for a Project-based Learning task. Students can easily refer to the chart to know what group they are in or where they need to be throughout the math block. Similar to agendas, the daily schedule can be provided on a Google slide or PowerPoint slide that you project or that students can access on their tablets or computers.

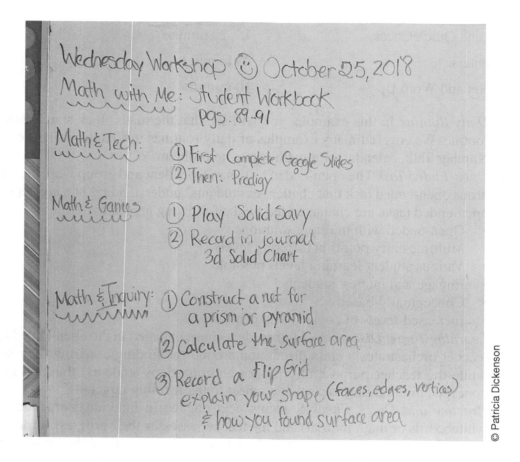

© Patricia Dickenson

Timers can be used to signal the rotation of your students throughout your schedule. Students can be taught to respond to the timer when it goes off and transition to the next group or activity on the chart or slide without being told verbally. Expectations must be taught explicitly for transitions and reinforced daily at the beginning, but once your students get used to moving from center to center they will be able to do this automatically. By having your students independently monitor their actions, you are building self-monitoring and independence which are important 21st-century skills.

B. Developing systems for organizing, collecting, and documenting student work

Organization is not something we all do naturally; when it comes to students, you will find this to be extremely true. Therefore, you need to teach your students explicitly how to organize their written work, keep records, and store digital creations.

Math Journal—One way to streamline mountains of student work is to have everything recorded in a single book or math journal, which can be a composition or spiral notebook. We like having a composition book as pages cannot be easily torn out and with a table of contents to start, students' notes become organized. The benefit of a math journal is that you can collect it periodically to check on students' thinking and look for potential misconceptions. You can also use journal to have students reflect on their learning and ask you questions. Assigning a grade for journal work can be a good motivator to stay on task. Also, you can keep journals in the class-room on a shelf or in cubbies so they are never left at home by accident.

Math journals can be used to record any thinking or writing. You can teach students to use dif-ferent headings within their journal to note specific types of thinking like:

- Daily Math
- Group Thinking
- My Thinking
- Quick Writes
- Reflections
- Jot Thoughts
- Problem of the Day

Always have students write a heading with the date and title of their work so it remains organ-ized and then you can later decipher the activity related to their response. Again, you must explicitly model and teach how to make a heading on the page of paper.

In the intermediate grades, it is more practical for student to organize single pages of lined or graph paper in a binder. When using this method, ask students to come with dividers or have them create tabs with book-marking stickers found at a stationery supply store. Sections might include:

- Title of the project or the name of the unit
- Notes
- Journal
- Problems
- Reflections
- Vocabulary/Dictionary

Pockets are a great way to help students organize homework with one pocket being a "To Do" pocket while the other be the "Completed Work" pocket. Pockets can also be used for current or ongoing investigations and can be marked with the title of the investigation or project. Pockets, report folders, and large envelopes can be used for storing students' findings and ongoing data. Again, these can be collected, scanned, or uploaded to become digital records.

Digital Math Journal—If you are ready to go digital and ditch the paper trail consider how you want students to organize digital files, since there will be images, group work, project-related work, and individual documents that need proper storage and labeling for future access. Create folders for each of your students within Google classroom and make sure that students organize and submit their own labeled work into their designated folders. Some applications store stu-dents' work within their own files which you can manage as the teacher.

Organizational systems like labeling and filing must be explicitly taught at the start of the year as well as how to access and be responsible for technology use. Lessons should be dedicated during the first few weeks of school to address topics such as:

- Checking out tablets or computers
- Logging in to applications

- Creating documents
- Labeling files
- Sharing documents
- Proper care and treatment of devices
- Appropriate communication and netiquette
- Digital Portfolios

Collecting Work—Gathering evidence informs our instruction, future planning, and documentation when reporting student progress to parents through conferences, grading, and report cards. Students constantly produce data and one of our jobs is to identify evidence from this data to document learning progress. You might wonder, *does everything need to be collected and graded?* From our experience, grading everything students produce is not practical; however, strategically gathering evidence of student learning that shows progress toward the standard and or evidence of math skill development is critical. For example, if your student learning goal is for students to be able to create an array and a corresponding expression, then taking digital pictures of students' arrays and providing an opportunity to create voice-over recordings of the related multiplication would be valuable evidence.

> Gathering evidence informs our instruction, future planning, and documentation when reporting student progress to parents through conferences, grading, and report cards.

Digital Student Evidence—Student work can be collected in many different forms, both paper and digital. While paper can be easily manipulated, digital evidence is easier to collect and store. We suggest gathering both types of evidence. If you give your students a student number from 1 to 30 at the beginning of the year and require students to put this number on every piece of paperwork alongside their name in the right hand corner, you can easily organize the work numerically to grade and record. Digital work can be collected, stored, and shared easily using applications like Google Classroom and Gradelink. Not only can students easily see their work and receive feedback, but parents can also sign into their students' accounts and view their work. Student numbers can also be used as the same number when it comes to assigning computers or tablets.

Digitizing images of 3-dimensional evidence is another way to document student work. For example, a student's ability to build collections of 10 up to 100 can be captured in pictures through your tablet or phone. Moreover, if a student can build collections to 100 and then count by 10s, this can be recorded in a video. Students can reflect on their learning in writing to go with the pictures or videos. Of course, in the case of Project-based Learning, students will likely create digital or physical artifacts that you can collect or document digitally.

In Google Classroom, students have their own folder and can collect and organize their work. Teaching students how to label their own digital files and organize them into digital folders must also be explicitly taught. Just like paper organization, digital organization is not innate. Students can also take pictures of their written work to scan into digital files. Free scanning tools are available online that create a clear and legible copy. See the link below for a free digital scanner that we like to use.

Photo Scan: https://www.google.com/photos/scan/

C. Tracking student progress

As teachers, an important aspect of our job is documenting student achievement. Schools often have school-wide digital programs for collecting and recording student progress and generating report cards. Knowing what your school provides is the first step. Find out what record-keeping programs are already available to you and make use of them to record data. Also, take any opportunities provided to learn more about the function and use of these data tools.

In addition, you can make simple spreadsheets on a program like Excel or Google Sheets to give you a place to record assignments and record students' achievement. Of course, this means boiling down your evaluation of student progress to a number or a letter. If you think back to the many rubrics we have provided in the many chapters across this text, you can use the numerical evidence from rubrics to record growth and progress. We have provided a simple data recording sheet below to get you started.

In Chapter 4, we discussed anecdotal notes which are your written qualitative comments about student progress. If you have these comments digitized, they provide another way to document student learning and may help to expand on other quantitative assessment data you have gathered.

Make the Tech Connection: Google Forms & Sheets

Creating a simple form to record student notes can produce a spreadsheet of information that you collect throughout the school year. A google form is a survey where you record information in a textbox. When you look at the data you will see a collection of responses that you created. Data can be organized by student name or date.

You can make a copy of the form that we have created to keep track of your students. Feel free to include additional information on the survey as you desire.

 Snag It: https://goo.gl/zjf1YE

Student Portfolios

An excellent way to gather and record student progress is to develop portfolios throughout the year. A portfolio is an assessment tool that consists of individual student work to demonstrate learning, whether developmentally across time or a showcase of best work. The content of the portfolio is usually determined by its purpose. If you are using the portfolio to show growth in mathematics, you would have students select pieces that demonstrate growth. If the portfolio is being used as a collection of work to represent a significant project, as in Project-based Learning, then the student will select particular pieces demonstrating the process to the final product. Perhaps the portfolio is being used to showcase students' best work, then the content would be pieces that demonstrate high quality work.

Digital portfolios allow for all forms of work to be collected, such as pictures, 3-D creations, papers, presentations, and videos; however, portfolios can also be created from collections of paper copies of student work enhanced with digital pictures. Teachers can use either of these types of portfolios when conferencing with both students and parents about the learning that has taken place.

Portfolios enhance students' metacognition by including purposeful reflection on what has been learned and explanation for selection of work. Engaging your students in reflective thinking forces them to think more deeply about their own thinking. It is a powerful tool to shape students' beliefs about themselves and the power they have over their own learning. Reflection of this kind is also a window into students' thinking and can provide insight into valued activities as well as beliefs and attitudes of your students in relationship to their own individual learning.

If you are using a portfolio as an ongoing record of student work, have students take key samples of their work at the end of a unit to put into their digital or paper portfolios. Students sift through their notebooks, digital folders, or binders to identify a recent example of work they believe represents significant learning or growth. This could include:

- Data from investigations
- Representations
- Written explanations
- Reflections
- Pictures of 3-D models
- Video
- Rubric assessments
- Self-assessments
- Reflections

If this is non-digital data, these samples can be placed into a student's portfolio, which can be large binder or individual folder kept in a designated spot in the room, such as a crate or file drawer. If using a digital portfolio, files can be organized on a student's individual flash drive or documents within a student's computer file to highlight their work and reflection. As a teacher, you can also set up your own web page where you can host individual files and make work available through an individualized shared link. Students would only be able to access their own work samples and reflection.

In some cases, teachers want control over the selection of work in a portfolio; however, we believe allowing students to select for a portfolio is even more valuable to student learning. When selecting for the portfolio, we suggest asking students to choose a piece because it displays one or more of the following:

- ❑ Significant math concepts learned
- ❑ Accomplishment of a math skill
- ❑ Mathematical thinking

❏ Evidence of teamwork
❏ Key parts of an investigation or project
❏ Final product or presentation
❏ Something for which they are proud
❏ A product or model they made

Once students select the item for the portfolio, they should reflect on the learning or experience around which the portfolio item was created using specific given prompts. These can be to responded to in writing or captured orally. Students' responses are placed alongside the chosen work sample in the portfolio, whether digital or paper. The process of selecting a sample, reflecting on the significance of the document, and providing a written or oral (digitally captured audio or video) reflection to go along with a selected piece of work assists students in recognizing their own learning and growth, encourages self-actualization, and builds self-efficacy.

You can find below an example of a generic portfolio reflection form you can use with students. You can modify this form in many different ways to suit your students' reflection needs.

Reflection Form	
Why did you select this piece?	
What did you do or make?	
How did you do or make it?	
Who did you collaborate with?	
What did you learn?	

🛍 Snag It: Make a copy of the Reflection Form shorturl.at/ryU58

Digital Portfolios are also becoming increasingly popular in upper elementary and secondary classrooms. With a digital portfolio, students create a website or a blog to share evidence of student learning throughout the school year. Their home page can feature information about themselves and math goals for the year. Students can be directed to create a page to represent each unit in their math curriculum. Templates are built into each page of a website and images can be easily uploaded from classroom folders or desktops.

Make the Tech Connection: Google Sites

Having a digital portfolio creates an archive of students' work on the web in a physical space for review, sharing, and reflection. Our students love creating a website to share their work with parents and peers. The excitement of creating a webpage will kick student motivation into overdrive. We have our students share an image, their math goals, and their top ten favorites on their home page.

Check out one of our students' web pages. https://goo.gl/yZi1N8

Make the Tech Connection: Save to Google Drive

This Chrome extension will take snapshots of any images on the web so your students can post these images on their website or blog. Rather than having students download and save pictures on a cluttered desktop, this tool will allow students to simply click on the drive icon in their web browser and automatically save these images to their drive. Then students can easily locate their images to include in their webpage.

D. Communicating with students and parents

It is important to view parents positively and consider them as partners in their children's education. Together you can provide support for children's success. Communicating with families is a part of this process and leveraging technology allows you to communicate about topics you are studying, projects, field trips, needs for supplies, or parent participation. You can also encourage parent participation by providing questions for parents to ask their student at home related to school and current learning. Home-school connections are powerful in engaging families and students alike.

Often schools have digital systems used school-wide to communicate with parents. It is important to find out what your school uses and regularly harness it to communicate with families. Communicating with students and parents is valuable and enhances family involvement and support by providing access to the classroom. Here are a few other ways to communicate or involve families:

- Remind.com is a free and easy way to communicate such things as reminders, upcoming deadlines, homework, and events. Parents and students can subscribe and then receive notices you send out as one-way communication. Each person subscribes from their end to your account and then they receive your communications.
- Other applications, like Seesaw and Edmodo, allow parents to subscribe to their students' accounts so they can access and see their students' work. Google classroom has a parent feature that allows parents to sign into their child's account and view class materials.
- Monthly newsletters, whether digital or paper, provide your families with an update of what you are learning and how they might be involved. Parents appreciate ongoing communication and often feel more connected to their child's learning by knowing more about your class.
- Plan events that invite parents to participate. Parents can be part of a panel who hear the final presentations at the culmination of a Project-based Learning task or can assistant in running a math center.
- Provide a link to a student's electronic portfolio or videos and have the parents reflect on their child's learning.

E. Arranging your classroom

How we arrange our classroom communicates much about our beliefs. If you organize your desks in groups, you are communicating that you value collaboration. If you ensure your everyday materials (e.g., paper and manipulatives) are student-accessible, it communicates that you value student autonomy and choice. So, as we think about how to organize our classroom space, it is important to consider a few questions:

- ❑ How can I arrange seating to foster teamwork and build collaboration?
- ❑ How can I create a space where students can easily move, see comfortably, or sit in more than one area?
- ❑ Where is the best location for students to have easy access to tools and supplies, like paper, pencils, markers, scissors, counters/manipulatives, and calculators?
- ❑ Where should games and other math center materials be placed for easy access?

❏ Where should technology be located to ensure easy access, safety, security, and recharging?

❏ How can I display student work so that it can be referenced, valued, and appreciated?

❏ How can I display charts, expectations, and records of past learning for accessibility?

Once you begin to formulate ideas about your learning space, you can move forward to the planning phase. To begin planning your classroom space:

1. Make a sketch of your classroom.
2. Organize the furniture in your sketch so that it fulfills your beliefs about classroom interaction and accessibility. Include enough seating for your maximum possible number of students.
3. Determine where materials will be kept and how they will be made available.
4. Consider the location of charts, posters, expectations, and student work. Ensure there is equitable space for displaying student work.
5. Consider where you plan to put charts or posters that students will use for reference (e.g., Hundreds Charts, Multiplication Chart, math center rotation schedule).
6. Identify where and how the technology will be stored and managed in the room. Again, ensure easy accessibility and space for students to move around and between desks and chairs.

There are digital options to help you with the visual layout of your classroom. You can use a PowerPoint slide to organize the layout by putting shapes on a slide that match the layout and furniture of your classroom. You can also use free tools to do the same thing.

 Make the Tech Connection:

Check out this free tool to organize your classroom layout. Classroom Architect. http://classroom.4teachers.org/

Once you have planned your organizational strategy, you are ready to begin the physical work of putting your room together. Remember that your walls are tools for learning. What you hang on your classroom walls should speak of students' learning, including their words and ideas. Of course, include your own charts too, but make sure that your walls are balanced and that student work is evident. Capturing student conjectures on charts or displaying their work in designated spaces on the walls shows you value students' ideas. We recommend you keep your walls fresh by replacing student work weekly.

Effective classrooms encourage students to thrive and engage wholeheartedly in mathematics. Here are a few reminders of effective mathematics classrooms.

Effective Math Classrooms are	Effective Math Classrooms are NOT
• Welcoming and connected to students and parents • Busy with activity and student talk • Organized and accessible with manipulatives and materials available to students • Structured for movement • Visually stimulating and provide visual reinforcement of learning • Organized for interaction and collaboration • Efficient with systems for collecting, distributing, and showcasing student work • Well-planned • A place where students and teachers are energized to learn	• Unwelcoming or isolated from families and students • Silent and still • Teacher-centered and controlled with materials behind locked cabinets • Dull and uninteresting • Movement-limiting • Disorganized and focused on independent learning • Stifling and uncreative

Setting Goals in Your Math Practice

Goal setting is an effective way to improve students' achievement, and it can also improve your own teaching practice (Marzano, Pickering & Pollock, 2001). Making steps toward growth requires time set aside to reflect on your overall practice and identify goals for improvement. Whether you are a brand new teacher or a veteran teacher, at the end of every school year it is important to take stock of where you are in your math teaching and purposefully reflect on your next steps through goal setting.

Goal setting includes four important steps that should repeat yearly:

1. Reflect on your practice
2. Identify 1–3 areas of needed growth
3. Set specific goals
4. Develop an action plan

Reflect & Identify Areas for Growth There are many significant areas to consider in your own development as a math teacher and below we provide a list for reflection. Consider each point carefully while identifying 1–3 areas for growth. You know yourself, so set achievable goals that you really believe are possible.

- ❏ What are my strengths?
- ❏ What areas need growth?
- ❏ To what degree am I
  - ❏ Incorporating the Big 5 pedagogies?
    - ❏ Daily Routines
    - ❏ Open-Ended Tasks

        ❑ Project-based Learning
        ❑ Problem-based Learning
        ❑ Math Centers
    ❑ Engaging students in group work?
    ❑ Incorporating technology?
    ❑ Encouraging students to share their math thinking?
    ❑ Incorporating math discussions?
    ❑ Developing students' academic language in math?
    ❑ Incorporating manipulatives?
    ❑ Requiring representations?
    ❑ Using assessment to drive instruction?
    ❑ Matching tasks to students' learning interests?
    ❑ Matching tasks to students' learning needs?
    ❑ Differentiating instruction for my advanced students?
    ❑ Differentiating instruction for my struggling students?
❑ What new strategies or teaching pedagogies have I implemented consistently this year?
❑ Who have I sought at my school or district for math teaching support?
❑ What math professional development or conferences have I attended?

Goal Setting & Action Plan Once you have considered these questions and identified 1-3 target areas, the next step is to identify actions and evidence to support achieving your goals. We have created a template for you to use following four steps:

Step 1. What is your goal? Describe the focus in clear language that specifically identifies what you will be working towards. Why is it important?

Step 2. Describe the activities and how you will use them in detail.

Step 3. Give yourself a dated deadline for when you expect to have your activities implemented.

Step 4. Identify evidence you can collect to affirm you have met your goal.

Goal Setting Organizer Example—Ms. Peterson's 2nd grade

Step 1. Goal	<ul><li>I will incorporate Daily Routines at the start of every day in specifically two forms: Number Talk and Calendar.</li><li>Daily Routines benefit students as they reinforce math skills and concepts regularly, develop mental math strategies, and provide ongoing practice.</li></ul>
Step 2. Activities	<ul><li>I will include both Number Talks and Calendar daily</li><li>Number Talks will take place at the start of the math block. Students will solve 1-3 given problems mentally.</li><li>Calendar will occur at the start of my instructional day. Students will solve a money problem, use a 100s Chart to chant number patterns, build tens and ones, and bundle days of the year.</li></ul>

Step 3. Deadline	• I will have implemented these two types of Daily Routines by Oct 31.
Step 4. Evidence for Meeting Goal	• My daily schedule should reflect Number Talks and Calendar. • Number Talks and Calendar will be written in the daily agenda posted on the board • I will find evidence on the board showing student solutions from Number Talks and see a visible calendar in our class meeting corner with prompts on the wall for counting and daily math work around money, days of the year, and patterns.

Growth does not come without intentional planning. Once you have gone through this process and see evidence of growth, you will experience the satisfaction of knowing you have set and met your goal. If for some reason you have not, don't beat yourself up; instead, extend yourself some grace and reset your goals. If you are struggling, select fewer goals and make them achievable. You might also elicit support from a colleague for accountability. It is often easier to make strides forward when you are walking alongside someone else.

🛍 Snag It: Get your own Goal Setting Organizer here

shorturl.at/bzIUW

Fostering a Mathematical Mindset

We started this chapter by talking about your own mindset towards beginning something new. Mindset research (Dweck, 2006) should not only inform the way we approach problems but also how we teach. In teaching, we must help students develop a growth mindset by giving them experiences to note progress over time by goal setting and regular reflection, similar to your own process. This allows students to take ownership over their learning by helping them realize they have more power and control over their own success than they think. The growth mindset keeps us focused on the truth that our ability is not fixed; we have the ability to grow, learn, change, and develop beyond where we are today.

Developing a growth mindset means that we and our students

- See challenge as an opportunity
- Recognize that we are never finished learning
- Take stock in our strengths and weaknesses without comparing to others
- Don't allow others' beliefs to define our abilities
- Identify effort and reflection as the root of improvement
- Use failure as an opportunity to grow
- Value process over the product
- View ourselves as capable and changeable

Every time we problem-solve, we are exercising and developing a growth mindset. When we solve a problem, we are improving and increasing in our problem-solving abilities. Problem-solving becomes easier with opportunities and practice, and we develop greater competence and confidence the more we engage in problem-solving.

Problem solving is key to increasing student motivation, which is often wrapped in how students view themselves. For example, motivation can be derived by feelings of self-efficacy, or students' beliefs about whether they can succeed or not. Another way students view themselves is whether they believe intelligence, abilities, and talents are given at birth or if they can change and grow over time. So, when you hear a student say, "I'm not good at math," he is giving you insight into his belief about himself and his growth mindset. A student who views himself as "bad at math" already believes that he cannot improve and, therefore, has a fixed mindset. Those who have a growth mindset are more likely to succeed than those with fixed mindsets, since they take steps to improve and grow rather than staying in place, believing they have no control over their future (Dweck, 2006).

Fostering students' mathematical mindset is a critical function of our work as teachers. We must remember our role in shaping young minds, attitudes, and beliefs about math. In reality our own subconscious attitudes and beliefs can actually be transmitted to students; therefore, we also must be self-aware and adjust our view of math, for the benefit of both ourselves and our students.

As teachers and curriculum leaders, there are 10 characteristics we must develop in our students as math learners.

1. Children must persevere.
2. Children must critically analyze problems and reason about them.
3. Children must know how to approach problems and solve them in multiple ways.
4. Children must listen to each other's arguments and evaluate their validity.
5. Children must learn to make claims about what they think is true mathematically.
6. Children must use objects and symbols effectively to support their solutions and claims.
7. Children must make sense of their math knowledge by applying it to their daily lives.
8. Children must recognize patterns and structure in numbers and equations.
9. Children must look for repetition and use shortcuts when appropriate.
10. Children must continually reevaluate their reasoning to make sure they are on the right track.

(Adapted from the 8 Standards for Mathematical Practice, NGA & CCSSO, 2010)

Building Mathematical Identity

Beyond just shaping students' mindsets, fostering opportunities for students to develop their mathematical identity and self-conceptions needs to be the focus of our efforts. One way to support students' development of mathematical identity is to identify what being a mathematician is all about. Students need opportunities to generate what mathematicians do, how mathematicians think, and what mathematicians use. By specifically identifying and labeling these characteristics, students will know how their own actions and thoughts mirror those of mathematicians.

To develop students' mathematical identity, we recommend spending time at the beginning of your school year and throughout the first few months of school generating students' ideas about what it means to be a mathematician, based on their previous experiences. Have your students chart and draw responses collaboratively with their peers to capture their thinking about what it means to be a mathematician or do math. Once you begin this process, build on their thinking by revisiting frequently, naming the experiences and identifying the behaviors and ways of thinking that fit a mathematician's. Older students will have more experience than younger students when it comes to background knowledge, school experience, and home life; however, they may have had limited positive mathematical experiences and need help labeling actions as positive examples. These ideas will need to be shaped over time with new experiences generated by your own math classroom. Regardless, all students can draw from their past experiences and funds of knowledge. Younger students who may have less schooling experience can draw on their personal experiences at the start. As well, you can draw attention to these ways of thinking and being when you debrief meaningful learning experiences in your math block. Regularly add your students' collective ideas to a class chart or use a digital space such as a wiki or Padlet to keep a record of your discussions throughout the year as younger students develop new skills and experience new ways of experiencing math.

We've included a few foundational ideas to draw on during your discussions fostering your students' mathematical identity.

What mathematicians do

- Ask questions
- Analyze and solve problems
- Think deeply
- Collaborate with others
- Persevere
- Try many different ways to solve problems
- Know what tools to use
- Use a variety of resources and tools that match the task

How mathematicians think

- Question
- Use knowledge of numbers (place value and Base Ten)
- Use knowledge of operations (addition, subtraction, multiplication, and division)
- Use knowledge about shapes
- Use knowledge about graphs and lines
- Reason whether an answer makes sense
- Draw representations
- Wonder if there is another way to solve a problem
- Explain their solutions
- Argue their reasoning with evidence
- Listen and analyze others' arguments and evidence

What do good Mathematicians do?

They begin and try

They help others

They solve problems

They use strategies

They learn from their mistakes

They work independently

They concentrate

They show stamina

They keep trying – they persist

They choose the right tools

What mathematicians use

- Number lines
- Hundreds charts
- Rulers

- Manipulatives (Base Ten blocks, counters, virtual manipulatives)
- Calculators
- Graph paper and digital graphs
- Tangrams
- Geoboards
- Fraction pieces
- Computers and tablets
- Formulas

Make the Tech Connection: **Canva**

Create a digital poster for your classroom or have your students create one to share their ideas about developing a mathematical mindset.

We believe that using the Big 5 pedagogies not only develops mathematical learners but also supports the development of a students' mathematical identity. By developing habits of mind through engagement, real-world application, and technology-infused learning, you are supporting your students as they become competent mathematicians.

Supporting Inclusive Practice

Do you remember observing a classroom in action when one or two students were visibly disengaged or lost? Our goal is to prevent that from happening by engaging all students right where they are, teaching from the floor to the ceiling. The choices we make in designing instruction to reach all students will determine how they perform throughout the school year. By providing differentiation with tiers of support and scaffolding, students are more likely to flourish, enjoy math, and become academically proficient. It is vital to learn about your students, identify the types of math experiences that best support them in learning new concepts, and provide multiple ways for students to express what they know. This can be achieved if you differentiate instruction, assessment and "teach outside the box." Providing one way to learn about a math concept does not give you (the teacher) with an opportunity to see how a particular student learns best, nor does it provide your students with the chance to think differently about math. In addition, creating extensions to our lessons that expand and enrich our advanced students' experiences will also keep them from boredom, behavioral challenges, and disliking math.

Multiple ways to build on students' understanding of Surface Area:

1. Students wrapped a box in square unit paper to connect a real-life experience with the concept of surface area.
2. Students cut out nets to create polyhedrons and identify number of faces, vertices, and edges.
3. Students used marshmallows and toothpicks to construct a polyhedron.
4. Students used virtual graph paper to illustrate a net and determine the surface area.
5. Students played virtual games to identify polyhedron shapes and matching nets.

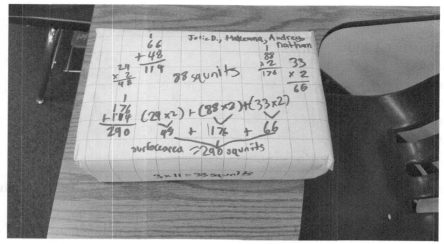

© Patricia Dickenson

Surface Area = 90 sq unit   By: Lupita

© Patricia Dickenson

© Patricia Dickenson

© Patricia Dickenson

In this book, we have covered many different ways to approach differentiation including tiered activities that provide a variety of entry points for students, scaffolding by using math tools, manipulatives, language stems, and strategies to make learning concrete and visual. What works for one student will most likely not work for another, so your job is to figure out what works best for each child and adapt your instruction to promote success. This makes you part detective and part scientist as you follow clues to the source of disinterest or cognitive difficulty. Then you must apply strategies and interventions to mitigate the problem and gather evidence to assess whether your intervention is making a difference or not in the student's learning.

We believe that all students should be able to access and engage content in any learning situation, regardless of ability. One way to do this is by using a framework called Universal Design for Learning (UDL). UDL states that, no matter what curriculum is used, students must be able to access it, barrier free.

UDL identifies three guiding principles when students learn. A teacher should:

1. Provide multiple means of engagement.
2. Provide multiple means of representation.
3. Provide multiple means of action and expression. (CAST, 2018).

Since every math learner will approach mathematical tasks differently, these principles guide how we present and engage students at the intersection of both pedagogy and technology. Let's explore each of these three principles and consider how they should influence our teaching and student learning.

Engagement This principle highlights the importance of teachers engaging and sustaining the attention of students in learning tasks within a learning community. This means that teachers must pay attention to organizing content around students' interests and developing ways to sustain their effort and persistence, while providing opportunities to self-regulate and monitor. This principle suggests varying learning demands and providing feedback, while also encouraging persistence and self-regulation. To do this, we must engage students by including choice, collaboration, goal-setting, self-assessment, and reflection. Engagement also comes from using authentic tasks that are interesting and meaningful within a supportive community.

Representation This principle governs the way content is presented to students. Representations of content should vary in the way content is perceived (visual), received (linguistic or nonlinguistic), or processed (cognitive processing through active versus passive engagement). For example, when math content is presented to students, it is often represented in numeric form. In Chapter 2, we discussed that numbers are symbolic and in the abstract form. Abstract concepts with symbolic notation are more difficult to grasp and every student in the same classroom will perceive the content differently depending on their own personal reasons, such as learning style, visual reception, past knowledge, or disability. Thus, students need variety in the way that information is presented. How content is structured should also engage students in actively processing of information.

Action and Expression This principle recognizes that all learners have differences in how they navigate learning and demonstrate knowledge. Teachers must provide tiered supports for students who need scaffolding during the learning along with alternate ways of expressing knowledge. Sometimes the variation comes in the form of tools or communication. For example, solving a problem requiring multiplication may be difficult for some students who struggle with memorizing multiplication tables. Even though multiplication practice continues, students can be given supports while completing the task, such as a multiplication chart or calculator. For students with a physical disability, holding a pencil to write an explanation may be difficult and using a voice to text feature on the computer would allow for easy expression of ideas instead of writing a response.

Universal Design for Learning in Action

Let's explore a UDL example in action. The concept is regrouping with subtraction and the problem is $45 - 6 =$ ___. If taught in a traditional way showing students numerically how to solve this equation on the board, a percentage of students will be lost and unable to understand. This concept relies and draws on students' knowledge of number and place value. To begin, situating the problem in a real-life context and providing visual supports with concrete representations is critical.

Standard:

CCSS.MATH.CONTENT.2.NBT.B.7

Add and subtract within 1000, using concrete models or drawings and strategies based on place value, properties of operations, and/or the relationship between addition and subtraction;

relate the strategy to a written method. Understand that in adding or subtracting three-digit numbers, one adds or subtracts hundreds and hundreds, tens and tens, ones and ones; and sometimes it is necessary to compose or decompose tens or hundreds.

Problem: There are 40 gummy bears with 10 bears in each bag and five loose gummy bears. The teacher needs to reward six children with one gummy bear each. How many gummy bears are left? Use regrouping to determine how many tens and how many ones.

Here are three different ways for students to learn the concept incorporating various adaptations across the three principles.

1. Virtual Manipulatives:
   a. You can use visuals like a virtual Base Ten tool (National Library of Virtual Manipulatives) to demonstrate another way to see regrouping visually. This method shows visually how to borrow and regroup Base Ten blocks and manipulate them to show students visually what is actually happening when they break apart a 10 bar and regroup. Students practice on tablets using this same tool as a follow-up to the teacher modeling subtraction problems and regrouping. This is a simple drag and drop method and does not require any other paper or pencil action by students. This is an adaptation for students who have difficulty expressing in traditional ways.

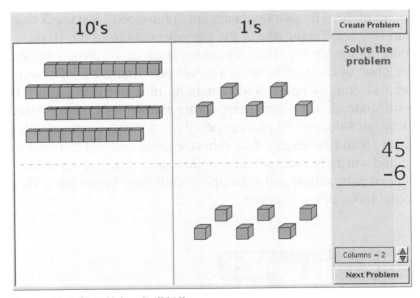

Source: Utah State University (2018).

   b. Another approach uses concrete Base Ten blocks or gummy bear counters under the document camera and projects the image of objects onto a screen. This is an alternative to virtual manipulatives, but is similar using concrete versus virtual objects. Engaging students by having them use counters or Base Ten blocks to solve additional problems with guidance adds to their understanding and follows the CRA method of instruction (see Chapter 2). Students can create their own problems using virtual manipulatives on their tablets to show how they solved their problem and record their explanations either orally or in writing. By having the teacher model regrouping using the Base Ten blocks, students can visualize the concept using real objects. As students work on their own with blocks, they receive concrete support while cognitively processing and benefit from hands-on methods while developing an understanding of the concept.

c. Finally, setting the problem in a real-life context with realia, or objects, and making students active and engaged supports students' understanding. When presented this way, students can access the information visually through participation bypassing a written problem. This works particularly well for students who have limited reading abilities or receptive language.

    i. For example, you can present students with four clear baggies with 10 gummy bears in each bag along with five gummy bears loose and not in a bag, to represent 45. Have four volunteer students come to the front of the room and each hold one baggie with 10 gummy bears inside each. You then ask for students' suggestions for how they could eat six gummy bears when there are only five loose ones. Inevitably, one student will say they can eat the five loose ones and take one gummy bear from one of the bags. This "borrowing" is regrouping and the teacher can explain under the document camera how they would need to open up a bag of 10 gummy bears and take all the bears out, breaking up a group of 10. The gummy bears are "regrouped" leaving 3 bags representing 30 and 10 ones. Taking one of the gummy bears from the 10 ones leaves nine bears loose alongside the three remaining bags of 10. When students realize the six are gone or have been eaten, you see how many are left, noting three groups of ten (30 gummy bears) and remaining nine ones (9 gummy bears). Follow up with students solving in groups other examples of reality-based word problems. Drawing solutions on chart paper gives students practice with support.

Students should be engaged in robust guided and independent experiences physically and virtually manipulating objects and drawing representations around the concept of subtraction and regrouping until they begin using the numeric form or symbolic form, of the equation.

Stop and Reflect

Think of a recent lesson you taught or observed. How could you have changed the lesson to exemplify one or more of the Universal Design for Learning principles?

_____

_____

Incorporating UDL principles while planning across your math block will enhance student engagement, support access and understanding of the content, and enable students to act upon and express what they know. For more information on UDL, you will want to spend time on the UDL Guidelines website at cast.org to view more descriptions and support for implementing UDL.

Let's explore how UDL aligns with the Big 5 pedagogies with infused-technology. As you can see, the pedagogies directly connect with the principles of UDL and add to content accessibility and student expression. These practices and the infused technology meet students right where they are, no matter what their individual needs may be and decreases the barriers that may keep them from learning.

Bringing It Together: Big 5, Technology, and Universal Design for Learning

Big 5 Pedagogies	Engagement	Representation	Action & Expression
Daily Routines			
Strategies *Number Talk* *Hundreds Charts* *Warm-ups* *Calendar Activity* *Math Journals* *Exit Tickets* *Counting Collections*	Tiered to learning level Collaborative or independent Fosters community Autonomy and choice Games Provides immediate feedback	Chants, visuals, repetition Interactive charts, calendar, games, problems Variety of materials for counting collections Strategy practice Digital presentation with virtual manipulatives Highlights patterns Reinforces procedural and conceptual knowledge Promotes group discussion	Multiple solutions Concrete or digital manipulatives Digital, oral, or visual representations Mental math Verbal, non-verbal, or visual solutions Varied ways to assess knowledge

(Continued)

Big 5 Pedagogies	Engagement	Representation	Action & Expression
Technology	Google Docs PowerPoint YouTube Kahoot	Interactive Number Chart Math Playground Interactive Number Line Letsrecap Google Docs PowerPoint	Voice to Text—Word National Library of Virtual Manipulatives https://letsrecap.com/ Shadow Puppet Adobe Spark Goformative.com Google Forms Woot Math Formative Padlet
Open-Ended Questions			
Strategies	Tiered to learning level Varied levels of questions & cognitive demand Develops persistence Authentic and interesting Collaborative Process valued as much as final solution Draws on background knowledge	Input using realia, pictures, digital images, video Multiple entry Points Varied levels of questioning Promotes group discussion Concrete or digital manipulatives Practices conceptual and procedural fluency Conceptually based Tiered support	Multiple methods and multiple solutions paths Digital representations and charts Digital recordings of solutions

(Continued)

Big 5 Pedagogies	Engagement	Representation	Action & Expression
Technology	https://flipgrid.com PowerPoint Google Docs Adobe Spark Recap	Text to Speech—Word Google Docs Flipgrid National Library of Virtual Manipulatives	Voice to Text—Word Google Docs Seesaw Adobe Spark Recap Padlet
Problem-Based Learning			
Strategies	Tiered to learning level Authentic Reality-based problems Collaborative Develops persistence Practices self-regulation Potentially interdisciplinary	Input using realia, pictures, digital images, video Multiple entry points Varied levels of questioning Promotes group discussion Use of multiple tools Practices conceptual and procedural fluency	Multiple methods and solution paths Modeling by graphing, drawing, representing thinking Explanations written or digitally presented
Technology	Padlet Google slides Adobe Spark Recap	Google Docs Text to Speech—Word Popplet Sutori Padlet	Google Docs Voice to Text—Word Adobe Spark Seesaw Desmos Google Drawing Recap Shadow Puppet Create a Graph Padlet

(*Continued*)

Big 5 Pedagogies	Engagement	Representation	Action & Expression
Project-Based Learning			
Strategies	Tiered to learning level	Investigation with tiered support	Collaborative presentation
	Authentic and meaningful tasks	Cooperative groups with mixed abilities	Multiple investigations with varying results
	Student-driven or teacher-driven Question	Promotes group discussion	Modeling by graphing, drawing, representing thinking
	Reality-based investigations	Tiered support with teacher conferences	Explanations written or digitally presented
	Collaborative	Ongoing sense-making and documentation	
	Interdisciplinary	Various tools	
		Graphic organizers	
Technology	Google Docs	Google Docs	Google slides
	PowerPoint	Popplet	Voice to Text - Word
	Recap	Kidspiration	PowerPoint
	Adobe Spark	Text to Speech—Word	Canva
	Padlet	https://flipgrid.com	Seesaw
		National Library of Virtual Manipulatives	Sway
			Recap
			Create a Graph
			Kidspiration
			Padlet
Math Centers			
Strategies	Tiered to learning level	Input using realia, pictures, digital images, video	Modeling by graphing, drawing, representing thinking
	Interactive	Concrete or digital manipulatives	
	Autonomy and choice through menus		

(Continued)

Big 5 Pedagogies	Engagement	Representation	Action & Expression
	Collaborative or independent	Practices conceptual and procedural fluency	Explanations written or digitally recorded
	Student-centered	Computer-driven games that are adaptive	Multiple solutions
	Individualized as needed		Concrete or digital manipulatives
	Rotations and varied activities	Teacher center for support	
	Multiple Intelligences		
	Hands-on learning		
	Games		
Technology	Google Docs	Google Docs	Google Docs
	Adobe Spark	Interactive Number Chart	Seesaw
	Animoto	Math Playground	Voice to Text—Word
	Seesaw	Interactive Number Line	Goformative.com
	Recap	Text to Speech—Word	Animoto
	Padlet	National Library of Virtual Manipulatives	Adobe Spark
		STmath	Seesaw
		Brainpop	Desmos
		PBS Kids Math	Google Drawing
		Dreambox	Recap
			Shadow Puppet
			Create a Graph
			Padlet

Developing Digital Literacy

At this point, you are ready to implement technology as a part of your teaching plan. As you do this, reflect on how you develop students' mindset toward technology use and consumption. Remember that digital learning is more than just going online and using digital tools. Students must know how to wield this power and information gathered in responsible ways. There are many important cognitive skills required as students navigate information, interpret visuals, use tools, and interact with others. This is all part of what is considered students' digital literacy development, and as teachers we are the ones who need to provide experience and support students' growth just as in any other academic subject.

We have outlined four key factors in developing students' digital literacy based on the 21st-century skills.

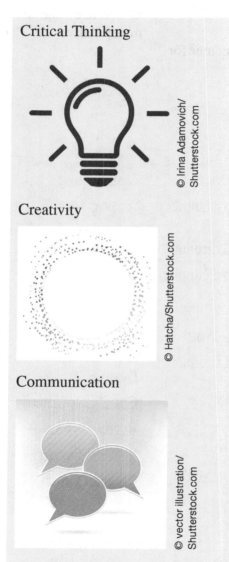

Critical Thinking

Students must be able to sift through articles, data, or visual representations and think critically about the content and whether it is reliable and trustworthy. There is an overwhelming amount of information on the Web and just because it can be accessed doesn't mean that it is reliable and true. Critical thinking is needed for evaluating information and decisions must be made about its value and usability.

© Irina Adamovich/Shutterstock.com

Creativity

Students must learn how to think creatively about information, make quality products with technological tools, and publish their own works responsibly. They need help to know what tools are appropriate and most beneficial to achieving their creative goals. Teachers must also provide a wide range of opportunities for creative expression using technology.

© Hatcha/Shutterstock.com

Communication

Students must become aware of their digital footprint and know how to act responsibly in communicating with others, whether in the immediate environment or in the world at large. Communication no longer is limited to a phone conversation, but rather is represented in many forms across technology. Students must be aware of the nature of communication and its power to do good or harm and learn to use digital communication effectively to accomplish tasks and personal goals. Communication globally to countries beyond our own provides a world of opportunity that motivates and authenticates student learning.

© vector illustration/Shutterstock.com

Collaboration

© Billion Photos/
Shutterstock.com

Students must experience working with others as they seek answers to problems, explore information, and collaborate on new projects. Exposure to a variety of tools and learning how to use these tools provides students with the foundation to explore and present their collaborative ideas to audiences both near and far. Communicating through collaborative tools (e.g., Skype, Google Hangouts, and Twitter) provides a means for greater collaboration that goes beyond the four walls of the classroom.

Source: Adapted from Dowd (2017).

We must ensure students know how to harness technology for both power and information as a natural part of their learning experience. Students should see that technology is not just an add-on to their learning, but rather a natural embedded part of their ways of thinking and as an integral part of the learning experience.

Summary

In this chapter, we discussed implementing the Big 5 pedagogies by organizing, setting goals, fostering a mathematical mindset, along with incorporating inclusive practice and developing digital literacy. When organizing a math instructional block, we must consider timing and organization of daily tasks as well as how to develop systems for collecting and storing student work. When using either digital or paper methods, organization must be taught explicitly and reinforced until systematic. Tracking student progress is also a critical part of teaching and requires multiple methods of assessment as well as collection and storage of data. While it is important to reflect and set goals for our own growth, it is also critical to allow students opportunities to reflect on progress to promote the development of positive mindsets and mathematical identity. Providing opportunities for success in math also means eliminating barriers to learning by incorporating principles of Universal Design for Learning. Furthermore, developing students' digital literacy through critical and creative thinking, along with communication and collaboration, will enhance students' 21st-century skills and enable them to be responsible and respectful citizens.

Additional Activities/Discussion Questions

1. Reflect on your mathematical identity development by remembering experiences both in and outside of school that shaped your view of math, both positively and negatively. How might these experiences influence your work as a teacher?

2. Plan a lesson that builds students' digital literacy around one of the 4Cs. Discuss how it builds students' digital literacy.

3. Now that you have completed the reading of this book, plan a unit of curriculum for ten days of instruction using at least one of the Big 5 pedagogies. Keep in mind the learning progressions, as discussed in Chapter 2. Make sure to include pertinent technology as well as your assessment plan throughout, including a rubric for the final product or solution.

Instructor Activities

1. Engage your students in developing lesson plans around the Common Core Standards for Mathematics that embed at a minimum one of UDL principles. Have students justify how they used differentiation by making direct connections to the three UDL principles. Have students micro-teach their lessons during class.

2. Present several lesson plans to students and have them analyze them for principles of UDL in small groups. Have students then select appropriate technology tools and apply them to improve the lesson plans.

3. Ask students to reflect on a product from your course and select one for a written reflection. Use a Google form and provide prompts similar to the reflection form to prompt students' reflections. Not only will this exercise assist your students in reflecting on their learning, but you will also gather data on their learning.

4. Present lesson vignettes that include students with various learning challenges. Have your students discuss in groups how they would use technology as a means to differentiate access to meet the students' needs. They can use tools in the Bringing It Together matrix.

5. Have students create their own e-portfolio and select and reflect on three assignments from across your course that represent significant learning. Have them write a reflection to go with each about why the selected pieces are significant.

Bibliography

Adelman, C. (1999). Answers in the tool box. Washington, DC: U.S. Department of Education.

Anderson, L. W., Krathwohl, D. R., Airasian, P. W., Cruikshank, K. A., Mayer, R. E., Pintrich, P. R., ... & Wittrock, M. C. (2001). A taxonomy for learning, teaching, and assessing: A revision of Bloom's taxonomy of educational objectives, abridged edition. *White Plains, NY: Longman.*

Armstrong, T. (1999). *7 kinds of smart: Identifying and developing your multiple intelligences.* Plume Books.

Ausebel, D. P. (1968). *The psychology of meaningful learning.* New York: Grune & Straton.

Barron, B. J., Schwartz, D. L., Vye, N. J., Moore, A., Petrosino, A., Zech, L., & Bransford, J. D. (1998). Doing with understanding: Lessons from research on problem-and project-based learning. *Journal of the Learning Sciences, 7*(3–4), 271–311.

Barrows, H., & Kelson, A. C. (1995). *Problem-Based Learning in Secondary Education and the Problem-Based Learning Institute* (Monograph 1). Springfield, IL: Problem-Based Learning Institute.

Bell, S. (2010). Project-based learning for 21st century skills: Skills for the future. *The Clearing House, 83,* 39–43.

Blackwell, L. S., Trzesniewski, K. H., & Dweck, C. S. (2007*). Implicit theories of intelligence predict achievement across an adolescent transition: A longitudinal study and an intervention. Child Development, 78*(1), 246–263.

Bloom, B. S. (1971). Mastery learning. In J. H. Block (Ed.), *Mastery learning: Theory and practice* (pp. 47–63). New York: Holt, Rinehart and Winston.

Boaler, J. (1998). Open and closed mathematics: Student experiences and understandings. *Journal for Research in Mathematics Education, 29*(1), 41–62.

Boaler, J. (2013). Ability and mathematics: The mindset revolution that is reshaping education. *Forum, 55*(1), 143–152.

Blumenfeld, P. C., Soloway, E., Marx, R. W., Krajcik, J. S., Guzdial, M., & Palincsar, A. (1991). Motivating project-based learning: Sustaining the doing, supporting the learning. *Educational Psychologist, 26*(3–4), 369–398.

Bolyard, J., & Moyer-Packenham, P. (2012). Making sense of integer arithmetic: The effect of using virtual manipulatives on students' representational fluency. *Journal of Computers in Mathematics and Science Teaching, 31*(2), 93–113.

Burrill, G., & Kennedy, D. (1997). NCTM and the national standards for mathematics education. In *Improving student learning in mathematics and science: The role of national standards in state policy*. National Academy Press: Washington, DC. Retrieved from https://www.nap.edu/read/5844/chapter/5

California Department of Education (2013). *California Common Core State Standards: Mathematics*. Retrieved from http://www.cde.ca.gov/be/st/ss/documents/ccssmathstandard aug2013.pdf

California Department of Education (2015). *Overview of the standards chapters of the mathematics frameworks*. Retrieved from http://www.cde.ca.gov/ci/ma/cf/documents/mathfwoverview.pdf

California Department of Education (2014). *Common Core State Standards systems implementation plan for California*. Retrieved from http://www.cde.ca.gov/re/cc/

California Department of Education (2016). *What are the Common Core Standards?* Retrieved from http://www.cde.ca.gov/re/cc/tl/whatareccss.asp

California Department of Education (2010). *Improving education for English learners: Research-based approaches*. Sacramento, CA: CDE.

Carpenter, T., Fennema, E., Franke, M. L., Levi, L., & Empson, S. B. (1999). *Children's mathematics: Cognitively guided instruction*. Portsmouth, NH: Heinemann.

CAST (2018). Universal Design for Learning Guidelines version 2.2. Retrieved from http://udlguidelines.cast.org

Chapin, S. H., O'Connor, C. & Anderson, N. C. (2009). *Classroom discussions: Using math talk to help students learn* (2nd edition). Sausalito, CA: Math Solutions.

Cheng, R. W., Lam, S. & Chan, J. C. (2008). When high achievers and low achievers work in the same group: The roles of group heterogeneity and process in project-based learning. British Journal of Education Psychology, *78*, 205–221.

Common Core State Standards (CCSSI). Common Core State Standards for Mathematics (CCSSM). (2010). Washington, DC: National Governors Association Center for Best Practices and the Council of Chief State School Officers. http://www.corestandards.org/wp-content/uploads/Math_Standards.pdf

Cordova, D. I., & Lepper, M. R. (1996). Intrinsic motivation and process of learning: benefitical effects of contextualization, personalization, and choice. *Journal of Educational Psychology*, *88*(4), 715–730.

Desilver, D. (2017). U.S. students' academic achievement still lags that of their peers in many other countries. *Pew Research Center*. Retrieved from http://www.pewresearch.org/fact-tank/2017/02/15/u-s-students-internationally-math-science/

Dewey, J. (1938). *Experience and education*. New York: Simon and Schuster.

Dochy, F. Segers, M., Van den Bossche, P., & Gijbels, D. (2003). Effects of problem-based learning: A meta-analysis. *Learning and Instruction*, *13*, 533–568.

Dowd, E. (2017). Skills for today: Digital literacy & the importance of the 4Cs in a global context. *P21 Partnership for 21st Century Learning*. Retrieved from http://www.p21.org/news-events/p21blog/2172-digital-literacy-a-the-importance-of-the-4-cs-in-a-global-context

Dweck, C. S., (2006). *Mindset: The new psychology of success*. New York: Random House.

Ellenberg, J. (2015). *How not to be wrong: The power of mathematical thinking*. Penguin: London.

Fong, A., Jaquet, K., & Finkelstein, N. (2014). Who repeats algebra I, and how does initial performance relate to improvement when the course is repeated? (REL 2015–059). Washington, DC: U.S. Department of Education, Institute of Education Sciences, National Center for Education Evaluation and Regional Assistance, Regional Educational Laboratory West. Retrieved from http://ies.ed.gov/ncee/edlabs

Franke, M. L., Webb, N. M., Chan, A. G., Ing, M., Freund, D., & Battey, D. (2009). Teacher questioning to elicit students' mathematical thinking in elementary school classrooms. *Journal of Teacher Education, 60*(4), 380–392.

Gardner, D. P., Larsen, Y. W., Baker, W. O., Campbell, A., Crosby, E. A., ... Wallace, R. (1983). *A nation at risk*. National Commission on Excellence in Education (No. 065-000-0177-2). Washington, DC. Retrieved from http://files.eric.ed.gov/fulltext/ED226006.pdf

González, N., Moll, L. C., & Amanti, C. (Eds.). (2006). *Funds of knowledge: Theorizing practices in households, communities, and classrooms*. Routledge: London.

Grant, M. M. (2002). Getting a grip on project-based learning: Theory, cases and recommendations. *Meridian: A Middle School Computer Technologies Journal, 5*(1), 83.

Hattie, J. A. C. (2009). *Visible learning: A synthesis of over 800 meta-analyses relating to achievement*. New York, NY: Routledge.

Hmelo, C. E. (1998b). Problem-based learning: Effects on the early acquisition of cognitive skill in medicine. *Journal of the Learning Sciences, 7*(2), 173–208.

Hmelo-Silver, C. E. (2004). Problem-based learning: What and how do students learn? *Educational Psychology Review, 16*(3), 235–266.

Honomichl, R. D., & Chen, Z. (2012). The role of guidance in children's discovery learning. *Wiley Interdisciplinary Reviews: Cognitive Science, 3*(6), 615–622.

House, J. D. (2011). Effects of classroom computer instruction on mathematics achievement of a national sample of tenth-grade students: Findings from the education longitudinal study of 2002 (ELS: 2002) assessment. *International Journal of Instructional Media, 38*(4), 391–400.

Hunter, M. (1982). Mastery teaching. El Segundo, CA: T.I.P PUblications.

Jones, B. F., Rasmussen, C. M., & Moffitt, M. C. (1997). Real-life problem solving.: A collaborative approach to interdisciplinary learning. Washington, DC: American Psychological Association.

Joyce, B. R., & Showers, B. (2002). Student achievement through staff development.

Kazemi, E. & Hintz, A. (2014). *Intentional talk: How to structure and lead productive mathematical discussions*. Portland, ME: Stenhouse Publishers.

Kelemanik, G., Lucenta, A., & Creighton, S. J. (2016). *Routines for reasoning: Fostering the mathematical practices in all students*. Portsmouth, NH: Heinemann.

Khan Academy. (2018). *Khan Academy introduces new mastery learning features*. Retrieved from https://www.prnewswire.com/news-releases/khan-academy-introduces-new-mastery-learning-features-300708027.html

Kiewra, K. A. (1987). Note taking and review: The research and its implications. Journal of Instructional Science, *16*, 233–249.

Klein, D. (2003). A brief history of American K-12 mathematics education in the 20th century. Retrieved from http://www.csun.edu/~vcmth00m/AHistory.html

Legal Information Institute (1992), Tenth Amendment. Retrieved from https://www.law.cornell.edu/constitution/tenth_amendment

Lesh, Richard, and Helen M. Doerr. 2003. "Foundations of a Models and Modeling Perspective on Mathematics Teaching, Learning, and Problem Solving." In Beyond Constructivism: Models and Modeling Perspectives on Mathematics Problem Solving, Learning, and Teaching, edited by Richard Lesh and Helen M. Doerr, pp. 3–34. Mahwah, NJ: Lawrence Erlbaum Associates

Lesh, R., & Lehrer, R. (2003). Models and modeling perspectives on the development of students and teachers. *Mathematical Thinking and Learning, 5*(2–3), 109–129.

Lester, F. K., & Cai, J. (2016). Can mathematical problem solving be taught? Preliminary answers from 30 years of research. In Felmer, P., Kilpatrick, J., & Pehkonnen, E. (Eds.), *Posing and solving mathematical problems: Advances and new perspectives* (pp. 117–135). Buenos Aires, AR: Springer.

Koehler, M., & Mishra, P. (2009). What is technological pedagogical content knowledge (TPACK)?. *Contemporary issues in technology and teacher education, 9*(1), 60–70.

Loveless, T. (2008). The misplaced math student. *The 2008 Brown Center Report on American Education: How well are American students learning.*

Martin, L., & Gourley-Delaney, P. (2014). Students' images of mathematics. *Instructional Science, 42*(4), 595–614.

Marzano, R. J., Pickering, D. J., & Pollock, J. E. (2001). *Classroom instruction that works: Research-based strategies for increasing student achievement.* Alexandria, VA: ASCD.

Maxwell, C. (2016). *What blended learning is—nd isn't.* Retrieved from https://www.blendedlearning.org/what-blended-learning-is-and-isnt/

Mishra, P., & Koehler, M. J. (2007, March). Technological pedagogical content knowledge (TPCK): Confronting the wicked problems of teaching with technology. In *Society for Information Technology & Teacher Education International Conference* (pp. 2214–2226). Association for the Advancement of Computing in Education (AACE).

Moll, L. C., Amanti, C., Neff, D., & Gonzalez, N. (1992). Funds of knowledge for teaching: Using a qualitative approach to connect homes and classrooms. *Theory Into Practice, 31*(2), 132–141.

Moschkovich, J. (2013). Principles and guidelines for equitable mathematics teaching practices and materials for English language learners. *Journal of Urban Mathematics Education, 6*(1), 45–57.

Moschkovich, J. (1999). Supporting the participation of English language learners in mathematical discussions. *For the Learning of Mathematics, 19*(1), 11–19.

Moyer, P. S., Niezgoda, D., & Stanley, J. (2005). Young children's use of virtual manipulatives and other forms of mathematical representations. In W. J. Masalaski & P. C. Elliott (Eds.), Technology-supported mathematics learning environments (pp. 17–34). Reston, VA: National Council of Teachers of Mathematics.

Mullis, I. V. S. Martin, M. O., Foy, P., & Arrora, A. (2012). TIMSS 2011 International results in mathematics. *International Association for the Evaluation of Educational Achievement.*

Library of Congress Document #2012947308, pp. 1–503. Chestnut Hill, MA: Boston College.

Natasi, B. K., & Clements, D. H. (1991). Research on cooperative learning: Implications for practice. *School Psychology Review*, *20*(1), 110–131.

National Council of Teachers of Mathematics (2014). *Principles to actions executive summary*. Retrieved from https://www.nctm.org/uploadedFiles/Standards_and_Positions/PtAExecutiveSummary.pdf

National Council of Teachers of Mathematics (2014). *Students need procedural fluency in mathematics*. Retrieved from https://www.nctm.org/News-and-Calendar/News/NCTM-News-Releases/Students-Need-Procedural-Fluency-in-Mathematics/

National Education Association. (2010) Preparing 21st Century Students for a Global Society: An Educator's Guide to the Four C's.

National Education Association. (2020). *English language learners*. Retrieved from https://www.nea.org/resource-library/english-language-learners

National Governors Association, Council of Chief State School Officers, & Achieve (2008). *Benchmarking for success: Ensuring U.S. students receive a world-class education*. Retrieved from http://www.edweek.org/media/benchmakring%20for%20success%20dec%202008%20final.pdf

National Governors Association, Council of Chief State School Officers (2010). *Common Core State Standards Mathematics*. National Governors Association Center for Best Practices, Council of Chief State School Officers, Washington D.C. Retrieved from http://www.corestandards.org/wp-content/uploads/Math_Standards1.pdf

National Governors Association Center for Best Practices, Council of Chief State School Officers (2010). *Common Core State Standards*. Washington D.C.: National Governors Association Center for Best Practices, Council of Chief State School Officers. Retrieved from http://www.corestandards.org/about-the-standards/development-process/

National Governors Association Center for Best Practices & Council of Chief State School Officers (2010). The development process. *The Common Core State Standards Initiative*. Washington D.C. Retrieved from http://www.corestandards.org/about-the-standards/development-process/

National Math Council (2004) (from Chapter 7)

National Mathematics Advisory Panel. (2008). Foundations of success: The final report of the National Mathematics Advisory Panel. Washington, DC: U.S. Department of Education.

National Research Council (2001). *Adding it up: Helping children learn mathematics*. J. Kilpatrick, J. Swafford, and B. Findell (Eds.). Washington, DC: National Academy Press.

Nunes, T., Bryant, P., Evans, D., & Bell, D. (2010). The scheme of correspondence and its role in children's mathematics. In BJEP Monograph Series II, Number 7-Understanding number development and difficulties. *British Psychological Society, 83*(99), 83–99.

The Partnership for 21st Century Learning (2015). *P-21 Framework definitions document*. Retrieved from http://www.p21.org/storage/documents/docs/P21_Framework_Definitions_New_Logo_2015.pdf

NCTM (2000) Principles and Standards for School Mathematics (2000). *Executive summary. Principles and standards for school mathematics.* Retrieved from https://www.nctm.org/uploadedFiles/Standards_and_Positions/PSSM_ExecutiveSummary.pdf

Project Tomorrow (2017). Trends in Digital Learning: Building teachers' capacity and competency to create new learning experiences for students. Irvine, CA: Project Tomorrow.

Puentedura, R. R. (2006). Transformation, technology, and education. Retrieved from http://hippasus.com/resources/tte/

Reimer, K., & Moyer, P. S. (2005). Third-graders learn about fractions using virtual manipulatives: A classroom study. *Journal of Computers in Mathematics and Science Teaching, 24*(1), 5–25.

Richmond, E. (2016). How do American students compare to their international peers? *The Atlantic.* Retrieved from https://www.theatlantic.com/education/archive/2016/12/how-do-american-students-compare-to-their-international-peers/509834/

Rittle-Johnson, B., Schneider, M., & Star, J. R. (2015). Not a one-way street: Bidirectional relations between procedural and conceptual knowledge of mathematics. *Educational Psychology Review, 27*(4), 587–597.

Rittle-Johnson, Schneider, & Star (2015). *Not a one-way street: Bidirectional relations between procedural and conceptual knowledge of mathematics. Education Psychology Review, 27,* 587–597. Doi:10.1007/s10648-015-9302-x

Roberts, J, & Inman, T. (2007). *Strategies for differentiating instruction best practices for the classroom.* Waco, Texas: Prufrock Press Inc.

Shulman, L. S. (1986). Those who understand: Knowledge growth in teaching. *Educational Researcher, 15*(2), 4–14.

Simons, K. D., & Klein, J. D. (2007). The impact of scaffolding and student achievement levels in a problem-based learning environment. *Instructional Science, 35,* 41–72. doi: 10.1007/s11251-006-9002-5

Snipes, J., & Finkelstein, N. (2015). Opening a Gateway to College Access: Algebra at the Right Time. Research Brief. *Regional Educational Laboratory West.*

Soto, I. (2012). *ELL shadowing: A catalyst for change.* Thousand Oaks, CA: Corwin.

Steen, K., Brooks, D., & Lyon, T. (2006). The impact of virtual manipulatives on first grade geometry instruction and learning. Journal of Computers in Mathematics and Science Teaching, 25(4), 373–391.

Stein, M. K., Smith, M. S., Henningsen, M. A., & Silver, E. A. (2009). *Implementing standards-based mathematics instruction: A casebook for professional development,* (2nd Ed.). New York, NY: Teachers College Press.

Stevenson, H. W., Chen, C., & Lee, S. Y. (1993). Mathematics achievement of Chinese, Japanese, and American children: Ten years later. *Science,* 53–58.

Sullivan, P., & Lilburn, P. (2004). *Open-ended maths activities.* Melbourne, Victoria: Oxford Press.

Sullivan, P. Warren, E., White, P. (2000). Students' responses to content specific open-ended mathematical tasks. *Mathematics Education Research Journal, 12*(1), 2–17.

TIMMS & PIRLS (2015). International results in mathematics. Boston, MA: Boston College. Retrieved from http://timssandpirls.bc.edu/timss2015/international-results/timss-2015/mathematics/performance-at-international-benchmarks/advanced-international-benchmark/#side

U.S. Department of Education (November, 2009). *Race to the Top program executive summary.* Washington, DC. Retrieved from https://www2.ed.gov/programs/racetothetop/executive-summary.pdf

U.S. Department of Education, Office of Public Affairs (2004). *A guide to education and No Child Left Behind.* Retrieved from https://www2.ed.gov/print/nclb/overview/intro/guide/guide.html#act

Utah State University (2018). *National library of virtual manipulatives.* Retrieved from http://nlvm.usu.edu/en/nav/vlibrary.html

Verschaffel, L. (1999). Realistic mathematical modeling and problem solving in the upper elementary school: Analysis and improvement. In J.H.M Hamers, J.E.H. Van Luit, & B. Csapo (Eds.), Teaching and learning thinking skills. Context of learning (pp. 215–240). Lisse: Swets & Zeitlinger.

Metacognition and Mathematics Education (PDF Download Available). Available from: https://www.researchgate.net/publication/226914839_Metacognition_and_Mathematics_Education [accessed Apr 19 2018].

Vygotsky, L. S. (1978). *Mind in society: The development of higher psychological processes.* Cambridge, MA: Harvard University Press.

Webb, N. M., Franke, M. L., Ing, M., Wong, J., Fernandez, C. H., Shin, N., & Turrou, A. C. (2014). Engaging with others' mathematical ideas: Interrelationships among student participation, teachers' instructional practices, and learning. *International Journal of Educational Research, 63,* 79–93.

Webb, N. M., & Palincsar, A. S. (1996). Group processes in the classroom. In Berliner, D., and Calfee, R. (Eds.), pp. 841–876. *Handbook of Educational Psychology,* New York: MacMillan.

Wells, P. J., & Coffey, D. C. (2005). Are they wrong? Or did they just answer a different question? *Teaching Children Mathematics, 12*(4), 202.

Wiggins, G. P., & McTighe, J. (2005). *Understanding by design.* Alexandria, VA: ASCD.

Wilson, W. S. (2009). Elementary school mathematics priorities. *AASA Journal of Scholarship & Practice, 6*(1), 40–49.

Wirkila, C., & Kuhn, D. (2011). Problem-based learning in K-12 education: Is it effective and how does it achieve its effects? *American Education Research Journal, 48*(5), 1157–1186.

Witzel, B. S. (2005). Using CRA to teach algebra to students with math difficulties in inclusive settings. *Learning Disabilities: A Contemporary Journal. 3*(2), 49–60.

Woodward, J. (2004). Mathematics education in the United States past to present. *Journal of Learning Disabilities, 37*(1), 16–31.

Appendix

Model: Technology Inventory plan

Technology Access

As access to technology is different across classrooms and school campuses, we recommend that you begin to think about technology tools at your school site by first completing a technology inventory. Create a spreadsheet or table to list the school inventory. You can create a key to rate the quality of resources available and the location of these resources.

Where should you begin?

- Classroom Inventory:

    - Computer(s): size, year, model, accessories (CD drive, video camera, audio).

    - Software availability and version: MS Word, Excel, PowerPoint, AppleWorksteacher and student computers, printers, Elmo, overhead projector, etc.

    - Internet access and limitations: speed, functionality, uses, privacy.

    - Attendance and grading tools for teachers, parents and school personnel

    - Resources such as Smartboard, electronic curriculum resources, clickers, Elmo, etc.

    - How do you access data/test scores?

- Student/School Inventory:

    - List specific instructional software: games, typing, sketchpad

    - Access to internet: computer lab, library, lab top and tablet

- Computer and laptops: Where do students have access? What is the student/computer ratio? How often do they have access? What is the process for getting access to the computer/internet?

- Other technology: projector, doc camera (ELMO), printer, scanner

- How do students view videos?

- District Policy & Procedures:

  - Does the district have a technology department? How do you report and resolve technical issues/problems?

  - Can you access Web 2.0 tools at your school? Are social networking tools available? What is the process to receive access to blocked sites?

  - Does your district have an internet/computer policy that must be signed by parents before students can use the computer/internet?

  - Does your school district have a website and can your students access a teacher website or blog?

  - Do students have access to email and can they create a blog?

  - What professional development is available for technology use?

- Action Plan:

  - List at least 5 ways you would use these resources in your classroom instruction.

  - What are some of the challenges you might encounter for using technology in the classroom?

  - What are some possible solutions you might develop to overcome some of the technical challenges at your school site?

  - What is a personal goal you have for learning or implementing technology in the classroom?

  - You cannot make changes to a submitted item, but you can submit additional information or attachments.

After completing the inventory of your school technology resources you can now determine how to best utilize technology as a tool for student use. Depending on the number of devices to which your student have access, Table 3.3 provides recommendations for implementing technology in your classroom.

Table 3.3: Proposed Model for Technology Integration (Based on class size of 30 students)

Number of Devices	Recommended Model	Implementation
0-6	BYOD (Bring your own Device)	Set fair and firm rules where students place device at the corner of their desk with volume off screen down until directed for use. Great for polling, research, backchannel, and response tools.
7-12	Small group/station	Students use devices in small groups with each group of 3-5 students having access to one device. Collaborative use with students rotating use by timer or group roles.
15-29	Peer collaboration	Peer projects, research and polling. Work cooperatively with a peer to share device and report findings to larger group. Synthesize ideas and write collaboratively using web tools and writing tools.
30	One to One	Complete tasks autonomously such as note-taking, research, individual projects and assessments.

We have found in our work with teachers that one of the biggest deterrents to using technology in the classroom is the management that comes with it.

MUST DO: Our recommendations before you introduce technology in the classroom

1. **Establishing Norms:** What are the norms to create a tech-centric classroom where students work cooperatively?

2. **Establishing Rules:** What rules will you want to establish for implementing technology in the classroom?

MAY DO: Optional strategies to increase classroom management of technology devices in the classroom.

1. Assign each student to a device by number.

2. Create a desktop icon that students can click on to access your website.

3. Bookmark class websites/online resources you would like students to access in your browser.

Getting Started with Google Slides

Google Slides provides you with the means to: Collaborate.

Google Slides provides you with a way to: share your work so students have access to class notes and resources.

Google Slides provides your students with a way to create content.

Check out our Youtube Channel for Google Tools Tips & Tricks:
https://bit.ly/2JE4Qlt

If you need support with any google presentations or tools send an email to: thewiredprofessor@gmail.com

Getting Started:

You and your students must have a Google Account to use this resource.

Once you have a Google Account be sure your students also have access and you are able to share resources with them.

You can either send your students a LINK to the file or you can add their email addresses and they will be notified. If you have folders you already share with them you can put this in the folder.

Be sure each of your students make a copy and RENAME their file so that each student is working on their own Google Slide!

*Be Sure your VIEW is not set at 100% or you will not be able to move the manipulative pieces that are in the grey area (I set to 80%)

Step 1: Get accessing the Google Slide Show:
https://goo.gl/v1in7B

Step 2: Make a Copy of the Google Slide show and save to your Google Drive.

Step 3: Share your copied file with your students. Be sure they also make a copy. They should write their last name and first initial.

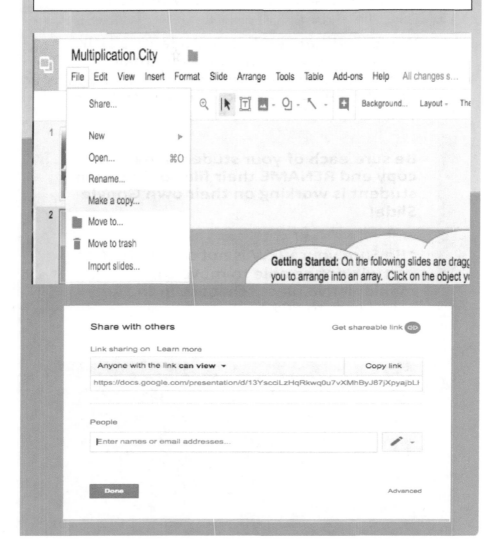

You will receive a link to a Google Slide presentation which your students will copy for their use. If your students have never used this product please give step-by-step directions. Students are likely to have dragged objects if they use IPADS or a Smartphone.

Model how to make an array and write an equation. Set expectations based on your students readiness. You can create or delete objects based on your students' abilities.

My Math Talk Sentence Starters

1. I agree with you because...

2. I disagree with you because...

3. Can you explain how...

4. So I hear you saying that...

5. Your strategy reminds me of...

6. My strategy was to...

7. To add on...

8. I wonder...

9. How did you...

10. What would happen if...

Calendar Math   Name_____

Today Is:	Number Word	Even or odd?

Tens Frame for Today

One less   One more

____ ◯ _____

Ways to make

Number Bond

Tally Marks

Money

Name_____ Calendar Math

Today's Number	Factors	Multiples
Prime or Composite		

Ways to Make Area:

Ways to Make Perimeter:

Division	Fraction	Decimal	Percent

Daily Big Number
Standard Form:

Expanded Form:

Word Form:

Data Set: _____

Make An Equation

Number Talk Planning Guide

Math Concept & Goal:

Number Talk Type: (Image, Number String, Ten Frame, Other):

Academic Language:

Next Steps: Exit ticket, Anchor Chart, Journal or Exit Ticket

Possible Solutions: Record all the ways of showing

Questions To Guide Student Discussion:

NOTES:

Name	Date

Counting Collections: Scavenger Hunt:
Identify arrays in your class and record a number sentence to represent each array.

1.	2.
3.	4.

Math Talk Moves

Revoicing
You can restate what someone is saying by summarizing or rephrasing his/her words.

Repeating
To Show you understand what someone is saying repeat what you heard.

Reasoning
Compare your thinking to what someone else is saying

Adding On
Connect to what someone else is saying with your ideas.

Wait Time
Make time for others to think about the problem and respond

Revise Your Thinking
Make Changes to your thinking after listening to the ideas of others.

My Video Word Problem Checklist:

Student learning Target: Write and act out interesting and challenging word problems for my classmates to solve.

Group Roles:

Camera-person	Writer	Actor(s)
Editor	Props	Director

Maximum #:_____   Minimum #:_____

Story Title: _____

Problem Situation:_____

_____

Story Setting:	Characters:	Operation to Solve: $+ - \times \div \$$

This is how you solve the problem:

©Dr. Patricia Dickenson doctorofed.com

Camera image and star border © Shutterstock.com

Open-ended tasks Planner:

Mathematical Goals:	Standard/Practice Standards:

The Task:

How will you present the task and hook the learner?

Anticipated Strategies & Misconceptions:	Questions to support student thinking:
Approach for class sharing/discourse:	Questions to Support Student Sharing:

Learner Outcomes & Plan to Integration Technology:

Math Centers Planning Sheet

Teacher Center: Small Group Work

Group 1:		Group 2:	
1. 2. 3. 4. Focus:		1. 2. 3. 4. Focus:	
Group 3:		**Group 4:**	
1. 2. 3. 4. Focus:		1. 2. 3. 4. Focus:	

Journal	Computers	Independent Work

Games	Problem Solving	Inquiry/Projects

Notes:

Project-Based Learning Planning Template

Teacher Name:	Grade Level:	Project Title:

Content Standards Addressed: (National Math Standards or Common Core/NGSS)

Cross-Curriculum Connections: What other standards and subjects will you address in this project and what connections will be made in these disciplines.

Stage 1: Setting the Stage

Driving Question: the question that drives the work	
Project Summary: (what students will do, learn and accomplish by the end of the project)	

21st Century Skills: (to be taught and assessed) Based on 4C's Framework	Creativity:	Critical Thinking:
	Collaboration:	Communication:
The Hook: How will you engage the students and spark their interest		
Resources & Materials	Material/Equipment: Technology: Community/Onsite people:	

Stage 2: Goals & Target to Support All Learners

Learning Outcomes & Targets:
What targets will students meet to be able to complete the project

Instructional Strategies:
What will you provide to support student learning and scaffold information with materials and lessons aligned to learning outcomes and assessment.

Checkpoint:
How will you ensure all students are on track and moving toward the learning goal.

Problem-Based Learning Planner

Teacher Name	Grade

Content Standards Addressed:(National Math Standard or Common Core) Other Subject area standards	

Mathematical Goal: Students will be able to….	Standard for Mathematical Practice:

Informal Math Knowledge: Students can…	Formal Math Knowledge: Students need to know…

The Task & Hook: State the problem and how you will hook students	

Possible Solutions: (include all pictures, models, representations)	

Possible Errors & Misconceptions:	

Language Demand	Scaffolding Strategies

Time	Group Roles & Process	Evidence Collected
min		

Time	Individual Process	Evidence Collected
min		

Time	Share Out Roles & Process	Evidence Collected
min		

Notes, Resources & Materials Needed:

Weekly Blended Learning Log
(This form is due each Monday)

Name _____   Date _____

Please name two or three activities/topics that you worked on this week:

_____

Complete the **line graph** below to record your activity for the week. Place a dot to show the number of minutes each day. You may round to the nearest five minutes. When you're done for the week, connect each dot to the next with a straight line.

	Mon.	Tues.	Wed.	Thurs.	Fri.	Sat.	Sun.
90							
80							
70							
60							
50							
40							
30							
20							
10							
0							

You completed_____ minutes at home this week.

Reflection:
What did you learn this week? What questions do you still have? What do you want to learn more about?

_____
_____
_____

Parent Comments & Signature _____

My Math Journal Table of Contents

Date	Title	Pages	Grade I deserve/earned

My Tour Around the World

Name   Class   Date

#1Destination: (Name and location)
- _____
- _____

Estimated Distance from home to destination:
_____

Actual Distance found via Google Maps:
_____

Fraction: (Estimate/Actual)
_____

Difference & Compare
_____

#2 Destination: (Name and location)
- _____
- _____

Estimated Distance from home to destination:
_____

Actual Distance found via Google Maps:
_____

Fraction: (Estimate/Actual)
_____

Difference & Compare
_____

Math Facts About Place:
1. _____
2. _____
3. _____
4. _____

Picture/Illustration:

Geometry Concepts:
_____
_____

Math Facts About Place:
1. _____
2. _____
3. _____
4. _____

Picture/Illustration:

Geometry Concepts:
_____
_____

Index